THE WELL OF SACRIFICE

DONALD EDIGER THE WELL

OF SACRIFICE

DOUBLEDAY & COMPANY, INC.

GARDEN CITY, NEW YORK

1971

Library of Congress Catalog Card Number 68–14216
Copyright © 1971 by Expeditions Unlimited, Inc.
All Rights Reserved
Printed in the United States of America
First Edition

Page 21 photo courtesy of M. F. Gazze

Design and decoration by M. F. Gazze

THIS ACCOUNT OF THE EXPEDITION
TO THE SACRED WELL OF THE MAYAS IS DEDICATED
TO THE MEMORY OF
F. KIRK JOHNSON, JR.
THE MAN WHO MADE IT POSSIBLE.

GRATEFUL ACKNOWLEDGMENTS are made to the following persons and organizations for their assistance to the expedition to the sacred well of the Mayas:

The late Dr. Eusebio Dávalos Hurtado of the National Institute of Anthropology and History of Mexico, Pablo Bush Romero, Oscar and Paul Bush, the Club de Exploraciones y Deportes Aquáticos de México and CEDAM International, Dr. Sol Heinemann, Fernando Barbachano, the Hon. Fulton Freeman, the Hon. John McKeithen, Adolph Kiefer, Ezio Cusi and Ezio Cusi, Jr., Dr. Ignacio Bernal of the National Institute of Anthropology and History, Sra. Josefina Martínez, the Hotel Mayaland, Barbachano Travel Service, the University of Texas at El Paso, Mr. and Mrs. Paul Basye, William A. McGregor, Robert Metcalf, Ray O. Peck, Peter Melo, David Tyson, Sarita Robinson, J. Walter Thompson, Srta. Guadalupe Grimaldi and the Hacienda Chichén, the government of Canada, the Louisiana State Police, the Tallahassee Police Department, the City of Campeche, the Hotel Baluartes, Petróleos Mexicanos, ALO-Cosmetics—Aloe

Creme Laboratories, *Argosy* magazine, W. R. Ames Company, American Oil Company, Clark Cortez Company, Dow Chemical, the Purex Corporation, Evinrude Motors, the Ford Motor Company, Gondas Corporation, Grove Manufacturing Company, Johns-Manville International, *The Daily Telegraph of London, Look* magazine, Nikon-Ehrenreich Photo-Optical, the Onan Corporation, Pacific Pumping Company, Pan American Airways, American Rolex Watch Corporation, Ryder Systems, *Saga* magazine, Seamless Rubber Company, E. R. Squibb & Sons, the Sullivan Machinery Company, Wallace & Tiernan, the Wilding Corporation, Pompano Federal Travel Service, Pompano Beach Bank and Trust Company, the Mai Kai Restaurant.

THE WELL OF SACRIFICE

1

THERE WAS a slow, steady rain the day our caravan arrived at Chichén Itzá. There was nothing unusual about the rain; early September is often wet in Yucatán. In our case, however, it may have been an omen, since we were here to invade the home of Chac, the powerful rain god of the ancient Mayas. It had taken our caravan of twenty-one vehicles exactly two weeks to make the journey from Florida to Yucatán, traveling through the Gulf states, through Texas, through the plains of northern Mexico, over the mountains and into the Valley of Mexico, over more mountains, on to the Gulf Coast of Mexico, then by ferry and washed-out roads and finally through the Puuc Hills and into Yucatán. The journey itself would hardly have been unusual except that it rained thirteen of the fourteen days, the rain culminating in a hurricane that met us on the thirteenth day in Mérida, just as we were preparing for the last short leg of the trip.

And now in Chichén Itzá we had the vestiges of the hurricane in the form of a drizzle. The hot air seemed to be composed entirely of gnats and drops of water. The tires slushed as they moved from the pavement onto the dirt road that led from the highway to the ruins of what was once the greatest capital in the hemisphere. "Highway" is a misleading term. It is a strip of pavement that runs from Mérida to the east coast of the Yucatán Peninsula, cutting through the dense scrub jungle like a dull knife. The villages that line the road seem to bear typographical errors for names: Tahmek, Hoctún, Xocchel, Yodzonot. Once off the main road the caravan rested for a few minutes in what appeared to be a vast plaza flanked by a pyramid, huge stone platforms and ancient buildings with endless rows of columns. The freshly cut grass provided the only color to the scene. The sky was gray with rain and the buildings that once rose in splendor were now brown or gray. It was impossible not to think of the rain as an ominous sign as our twenty-one vehicles, up to the hub caps in mud, paused in what was the most important city of the Maya civilization. The pause was to give workmen time to clear away some stones that lay between us and the *sacbe*, the road that led from the temple area of Chichén Itzá to our ultimate goal, the ancient and mysterious well of sacrifice.

Sweating in the humid air and looking at the desolate country around us, I wondered why the Mayas ever chose this place as the site of their greatest metropolis. On the other hand, maybe it actually was not the greatest; maybe it was not even a metropolis as we know the term. Those were but two of the many questions we hoped this expedition would help solve. In any case, *why* the Mayas chose this site is probably one of the last important questions about this strange people.

The entire Mayan civilization is a puzzle. We do not even know what the Mayas called themselves. (Maya derives from Mayapán, the name of the city that became the principal center after the fall of Chichén Itzá.) Quite likely they referred to themselves, as many primitive people do, as simply "the people." Where the people came from is another major mystery. Apparently the tribes that wandered across the land bridge from Siberia to Alaska moved slowly southward, some of them eventually being attracted to the lush rain forests in Guatemala and the state of Chiapas in Mexico. We do not know who the first settlers of the rain forests were nor whether they were the same people whom we later called the Mayas. Making the puzzle even more difficult to solve are the forest and jungle themselves, which closed in quickly on everything the early people built, either destroying it or mutilating it so thoroughly as to make archaeological research nearly impossible with its present tools.

In 1864 a small jade object turned up in Puerto Barrios, Guatemala. Though scarcely eight by three inches in size, the piece of jade was carved on both sides. On one side was a date corresponding to A.D. 320. Archaeologists believe the jade, known as the Leyden Plate, was made in Tikal. Wherever it was made, the hieroglyphics spell out the oldest Mayan date ever found.

Of course this does not mean that Mayan civilization suddenly sprang to life in 320. Among other things, the date reflects the fact that by that year the Mayas had developed a calendar more accurate than our own. Though the Mayan calendar was a couple of thousandths of a day more accurate than ours, it was considerably clumsier. Using it was like measuring a mile with a ruler instead of an odometer: the results may be more accurate, but rarely (especially in the case of primitive peoples) is such precision necessary. Still, the Mayas' achievement in calendrics is spectacular, and its existence in A.D. 320 means they must have been developing it for centuries.

It is not surprising that earlier Mayan hieroglyphic dates have not been discovered. The jungles of Guatemala are simply not conducive to preservation of artifacts. Vegetation is one of the archaeologist's worst enemies. Even in comparatively arid Syria, the Antiquities Department of that country has become alarmed over the thick bushes that have cracked the walls in the fortress of Saladin, one of the greatest relics of the Crusades in the Middle East. Officials of the department refer to the invading vegetation as the "green peril." If plants can crack the walls of a fortress in a dry country, it is understandable that they can smother the more fragile relics of a civilization in a humid climate. The surprise is not that earlier Mayan records have not been found, but that archaeologists have found such early ones at all.

It is an interesting footnote to Mayan history that no observatory has been discovered despite the Mayas' dependency on stellar observation in calendrics. Most experts think that the circular building at Chichén Itzá must have been an observatory of sorts, but there is no conclusive evidence of its purpose. Since all of Mayan life was well based on astronomy and calendrics, one would expect them to have had observatories in every city. But if they did, the edifices must have been square or rectangular, because the round building at Chichén Itzá is the only circular structure discovered in Mayan territory.

Mayas developed not only a wonderful system of calendars, but something much more subtle: zero, a concept that was not made part of European mathematics until many centuries later. Unlike an ultra-precise calendar, the zero is an extremely useful idea, especially for a people as commerce-minded as the Mayas.

Oddly, the Mayas seemed to have disliked, or disdained, circles. Their buildings were square or oblong, the symbol for zero was a shell, and they apparently made no particular use of the wheel. Archaeologists have found wheels on children's toys in several places in Meso-America, so it is probable that Mayas knew of the wheel. Why they never harnessed it remains a mystery. Perhaps it was because they lacked beasts of burden. Ancestors of the horse once inhabited North America but they became extinct before the continent was inhabited by man. Bison might have been domesticated, but they were far away from Mayan territory, the nearest being in the zoo of the Aztec rulers, some eight hundred miles away.

Despite the lack of a wheel, the Mayas developed one of the finest highway systems of any ancient people. It was so good, in fact, that archaeologist Victor von Hagen says it was not bettered in this hemisphere until British colonists started building roads in the American colonies.

Maya roads were elevated highways that connected the major ceremonial centers. They cut through jungle, swamps, mountains and the plains of Yucatán. Known as white roads or sacbe in Maya, the highways were holy and travelers upon them were under divine protection. To molest a traveler on a sacbe was a sin.

The network of highways spread as the Mayas migrated from Guatemala and Chiapas northward to what are now the Mexican state of Yucatán and the territory of Quintana Roo. Remains of the roads are visible throughout the peninsula, more so in the north because there rains are less damaging and construction is more recent.

But why the Mayas migrated northward in the first place is another mystery. The climate, except for two or three months of the year, is nearly unbearable. The land is fairly flat, but it is covered with stone which is the visible portion of the limestone shelf that forms of the base of the peninsula. There is not one river or even a stream in northern Yucatán, the only surface water being found in sinkholes. These look like huge round sunken ponds, some measuring nearly 200 feet in diameter. The ancient Mayas in the northern half of the peninsula depended almost entirely on these sinkholes for their water supply. They never developed an irrigation system or thought to dig a well. The inhospitable land could have been made much more livable if they had dug only a few feet into the rocky ground, which is honeycombed with underground streams that would have provided an endless water supply. The Mayas chose to endure the land as they found it, obviously frustrated by heavy rains but without any way to get water after the rains stopped.

How it was that northern Yucatán prospered is as much of a mystery as why it was ever settled. Great cities rose from the intractable land: Uxmal, Izamal, Dzibilchaltún, Mayapán, Maní, Ticul and T'ho. As the cities to the south were engulfed by the jungle, the centers of the north rose in splendor, developing a style of architecture which many consider superior to any other in the Mayan territory. A Toynbeean view might hold that the cities prospered because their inhabitants had more obstacles to overcome.

The fact that the cities probably were not cities as we know them and that they were only very loosely allied makes it difficult to speak of "Mayan territory" or "Mayan civilization." The cities seemed to be held together by language and religion. Except in the case of Chichén Itzá and Mayapán, there is no indication

17

of a capital, and even these cities were probably not capitals in the present-day sense of a state or national capital. Rather, these cities—like the southern cities of Uaxactún and Tikal before them— were probably great religious centers to which neighboring villages looked for leadership and protection. Many archaeologists even dislike the word "city," preferring "ceremonial center." The two terms are not necessarily mutually exclusive, but the word "city" connotes a place with many inhabitants, and no one knows whether or not the ceremonial centers were inhabited. Virtually no homesites have been found or excavated. When I have asked archaeologists to estimate the population of Chichén Itzá at its height, I have heard answers ranging from fifteen thousand to three hundred thousand. Some archaeologists think that great populations might have lived on the outskirts of the ceremonial centers, but as far as I know, no large number of homesites have been found in outlying areas either. It is not surprising that the remains of houses are scarce. They were undoubtedly made of wood and held together with a loose limestone mortar. These materials would quickly perish under heavy rains, intense heat and substantial plant growth. Mayan temples (we assume that is what they were) and other great buildings stood longer. They are found as far south as the border of Guatemala and Honduras, in British Honduras and the territory of Quintana Roo, in the Mexican states of Tabasco, Chiapas and Yucatán and even hundreds of miles to the west in the state of Veracruz. The area cannot be called an empire because it had no supreme ruler, nor can it be called a federation since there were no close political ties throughout. Referring to the ceremonial centers as city-states would be fairly accurate except that the term implies great size and strength. Present-day Mayas in Yucatán use an old word that roughly refers to the areas in which Maya is spoken. The word is *mayab,* and it is the logical term for us to use, the test being that it is immediately understood anywhere in Mayab.

Of all the cities of Mayab, one stands out as the most sacred— Chichén Itzá. It may not have been the largest but it was the holiest. Its temples stretch for miles, from the restored group of buildings where our caravan was parked far into the bush. It would take decades to find all the remaining structures of the city and several centuries to restore them. Any man straying off the jungle trails around Chichén Itzá might find a ruin never before discovered. As in other ceremonial centers, virtually all the buildings have an apparent religious purpose. Chichén, however, embraces something even holier than its temples. This is the well of sacrifice.

From the open place where the caravan was parked, members of the expedition had a good view of the major restored structures. To our right was the building called *el castillo,* the Temple of Kukulcán, or simply "the pyramid." It is small as pyramids go, only about one third the size of the Aztec Pyramid of the Sun at Teotihuacán near Mexico City. To the builders of the Pyramid of Cheops in Egypt it would have only been a working model. (And ironically, much more is known of the Egyptian pyramid, although it is many centuries older.) The pyramid in Chichén Itzá became known as *el castillo* when Spanish conquerors needed a fortress to prove to Spain that they could hold the land they had occupied. Rather than going to the effort of building a castle, the conquerors planted the Spanish flag on top of the crumbling pyramid and wrote the king that they had the required fortress. Archaeological evidence indicates the pyramid was actually used for some sort of religious ceremony, apparently connected with the Feathered Serpent, called Quetzalcóatl in Mexico and Kukulcán in Mayab. The "Temple of Kukulcán" is somewhat of a misnomer inasmuch as the structure is actually several pyramids built one over another, and only the last stage probably had any connection with the Toltec king who called himself the Feathered Serpent.

Perhaps the eminence of Chichén Itzá comes from the blending of cultures in the city. Although it was the holiest city in Mayab, Chichén was the least Mayan. Evidence is conflicting concerning the number of times it was invaded and concerning the "nationality" of the conquerors. Apparently the city was invaded at distinct times by the "water witches," whom the Mayas called the Itzá, and by the Toltec forces of Kukulcán. There is every reason to believe that the man called the Feathered Serpent actually lived and that he journeyed more than eight hundred miles from his capital at Tula to conquer—or at least to dominate—Chichén Itzá. He ruled the city for an undetermined length of time, established a cult around himself and then left. But it was the Itzá who gave their name to the city, which had previously been known as Uucy-abnal. The Itzá were so closely associated with sacrifices in the sacred well that the city itself became known as Chichén Itzá, which in Maya means "at the mouth of the well of the Itzá." Even though some Mayas apparently despised the invaders, it is doubtful that Chichén Itzá would have become the mecca of Mayab without the influence of Kukulcán or the Itzá.

It was not long after our excavations began at the well that we learned more about the strange cults that the early foreigners introduced. The history of Chichén Itzá was revealed for us as sacrifices were recovered from the sacred well. For the well was a kind of time capsule inadvertently deposited over a span of fifteen centuries by men whose purpose was to propitiate the god Chac. The god's response to the sacrifices of riches and of humans has gone unrecorded, but in making the sacrifices the Mayas created more than a cache of treasure. They built up a concentrated depository of their own history. Nature sealed the capsule so securely that no one had been able to open it despite several major attempts. Now it was our turn to try. The vehicles now parked amid the ruins, the tons of equipment which they carried and the men who drove them, were here for one purpose—to break the seal that nature had imposed and to excavate the sacred well, thereby opening the time capsule of the Mayas.

Beyond the Temple of Kukulcán to the right was the Temple of the Warriors, its many rows of columns fading away in the background with the drizzle and mist now at the time of our arrival. Behind the Temple of the Warriors and out of sight at the moment was a group of mostly unrestored structures built

Chichén Itzá. A part of the Temple of the Warriors in the foreground and the Temple of Kukulcán beyond.

around what was apparently a market place. To the left of the caravan were the Platform of the Jaguars and the Tzompantli, the latter carved with row upon row of skulls. The skulls supposedly represent the men who lost their lives playing in the Ball Court, which stands behind the Tzompantli. Archaeologists used to think the losers of the ball games were sacrificed, but current evidence suggests that it may have been the winners who lost their lives—or at least the captain of the winning team. The inference is that it was considered a great honor to be sacrificed and that warriors competed for the privilege on the ball courts of Mayab. If it was thus, the practice stands out as one of the strangest incentive systems in history.

Peeking out over the treetops from the other side of the highway was the circular building believed to be an observatory. It is called the Caracol, which in Spanish means snail, whose shape the interior of the building suggests vaguely. The ancient Mayas of Chichén Itzá would undoubtedly be chagrined if they could know that two of the greatest buildings in their holiest city bear the name "Snail" and "Castle." But if those names are degrading, imagine their reaction if they knew we referred to one of Chichén's best-designed buildings—possibly a residence for priests—as the Nunnery. This building stands behind the Caracol and near it is the Iglesia, church in Spanish. These structures, along with the Grave of the High Priest, are some of the most impressive buildings on the southwest side of the highway.

Directly in front of us was the Platform of Venus, and we got a better view of it as the caravan finally began moving. Like so many other terms used to describe Maya culture, Platform of Venus may not be too accurate. It might not have been a platform and it might not have had anything to do with Venus. It does, however, have carved serpents' heads representing Kukulcán and the glyph representing Pop, the first month in the complicated Maya year. On one side of the building are astronomical symbols that gave archaeologists the idea that the structure had something to do with Venus, the planet whose cycle was important in calculating the Maya year. The building is low and flat, a form that suggested to archaeologists that it was used for ritual dances.

As we progressed the rain changed from a drizzle to a downpour and pounded on the top of the platform, flowing down the carved sides. Some of the relief surfaces, principally on the northwest side, still had remnants of red pigment, and as I watched the water rush down the side I wondered how many more decades the color would last.

The caravan stalled again just as the camper I was driving entered the sacbe that led from the Platform of Venus to the sacred well. All of us were already wet since the heat forced us to keep the vehicle windows open, and since it looked as though there was an impasse at the front of the caravan, most of us got out of the vehicles and sloshed through the mud. Nature had not provided us much of a welcome, but what could one expect at the home of a rain god? I found out that the present delay was caused by the three tractor trailers at the head of the caravan. These carried the heaviest equipment and had to get to the well first, in case the other trucks made the sacbe impassable with too many ruts in the mud.

I stood, dripping with sweat and rainwater, in several inches of mud on what may well be the oldest continuously used road in North America. Brushing gnats away from my eyes, I looked for the edge of the road and saw that like other sacbes this one was raised several feet above the ground. It was difficult to discern the elevation because the scrub jungle pushed its way up to and over the road bed, gnawing at the large square chunks of limestone that formed its foundation. Through the few clearings, however, I could see that the surface of the road was at least five feet above the ground around it. Since archaeologists are not sure when Chichén Itzá was founded, there is no way to tell how old the sacbe is. Probably its age is well over a thousand years. At one time is must have been straight, but now it contains several jogs, apparently caused by the shifting of foundation rocks in wet weather.

Over the roar of the engines I caught the high-pitched sound of birds that had taken shelter in the bush by the road. Lizards scurried on the ground, and within several minutes I had spotted three small snakes. The millions of insects that swarmed in the bush apparently provided food for the larger animals. Even in the rain the flowers along the road were exotically beautiful. There must have been two dozen varieties within a few feet of where I stood. Most of the flowers were delicate and small, the predominant colors red and yellow.

It seemed as though we were stalled on the sacbe for hours, but the delay was exaggerated in our minds because it came at the end of a thirty-five-hundred-mile journey. By word passed along, we learned that expedition members at the head of the caravan were now positioning the large tractor trailers for unloading. This required hacking down quite a bit of bush and dismantling a gate near the well. By getting the big trucks well out of the way, we could drive the campers on to the campsite while the former were being unloaded.

The exhaust fumes mixed with the wet air around us and forced us to cut the engines. In the quiet we could hear voices from the campsite several hundred yards away. Norman Scott's voice came through as though he were using a loud-speaker. One of the qualities needed of an expedition leader is the ability not necessarily to eliminate chaos, which is inevitable, but to rise above it. Scott was a genius at this. While twenty local workers chattered away, Scott shouted out his commands.

It developed that the crane would have to come in first to remove a concrete gate post that was blocking the way of the tractor trailers. But meanwhile the trucks could be parked to one side and the other vehicles could be let in. We were rolling at last.

We ran through the mud back to our vehicles and started them. Then there was another delay while Scott and the local foreman debated in what order they should be parked. Finally this was decided. Slowly the caravan began to move again—for all of thirty feet. Then there was another stop, and another spurt forward. As I neared the end of the sacbe, I realized what was happening. As each vehicle pulled up near the campsite, Harold Martin stopped it to give the driver instructions. Finally it was my turn.

"The problem is this," Harold said as he poked his head through the window, "you've got to get that camper across that field of mud over there. The only way to do it is to put it in low, rev it up and let her go. Get over there beside that other camper as fast as you can." I nodded. "Whatever you do, don't stop."

Harold was pointing to what looked like a pool of mud some hundred yards in diameter. Beyond it, there was a slight incline which was drier. It was on this incline that the campers were being parked.

"Get going," Harold shouted.

I followed his instructions. I pushed in on the clutch and shifted into first. Then I floored the accelerator. My muddy left shoe, however, slipped off the clutch. The back wheels spun and sent a spray of mud onto a half-dozen workers waiting to give me a shove if I needed it. I didn't. Before I realized where I was going, I was halfway across the mud, concerned more now about stopping rather than about getting stuck. I slammed down on the brake pedal. The camper began to slide. It was out of control, but I managed to steer it vaguely in the direction Harold had pointed. Miraculously it ended up smoothly beside the other camper—not more than three feet from it, in fact. A perfect parking job. And doubly lucky, because as soon as the camper stopped, it began sinking in mud nearly a foot deep. Moving it again would have been nearly impossible.

Before long all the campers were lined up in a wide arc on the incline. There were eight small campers mounted on pickup trucks which the Ford Motor Company had provided the expedition, and there were three larger motor homes called Cortezes, which had been supplied by the Clark Cortez Corporation. These would be our living quarters and office space. The plan was to hook up electricity and install air conditioners on each camper. If we were lucky, water would be connected "as soon as we get around to it," as Scott put it.

Meanwhile, the area around the sacred well of the Mayas was beginning to look like a parking lot or construction site, depending which way one turned. Vehicles were rolling in at the rate of one every two or three minutes. The crane was now being used to unload the tractor trailers that were carrying heavy equipment like generators, compressors and industrial engines. The

This would be the expedition's home for many months.
The road to the Temple is in the background.

stake truck rolled in carrying eight large chunks of the material called Styrofoam, manufactured by the Dow Chemical Company, which looked like plastic foam. Another truck pulled in with some of the lighter gear such as electrical equipment and diving supplies. We had only two passenger cars, and these were station wagons. One served as sort of an executive's car and the other carried the film crew that was making a motion picture of the expedition. Scott himself rode in one of the two pickup trucks. The vehicle that probably had the least trouble negotiating the muddy sacbe was a jeep-like car with four-wheel drive called a Bronco.

As soon as the equipment was unloaded, expedition members began installing it. Jerry Kemler had picked a spot for the generator, which had an output capable of lighting a small city. Gordon Inman, meanwhile, was already choosing a site to pour concrete that would support a filtration system. Harold Martin was explaining to the local workers that we would need a shed covered with tar paper in which to keep our chemical supplies dry. It was already late in the afternoon and there was no indication that the rain would stop. Scott, however, obviously planned to get as much accomplished as possible in the few work hours remaining before sunset.

Mosquitoes and bugs had evidently got the scent of fresh humans in the area, and they swarmed around us as we splashed through mud to get the equipment unloaded. The insects were not the only menace in the area. I had just got out of my camper when a little man with a triangular face came up to me and introduced himself as Avelino Canul (a surname as common in Mayab as Smith is in the United States). He had been told to speak to me because he spoke only Spanish and I understood that language. The point he wanted to make was to advise us to beware of snakes, which he said often come out of the bush in wet weather. Just yesterday, he said, one of the caretakers at the ruins killed two rattlesnakes. The rattler, by the way, is the snake of the Feathered Serpent. They are occasionally found around Chichén but are generally rare here. Whether the story about the rattlers was true or not, Avelino had a point. Insects would be a source of constant annoyance, but snakes would be a source of danger.

In the excitement of arrival and unloading, we had almost forgotten the very thing that had lured us here, the sacred well. I decided it was time to take a look at it. I walked across the mud field onto which the local laborers were now pouring gravel and climbed on top one of the structures on the south side of the well. Several other expedition members joined me. We looked down.

It is easy to say that the well averages about 186 feet in diameter and that it is 116 feet from the top of the precipice to the deepest point, but these statistics only relegate the sacred well to the world of a draftsman. We saw it as a murky lake in the bottom of a round canyon, so large that one could hardly hear a shout from the other side. Its sides are strata of limestone, many of which jut out several yards. On these shelves are trees with roots shaped like brown snakes peering down at the water. The well is convex: we could stand at the edge and look down without seeing the limestone wall directly beneath us. Instead, some seventy feet below us, we saw the surface of the stagnant, pungent water. It has the odor of evil, appealing only perhaps to the thousands of bats that live between the limestone shelves. Compared with the fabled beauty of Olympus, this was a peculiar place for a god to choose as home.

This rain god supposedly died with the arrival of priests in the sixteenth century, but such is not the case. Chac may not have a formal place in the religion of contemporary Mayas, but they still believe he exists, and they fear him. We could see this ourselves as the laborers silently watched the unloading of our equipment. Many scientists and engineers thought we had little chance of excavating the well, even with our vast array of machinery. The Mayas thought so too, but for different reasons.

2

WE GOT quite a bit accomplished on the first day before darkness finally brought the unloading to a halt. Two of the three big trucks were unloaded, the bush was cut back to clear a wide area for the campsite, and the generator was put into operation to provide the campers with electricity. The real backbreaking work would come during the next few days, however. Despite the rain Scott hoped to start excavations within one week.

In only a few hours we had completely transformed the south bank of the well from a jungle clearing into a . . . well, it was difficult to say what at the moment. The campsite started at the end of the sacbe, some hundred yards from the precipice of the well. Standing at the end of the road, one faced the crane, an immense yellow piece of equipment that weighed thirty-five tons and which was capable of lifting twenty-five tons if the hydraulic boom was in a vertical position. The boom was a huge arm of steel that could be shortened or lengthened by the flick of a switch in the cab. Ironically, the word for boom in Spanish is *pluma,* which also means feather. The crane was currently positioned about ten yards from the precipice. There were actually two precipices, one only a few feet high that rose above a fifteen-foot-wide ledge which ran along the very rim of the well, at least on the south side of it. In order to get to the rim we had to jump down to the ledge or walk several hundred feet to the east where the first precipice petered out. Later in the expedition this double precipice caused a nearly insoluble problem.

On the ledge behind the crane was a slab of concrete that had been poured as a platform for the winch used by the National Geographic Society during its expedition in 1960 and 1961. Gordon Inman hoped to use the same area for the filtration tanks. Right now he was concerned over the possibility that the tanks might have been damaged en route. Scott, meanwhile, was eyeing an immediately adjacent area on the upper level for a booster pump.

If one stood at the end of the sacbe and turned right, he would be looking east. Since the road is elevated, the area east of the road is several feet lower. This muddy depression was the central area of the campsite, now being used for unloading and as a staging area for other operations. The campers were on the incline at the south side of this depression. Farther to the east beyond the staging area was a gate that sealed off the campsite from a road that led to the landing field a half mile to the north.

The terrain of the campsite was far from ideal. It was also dotted with ruins of buildings, so that in clearing away stones we were never sure whether we were not desecrating the remains of a temple.

The rain stopped around sunset, when we made our way from the campsite to the hacienda, the old Chichén hostelry, first for a pep talk from Scott and then for dinner. The evening at the hacienda would provide us an opportunity to get to know some of the technicians, like Gordon Inman, who had joined the expedition in Chichén Itzá instead of making the thirty-five-hundred-mile overland trip.

We were greeted at the hacienda by the top of the expedition's hierarchy—Scott, F. Kirk Johnson, Jr., and Pablo Bush Romero. Kirk had a bottle of beer in his right hand which he kept shifting to his left whenever he shook hands with anyone. Subsequently, throughout our story, I saw Kirk only twice without a beer in his hand, and both times he was under water. I'm afraid I took an immediate dislike toward Kirk, a Texas millionaire who liked expeditions nearly as much as he liked the jet set in Acapulco. Among many other attitudes that changed during the expedition was my opinion of Kirk.

Pablo Bush, however, looked like a hero. His white Bermuda shorts sagged slightly from the rain they had absorbed, but he appeared the classical picture of someone who goes on archaeo-

Workers brought wheelbarrows filled with rocks to brace the legs of the crane in order to keep it from tumbling into the well.

"Don Pablo Bush Romero . . . looked like a hero. . . ."

logical expeditions. His shoes were also white, and so were the socks that covered his legs to the knees. His shirt, too, was white, and he wore a pith helmet, which he removed as he entered the hacienda. From what I heard, Bush had been the driving force behind diving in Mexico for nearly two decades. He founded an organization called the *Club de Exploraciones y Deportes Acuáticos de Mexico* (literally, the Club of Water Explorations and Sports of Mexico). It was this organization, CEDAM, that teamed up with the National Geographic Society in 1960 and, according to Bush, was sponsoring our current expedition.

Mexicans referred to him as Don Pablo, using a title now usually reserved for somewhat elderly persons of importance. At sixty-two he still looked fairly athletic and he was saying that he was eager to start diving in the well himself. As he stood on the back veranda of the hacienda chatting with other expedition members, Bush looked like a Spanish grandee entertaining in a castle.

Scott's pep talk brought us back to reality. We had a monumental amount of work to accomplish in the next few days if we were going to begin operations in a week. Scott said he was confident we could do it. Our days would start with breakfast at the hacienda at seven-thirty or eight, followed by a daily eight-thirty meeting at the site. Lunch would be brought to the campsite and work would end at five-thirty. Dinner would be at the hacienda. We would be working six days a week, but this did not rule out the possibility of work on Sunday in an emergency.

"Once things get going in an orderly fashion and we start making some progress, I think we can get by with working a half day on Saturdays," Scott said near the end of his talk.

"One last point," he continued. "If anything should happen to me, the man in charge is my brother, Captain Sam Scott." Eyes shifted in Sam's direction. "In the absence of both of us, Harold Martin is the man in charge." Everyone glanced at Harold. "In the absence of all three of us, Bill McGehee is in charge." Everyone looked at Bill. "If none of us are around, Jerry Kemler is in charge." Everyone looked at Jerry. "I don't know *what* you'll do if something happened to all five of us."

The laugh that followed ended the talk and left us in good spirits for dinner. The hacienda obviously made a good profit from serving so many additional guests, but the staff apparently disliked the extra effort. Still, after eating on the road for two weeks, we were pleased to be in something of a homelike atmosphere. In fact, the hacienda had been the home of Edward Thompson, the American who had proved that the sacred well actually was a depository of Mayan treasure. It appeared that the staff had tried to Americanize its Mayan cuisine as much as possible, and at the time I deplored the effort, thinking that I would have preferred unadulterated local dishes. Later, however, I was grateful for their efforts. Yucatecan food is revered throughout Mexico, but it is not among my favorites. Something about fish wrapped in paper definitely puts me off.

Scott sat at a table with Inman and two other water experts from the Purex Corporation who had joined us in Chichén. There was also a representative from Ford at the table, and for the benefit of all of them Scott again went over his plan to explore the well.

Basically, there were two plans. He would first try to drain the well dry so archaeologists could work the bottom as a land excavation. If drainage proved impossible or too costly, he would clarify the water so the bottom could be excavated by teams of archaeologists and professional SCUBA divers. The first plan seemed preferable if the bottom could be completely dried. If not, the prospect of working in waist-deep slime was hardly any better than working under water.

Expedition members install the filter manifold.
Norman Scott at the far left.

Scott had brought to Chichén two centrifugal pumps, each capable of pumping more than two hundred thousand gallons an hour. Like most of our other equipment, these had been supplied by American-based corporations. The pumps came from the Pacific Pump Company of Oakland, California, and Ford provided the industrial engines to run them. Pumping the well was a theoretically simple undertaking, but made complex by a larger number of unknowns. First of all, the pump capacity referred to the ability to move water in a horizontal direction. We would have to move it seventy feet in a vertical direction, nearly straight up, from the surface of the water to the ledge around the well. From there, the water would have to be pumped away from the well. We felt sure the pumps could handle the job, but no one was willing to speculate on the actual rate at which they could discharge water from the well. The rate was crucial because some of the discharged water would undoubtedly seep back through the porous limestone into the well. The task of the pumps would be to pump water out faster than it seeped back. But if the rate of discharge were only slightly faster than intrusion, it might not be worth our while to continue pumping operations. Scott said the best he could realistically hope for would be to pump one hundred thousand gallons an hour. At that rate we could drain the well in about three and one half days. As the discharge rate declined, the drainage time would increase. Scott said he could easily afford to spend a week or even two at drainage but that beyond that length of time it would become too costly to continue with plan A.

Plan B was even more complicated. If Scott chose it, he would use one of the pumps to bring water to the filtration system which was being installed and handled by Inman and the other personnel from Purex's CHD Pool Division. To the ancient Maya (or even to some of the more sentimental archaeologists) it seemed like sacrilege to talk of treating the sacred well like a swimming pool. In fact, however, that is precisely how we would treat it. The job here, naturally, would be more complex because a swimming pool is a closed and easily controlled body of water while the well was subject to the forces of nature, including underground

35

water sources about which we knew very little. Size was another big difference. The well probably held more than eight million gallons. To illustrate the immensity of the unknowns, let me point out that we were not even sure of the exact amount of water in the well. It was impossible to render this in precise numbers because no one knew the exact shape of the bottom. It obviously sloped downward like a cone from the sides, making the middle the deepest part, but the degree of slope was unknown. So was the amount of water displaced by debris and mud. In other words, the educated guess of 8.5 million gallons might be off a million in either direction. The margin of error was important in plan A because it could affect the length of time required for drainage. It was less critical in plan B although it could still frustrate Purex engineers in determining the amount of chemicals to introduce for clarification.

Inman, with the benefit of having seen the well for the first time, outlined his end of the operation once more for Scott and the others. He liked the site of the ledge near the old winch for the filtration system. Once the concrete slab was poured, he could install four filtration tanks, each with a two-hundred-square-foot grid permeated with diatomaceous earth. One of the pumps would bring water from the well and send it through the four tanks where the diatomaceous earth could absorb impurities. Meanwhile, Inman said, he planned to introduce chlorine into the well to kill all forms of life, especially algae. If needed, he would also put a flocculant in the well that would cause particles to precipitate and fall to the bottom. Flocculation was reserved as a last-resort technique, however, since it would require leaving the well completely undisturbed for several days.

From beginning to end, Scott would have to make a choice between the two plans. It would be impossible to proceed with both of them simultaneously because the pumps would have to be used either for drainage or for bringing the water to the filtration unit. Once the water was filtered, or course, it would splash back into the well.

Inman was preoccupied with the possibility that the filtration tanks had been damaged en route. They were among the last

The pumps had to move the well water nearly straight up through these hoses to the terrain above.

pieces of equipment unloaded, and it had gotten dark before he had a chance to check them over. He wanted to install them immediately even though drainage would be attempted first.

Scott had knocked on a lot of doors before he found a company willing to undertake an operation as vast as purifying the water of the sacred well. Several executives laughed at him outright. Charles Wade, the head of the CHD Division, however, is an adventuresome type. He saw the promotion potential for Purex and studied the problem carefully. Then on Inman's advice, Wade decided to take a gamble. Wade's only price was that we take his eighteen-year-old-son, Fred, on the expedition. The boy was an enthusiastic amateur diver so Scott signed him on as a diver tender, a position which meant he would assist divers.

The only other debt that Scott paid in this way was to Adolph Kiefer, who said his son Jack wanted to go on the expedition. Scott had never seen Jack until the young man arrived by plane on September 5 in Pompano Beach, Florida, ready to start the journey to Mexico. His father had been instrumental in helping Scott get some of the industrial participation needed to conduct the expedition. Sportsmen will recognize Adolph Kiefer's name, since he is one of the greatest swimmers the United States has produced. He was a gold medal winner in the 1936 Olympics.

Jack had been on the Yale swimming team and had supposedly done some SCUBA diving. He was handicapped at the beginning by knowing no one on the expedition. His hair was wild and long, and he rarely spoke to anyone. Naturally Jack became a puzzle to many of the other expedition members.

"Do you know who he is?" one of the divers had asked one day on the trip.

"I hear his father's somebody important," another answered.

"Well, I'm sure he's not an important barber."

Now at the hacienda we were all getting to know one another a little better. Scott finished eating and went back out on the veranda. Some of us were already out there, and others came when they finished dinner. Members of Scott's organization, Expeditions Unlimited, numbered about two dozen, and there were seven others from Ford, Purex and Wilding, Inc., the latter being the film studio that was making a motion picture of the expedition. We were all so exhausted that the socializing was cut short to give us time for plenty of sleep before rising at about seven the next morning.

Rain had resumed again in that steady pattern that often means it will not stop for many hours. We had the prospect of working again in six inches of mud. The wind was also high, evidently from the tail end of Hurricane Beulah which we had encountered two days before in Mérida.

The big storm had taken a path almost identical to that of a hurricane in 1465, the worst in Maya history. Old people who had lived through it told the Spaniards about the hurricane so the accounts that have come down to us are probably fairly accurate. On that winter day in 1465 a tidal wave heaved water onto the island of Cozumel on the east coast of the Yucatán Peninsula and winds brought foam from the sea onto the land and toppled the thatched huts. Weaker parts of temples and buildings fell from the impact of the wind or were quickly undermined by the torrents of water. The hurricane bent inland after striking Cozumel, leveling houses and buildings, felling trees and driving animals from their homes in the jungle. Tulum, the temple city on the coast, was hit, then Cobá, and trees were picked up by the wind and thrown over the road that led from that city to Yaxuná, further inland. Chichén Itzá was among the next to feel the winds, which, according to legend, must have hit more than a hundred and fifty miles an hour. From Chichén the storm moved westward toward Mayapán, T'ho and Dzibilchaltún and finally southward to Kabah and Uxmal. The storm disappeared in the Gulf of Mexico after leaving much of Mayab in desolation. At least one archaeologist believes the great storm of 1465 contributed to the abandonment of Uxmal and the further decline of the Mayan civilization. The ancient Maya was certainly no stranger to hurricanes although this storm, coming in the winter, probably caught him by surprise. Hurricanes after the first of October are rare in the Caribbean area, and the chances are astronomical against a hurricane coming in December. Whether the storm of 1465 had the immense effect that some believe, it did obviously hinder the stability of an area already facing social and economical upheavals.

Hurricane Beulah also came into the peninsula at Cozumel, again felling trees and damaging nearly every building on the island. But as it moved inland, Beulah veered northward and lost some of its power. By the time winds reached us at Mérida, which was built on the ancient site of T'ho, they were no more than seventy-five miles an hour. Among other buildings on Cozumel, Don Pablo Bush's home had been wrecked by Beulah. Bush excused himself early, explaining he would have to fly home as soon as possible to survey damage and begin repairs. We felt doubly bad about Don Pablo's loss because he had told Scott several weeks earlier that members of the expedition were welcome to use the house on weekends.

Hoping that the rain and wind would stop by morning, we headed back to the mud flat that was presently our home.

Scott conducted the meeting in the morning in a light drizzle, and the session set the pattern for the future morning meetings. Scott introduced newcomers and then read off the list of assignments. Our staff archaeologist, Willie Folan, translated Scott's instructions to the local work force into Spanish. Then the local foreman, Avelino, translated the Spanish into Maya, a soft language full of glottal stops and "sh" sounds. All the laborers understood Spanish, but by translating the orders into Maya, Avelino left no doubt in their minds that the orders were coming from him.

"Willie, make sure the Mayas keep spreading gravel on this mud," Scott said. "Later on, we'll need some to help with the unloading, but co-ordinate that with Billy McGoo."

Everyone, including the workers, laughed. At first I thought the workers had laughed at "Billy McGoo," as we had, but later I realized that they were chuckling over something else Scott had said. He had called them Mayas, a term they would never apply to themselves. They called themselves *yucatecos* and others called them *indios*, Spanish for Indians. The workers were not only unoffended by Scott's term, but seemed almost to appreciate it. For lack of a better word, we all began calling them Mayas.

40

"... the local foreman, Avelino,
translated the Spanish into Maya. ..."

"I'm glad he didn't call them Mexicans," Folan said to me later. "Scotty would have seen twenty men walk off the job."

Folan was right. South of the border "Mexico" refers only to the state Mexico, its environs or the capital city. Outside the country, of course, all citizens are known as Mexicans in the same way all Americans are called Yankees outside the United States, but only Northerners are called Yanks inside the country. The distinction is especially important in the case of Yucatán because of the great political hostility between Yucatán and the rest of the nation. Even as our expedition was in progress, there was a serious suggestion by a Yucatecan politician for Yucatán to secede from Mexico. The source of hostility is complex but Yucatecans generally feel their state has received a long series of raw deals from the power structure in Mexico.

Slowly, as we worked through the rainy morning, some progress could be seen.

While the gravel was being spread, four Mayas were assigned to Bill McGehee to help with unloading, a task that seemed almost endless. Many of the local laborers had never seen equipment like ours before, and they often interrupted the spreading of gravel to watch it come out of the trucks. MeGehee also began setting up the locker to house the diving gear.

One of our two crane operators, Al Datz, worked at stabilizing the crane. This was quite a job because of the uneven terrain and its muddy surface. The crane, however, had four large podlike legs that could be lowered or raised hydraulically to balance the crane on rough ground. Sam Scott and his son helped with this delicate job of positioning a thirty-five-ton piece of machinery. It was Sam, by the way, who has first introduced his brother Norman to Kirk Johnson, who owned the airline on which Sam was a captain.

Once the crane was in position and once the Styrofoam was unloaded, Beasom Painter was put in charge of lowering the large pieces of plastic foam into the well. He was assisted by Norman's nephew, Austin. Once the Styrofoam was in the well, the plan was to connect the chunks so they would support a wooden raft. This raft would be the operation area for work directly in the well. One of the pumps would rest on it and divers would work from it.

The rain let up slightly by late morning, but rain itself was not the big problem. It was the viscous layer of mud that hindered us at every step. We could not really walk but only slosh around in the pudding-like earth. Some of the equipment seemed to slide into place, but most of it had to be lifted, carried and set down. The work would have been nearly routine, but now our legs were slipping out from under us. Some of us were so covered with mud that we wished it would begin raining hard once more just so we could rinse off.

Only the Maya laborers did not seem to mind the absurd

working conditions. I cannot explain what motivated them to work as hard as they did. Members of the expedition had their ambition fired by the hope that their efforts would lead to learning the secrets of the sacred well, but the Mayas were hardly interested in that. As a matter of fact, they were probably frightened by the idea of learning whatever secrets the well was hiding. Possibly they were working hard to keep their minds off the excavations that would follow. On the surface they were cheerful, but their frequent wary glances into the well gave them away. They were scared. But with one eye on the foreman and the other toward Chac, they put on a display of the same kind of diligence needed centuries ago to build the massive temples of another empire.

One of the youngest laborers, a boy who could not have been more than seventeen or eighteen years old, was helping unload plastic bags of soda ash that weighed nearly as much as he did. Another Maya lifted the bags down to the boy from the truck. The man on the truck teased him a couple of times by pretending to throw the bag down at him.

Then I saw the man on the truck slip and drop one of the bags on the truck railing. He scrambled to his feet and caught the bag before it fell overboard. But he was not fast enough to stop the soda ash from spurting out of a hole ripped in the bag when it hit the railing. At first the boy below thought the older man was again teasing him. When he looked up, the boy got a waterfall of soda ash in his face.

He spun around as though he had been shot and tried to shake the burning chemical from his head. It was probably all he could do not to scream out because the soda ash, which is similar to lye, was setting his eyes on fire. A couple of expedition members saw the accident and rushed over to help. An older Maya worker, however, had also seen the accident. As the boy approached the panic stage, the older man calmly reached for a canteen and took a big mouthful of water. He ran to the boy, pulled the latter's hands from his face and spit the water into the boy's eyes. The boy did not know what was happening. He blinked and shook his head. Then the old

43

man looked around for a clean piece of cloth. Seeing nothing at hand, he shoved his silky black hair into the lad's face.

The boy stood there for a minute, his hands at his sides. Then he raised one hand to wipe his forehead. His eyes were apparently no longer burning, and he thanked the old man for his quick help. In effect, the man washed the boy's eyes out and then put something in them to cause the eyes to tear; unorthodox though the technique was, it worked. Within ten minutes the boy was back on the job.

Not long afterward I learned that in pre-conquest times Maya parents sometimes punished their children by rubbing hot peppers in their eyes. The punishment must have been effective, but I wondered if the children might not have had their own remedy —like getting a playmate to spit in their eyes and rub them out with their hair.

The boy continued to work and was chuckling about the accident by time for lunch. And by then nearly all the chemicals were unloaded. This meant that high priority would be given to building a shed to keep the chemicals dry. Some, unlike the soda ash, were not in plastic containers.

Lunch was nearly intolerable. Only a pathologist could come up with an adequate description of the sandwiches prepared at the hacienda. The bread was soggy and in some cases muddy. A five-gallon container of tea had also been delivered to us, but its contents did not taste as good as the tea which some of the Mayas had brewed earlier. It was not an exotic flavor, but it was spicier than any other tea I had drunk. I made a mental note to ask them later what kind of tea it was.

While I was trying to eat, I could not help remembering an obnoxious German tourist whom I had run into at the bar in the Hotel Mérida several days ago. He had asked where our expedition was going, and I told him.

"Zat is ridiculous. How you make expedition to Chichén Itzá? You can go zere by road. Vat kind expedition is zat?"

I tried to explain that we were not looking for pyramids or the lost tombs of Mayan kings, but the explanation did not seem to register with him.

"Two years ago I went on expedition to Guatemala. Vee had to travel two days by mule. Now zat vas an expedition!"

I bet that mule would have choked to death on the sandwich I was trying to eat. But as I thought over the incident, I realized that many people do have a few wrong notions about archaeological expeditions. (And just when they find out a little about expeditions, Norman Scott changes the rules.) A streamlined, commercial expedition like ours was hardly what the German thought an expedition should be. On the other hand—and I had tried to explain this to the man—any other type of expedition was not likely to succeed as far as the sacred well was concerned.

The history of those who have tried to excavate the Mayan treasure that lay at the bottom of the well is the history of misinformation, failure and outright bungling.

One goes back to the sixteenth century to meet the man who first introduced the outside world to the well of sacrifice. He is Bishop Diego de Landa, the Catholic prelate responsible for giving the world more first-hand knowledge of the ancient Maya than any other man. Unfortunately, De Landa is also responsible for burning the Mayas' holy books as well as for promulgating lies about them. It is easy to forgive a Spanish priest for seeing Christian "evil" in the Mayas' barbaric rites. It is somewhat less understandable why he called the Mayas "tall of stature." In fact, the bishop could not have seen a shorter race of people in his life. Since he was writing for the Spanish court, maybe De Landa wanted the king to believe the savages whom the colonists were fighting were huge. If they had been, it would have helped to explain the many defeats that Spanish conquerors suffered at the hands of Maya warriors.

Spain first learned of the sacred well through the quaint writings of the bishop. He described some of the temples as "theaters" and called the sacbe a "handsome roadway." In nearly the same stroke of his quill De Landa casually mentioned that if Yucatán contained any gold at all, it would be found in the bottom of the cenote. That statement ordinarily would have sent conquistadors marching to Chichén in droves. But in fact they marched

right past it on the way to the already proven treasure of Moctezuma II.

About the only thing the conquerors did for the well was
to give it a name in Spanish. The Mayan word for sinkhole is
dzonot, which the Spanish pronounced "cenote." The well of
sacrifice became known as the *cenote sagrado de Chichén Itzá,*
"the sacred well of Chichén Itzá."

Many historians are willing to forgive De Landa for his
prejudices and inaccuracies. After all, his writings are still the
largest source of information we have from anyone who lived
with the Mayas so soon after the arrival of the Spanish. It is
also important to remember the circumstances in which his manu-
scripts were written. He was in Spain at the time, waiting to
be tried on charges of exceeding authority, and hoping that his
writings would help his defense. It is understandable that he
might portray the Mayas as large people, and emphasize their
devotion to paganism. The bishop, meanwhile, had devoted his
life to stamping out that paganism.

It is by what De Landa omitted that we surmise that the
Spaniards neglected the well. He records the distance from the
precipice to the water but not the depth of the water itself. That
indicates the Spanish probably dropped a rope, and possibly a
man, over the side but did not bother to explore the water. The
bishop recorded its width only as "more than 100 feet."

The information which De Landa has provided historians was
not known to exist before 1883 when his manuscript was discovered in the archives of Madrid. But even before its discovery
there had been mounting interest in the strange inhabitants of
Mayab. In 1785 a Spanish commission conducted the first archaeological expedition to the territory and succeeded in destroying
many ruins at Palenque by its crude techniques. Soon afterward,
Count Jean Frédéric Waldeck duped European scholars into be-
lieving the ancient Mayas had depicted elephants and liberty caps
in their sculpture. In England, Lord Kingsborough spent thousands of pounds in more than two decades trying to prove that the
Mayas were descended from the last tribes of Israel. Despite

his bias, Kingsborough compiled a large quantity of valuable information.

While Kingsborough was still working on his immense nine-volume *Antiquities of Mexico,* an American attorney, John Lloyd Stephens, and an English artist, Frederick Catherwood, were planning a trip to Yucatán and Central America. This journey and a later one resulted in two illustrated books by the men. Their writings and drawings were the first unbiased and objective accounts of the Mayas. The appearance of *Incidents of Travel in Central America, Chiapas and Yucatan* caused quite a stir in 1841, and two years later their *Incidents of Travel in Yucatan* rekindled interest in Chichén Itzá and ultimately in its sacred cenote.

> At four o'clock we left Pisté, and very soon we saw rising high above the plain the Castillo of Chichén. In half an hour we were among the ruins of this ancient city, with all the great buildings in full view, casting prodigious shadows over the plain, and presenting a spectacle which, even after all that we had seen, once more excited in us emotions of wonder. The camino real ran through the midst of them, and the field was so open that, without dismounting, we rode close in to some of the principal edifices. Involuntarily we lingered, but night was approaching, and, fairly dragging ourselves away, we rode on, and in a few minutes reached the hacienda.

That was Stephens' account of his arrival in Chichén Itzá on March 11, 1841. It parallels our arrival on September 19, 1967, so much that I felt as though we were repeating history. Stephens and Catherwood even stayed in the same hacienda in which members of our expedition ate two meals a day.

Their two books excited scholars in Europe as much as in the United States. In 1882 the French antiquarian, Désiré Charnay made the first known attempt to excavate the well of sacrifice. He failed largely because the dredging device he used closed as soon as it touched the bottom of the well, thus preventing the dredge from getting beneath the debris. Charnay was far from a failure, however, and he is credited with discoveries nearly a thousand miles away that led to solving many mysteries of Chichén Itzá. Our expedition discovered only a few days later just how important Charnay's studies were.

As our caravan drove into the area of restored buildings the day before, we had passed something like a gatehouse in which soldiers who guard the ruins are quartered. On the east side of this cottage lies a heap of rusted equipment. Few persons ever notice it and even fewer are aware of what the equipment is. It is the dredge and winch used to excavate the sacred well from 1904 to 1911. The man who used it was Edward Thompson, then the American consul at Mérida.

Thompson fell in love with Mayab and especially with Chichén Itzá. He made up his mind to excavate the well of sacrifice and wound up buying the hacienda and many acres around it, including the land on which the well is located. Thompson apparently was the first man who thought about draining the well. He studied the possibility of using windmill pumps but soon rejected it on grounds of expense. Instead he bought one of the most modern dredging devices of the day, known as an orange peel dredge, with a capacity of two and a half cubic feet. He let it out over the water on a pulley, then dropped it with the blades open. The heavy device fell through much of the debris, and when Thompson closed the blades, the bucket occasionally picked up mud rich in sacrificed artifacts. At first he hoisted the bucket to the top of the well, but since it took up to forty-five minutes for a round trip, he decided to work from a boat in the well itself, dumping his tailings in the water on the west side of the well. Thompson probably could have continued his excavations for a lifetime except that he made one crucial mistake. He exported the finds to the United States. (Some of them are still on display at Harvard University's Peabody Museum.) This so infuriated Mexican officials that the government declared it illegal to export pre-Columbian art. Mexico tried to make the new law retroactive in order to get back what Thompson had taken from the well. Litigation lasted for decades, and in the end Thompson lost his property at Chichén but won the right to keep the artifacts in

48

the United States. (In 1957 Peabody returned a good part of Thompson's artifacts to Mexico.)

Thompson's finds were impressive, especially the gold discs which depict the ritual of sacrifice, but what impressed archaeologists even more was his statement that he had recovered only a small percentage of the treasure that lay at the bottom of the well. Several Mexican archaeologists made proposals for excavating the well in the 1920s and 30s, and in 1954 a Mexican engineer, Edgar Espejo Evie, suggested that the well could be pumped dry or, alternatively, the water in it could be clarified. This was the first such proposal on record. Five years later the National Geographic Society teamed up with Don Pablo's organization, CEDAM, to conduct excavations under the direction of Mexico's National Institute of Anthropology and History. Bush wanted to work the well as an underwater excavation, using airlifts. On the recommendation of Edwin Link, who invented the Link Trainer, but who has more recently been connected with underwater innovations, Norman Scott was chosen for the job of running the airlifts. The expedition started in late 1960 and ended with ill feelings in early 1961. The working relationship between CEDAM and the National Geographic Society had deteriorated, and the National Institute claimed that airlifts were damaging the artifacts.

It was somewhat miraculous that Scott convinced the institute to authorize another expedition, but Don Pablo used his influence. Bush was a close friend of the institute's late director, Dr. Eusebio Dávalos Hurtado. Even more persuasive may have been the knowledge that despite two expeditions, there was still an estimated 80 per cent of the treasure left untouched. Moreover, Scott wanted to use an essentially Mexican plan, a variation of the one suggested by Espejo.

So here we were, drenched with rain and covered with mud, working with nearly two dozen superstitious laborers whose language we could not even speak. As I finished lunch, I wondered just what our chances were after so many others had failed.

If other expedition members had any doubts, they did not show them. It might even have been the desire to see some progress in the operation rather than the quality of sandwiches that caused expedition members to cut short their lunch hour. By now the rain would stop for a few minutes and then start again. We had got so accustomed to working in the rain that it was conspicuous by its absence. As work continued through the soggy afternoon, more progress did become apparent. The raft was being assembled in the water, concrete was being poured for the filtration tanks and for the personnel lift, sheds were being constructed at the main site and the unloading was nearing completion.

Gordon Inman was busy inspecting the last of the four filtration tanks. Luckily, all four were undamaged. On the other side of the campsite Dori Dowd and Ann Campbell were starting on the paper work that had accumulated for nearly three weeks. Jerry Kemler was making plans to hook up an "umbilical cord" that could carry electricity from the generator to the raft. Archaeologists, both Mexican and American, were conferring near the edge of the well. Operating the crane, Howard Williams worked without a pause as the big machine pulled up stumps, hauled rock, lifted personnel onto the growing raft and moved the tons of equipment to the floating platform in the middle of the smelly green water.

When I went for another glass of tea at midafternoon, I could see that things were definitely taking shape and progress was being made.

"How about a glass of tea?" I asked Scott as he passed by.

"What the hell are you drinking?" he said. "That's not our tea. That stuff belongs to the Mayas. We've got ours over there in that big can."

When I asked him what the difference was, Scott hesitated to explain. But when he finally did, I discovered that I had been gulping down tea made from the putrid, bacteria-laden water of the sacred well.

3

I RECOVERED from dysentery two days later, just in time to watch the permanent structures of the campsite being completed. Dori, who had dropped some medicine by my room at the hacienda, said Scott hoped to begin pumping operations tomorrow. That would be two days ahead of what he had originally expected.

I had noticed from the room that the weather was changing outside. There was no longer a steady downpour, but the constant rain was replaced with showers several times a day. Between the showers the sun came out, resulting in a blanket of steam that permeated the jungle, the houses and even the pores of our bodies. The fringes of Hurricane Beulah had long since disappeared to the west, and the air around us was motionless. Don Pablo had flown to Cozumel and begun repairs on his home. The newspaper from Mérida said Beulah, which everyone thought had spent her energy over the Yucatán mainland, picked up new strength in the Gulf and was currently slamming into Texas. Later I felt rotten when I learned that my uncle's house in southern Texas had been destroyed by the same hurricane which I had escaped.

We had arrived on Tuesday, and it was now Friday morning. I decided to eat a light breakfast and then go to the well by truck with the other expedition members after eating. When I got to the table, I did not feel as hungry as I thought. As I recall, breakfast consisted of a glass of water and a piece of gum. I left the table early so I would not have to watch the others gobble up food like *huevos rancheros,* eggs with a tomato and onion sauce on top. Finally we were ready to leave. Scott rode in the stake truck with Miguel González, a man from Mérida whom we had hired primarily to handle the purchasing of supplies that we would be buying locally, either in Mérida, the nearby port of Progresso or the major town east of us, Valladolid. The rest of us rode in the green pickup truck. The ride was not too bad on the highway but when we turned off onto the bumpy road that led around the ruins, I felt as though I were being homogenized. The problem was that Austin, Scott's nephew, was driving. Austin is probably a very good driver, actually, but he likes speed, regardless of the road he is driving on. The truck flew into the air with each bump and then slammed back on the ground, the wheels spinning in the mud and charging on to the next bump. Others thought it was all great fun or at least a never-fail method of waking up. Being out of bed for the first time in two days, I had a different attitude.

I eased myself out of the truck when we arrived at camp and staggered slowly to a spot in front of the office-Cortez where Scott was preparing to hold the morning meeting. It was a long meeting. Detailed instructions were given to the Mayas, first in English, then Spanish and then in what sounded like a mixture of grunts and "shs." Scott did not speak Spanish well, but he had a knack of making himself understood when talking to Miguel.

"Miguel. *Usted Mérida hoy. Compra partes para bomba. Diga en teléfono mí cuando sabe precios. Comprende?"* Scott said.

Miguel bore a pained expression as Scott was talking, but he understood perfectly what the expedition leader wanted. To the Yucatecan, Scott sounded something like this: "Michael. You

Detailed instructions were given to the Mayas, first, in English, then in Spanish and finally in Maya.

Mérida today. Buys parts for pump. Say in telephone me when you know prices." The grammar was terrifying, but there was a certain beauty in his succinctness.

After the meeting Scott told me why he was redoubling efforts to begin pumping by tomorrow. He said there was a slim chance that we would be able to pump and filter at the same time. If we could, plans A and B could go into effect simultaneously, meaning a substantial saving in time and energy. Expedition leaders had assumed that the pump, which had been lowered to the raft yesterday afternoon, would not be able to discharge water from the cenote without the help of a topside booster pump. But if the booster pump were not needed for that purpose, it could be used to run water through the filters. The cenote would then get shallower and clearer at the same time. The advantage would be that if we had to discontinue pumping, the water remaining in the well would be clear; but if we had to wait until pumping stopped in order to begin filtering, many days' work would be lost, the exact number depending on how long it would take to clarify the water. We could waste half a month if, after two weeks, we decided drainage was not feasible, since it might take us another two weeks to clarify the water. Scott said he hoped to give the pump on the raft a test run tomorrow. He knew it was capable of moving water up the seventy-foot precipice, but no one knew whether the water would have enough force behind it at the top to be pushed away from the campsite.

While Scott went below to oversee work on connecting a manifold to the pump on the raft, I surveyed the work accomplished in the last two days.

A fueling area had been set up at the end of the sacbe, and immediately beyond it was a shed where chemicals were stored along with spare hoses, buckets and shovels. The hoses were the same type of heavy fabric firehoses which fireman use to get water from hydrants to a blaze. Scott thought they would be ideal for our purpose; rigid pipe would have been difficult to connect down a seventy-foot precipice to the pump on the raft, especially if we ever had to move the raft.

Maya workers had built the chemical shed and two other sheds

54

Maya workers built the sheds with timber from the lean trees around the campsite.

in less than two days, using timber from the lean trees around the campsite. To cut the trees they used *coas*, a tool that looked like a machete with a savage hook on the end. It was the same tool they used in the fields to cut sisal, the principal crop of Yucatán. The workers wielded their coas as subtly as my grandmother would use a crochet hook, but the strength they put behind each swing was so great that branches up to four inches in diameter snapped with a single blow. The trick to building the sheds so quickly was finding branches with forks at just the right places. These forks, at a uniform height, held the crossbeams, which were lashed on with vines. When the vines dried, they contracted and the construction was made firm.

Meanwhile work continued on what most of us called the "Styrofoam raft." Actually it was a wooden raft with chunks of Styrofoam holding it up. If plan A were successful, the raft might wind up resting in mud at the bottom of the well. If not, it would become the heart of operations under plan B. The raft was designed to support not only diving operations but screening as well. If plan B were employed, airlifts would vacuum the bottom of the well and disgorge mud and silt onto screening tables on the raft. Although it had nearly a thousand square feet of deck space, we were still working in close quarters on the raft. One problem that had to be solved was how to prevent the water from the screening tables from getting to the machinery on the raft. Scott and Harold Martin figured they would try to build troughs that would channel the water over the side of the raft. Right now, the screening tables were being set up and the manifold was being connected to the pump. Later, construction would begin on a diving locker.

Topside, workers were pouring another slab of concrete for the H-frame that would hold the fire hoses at the top of the precipice directly in front of the filtration site. The H-frame was in effect a cradle for the topside manifold that channeled the four fire hoses from the raft back into one eight-inch aluminum pipe. At the east side of the campsite there was an A-frame that would support a personnel lift to enable expedition members to go from the camp to the raft without having to rely on the crane.

Scott was already trying to curtail the number of trips to the raft in order to free the crane for other duties. Banking on the crane for transportation was hardly the safest thing to do since the crane operator was unable to see his payload after it disappeared over the ledge. This meant that another expedition member, Beasom Painter, had to stand on the precipice, follow the load and give signals to Howard Williams, the crane operator. A mistake in signals or even a slight error in judgment could mean the basket could miss the raft and land in the water. Beasom used the largest of the remaining stone structures around the well as a vantage point; apparently this had been a ritual steam bath.

In the midst of the work going on around them, the archaeologists looked as though they were waiting for something to happen. It was obviously frustrating for them not to know if they were going to work in a land or underwater excavation. Victor Segovia perched close to Beasom and took notes. His superior from the Mexican National Institute, Dr. Román Piña Chan, took the opportunity to take a close look at the remains of structures around the well. These had never been studied, and the steam bath was the only structure with a known function. This was surmised from the round opening in the top similar to others found on ancient baths throughout Mexico. Just how the bath fit into the ritual of the well, however, remained a mystery. To the right of that structure was a platform that extended several feet over the precipice. It has commonly been referred to as an altar although no evidence exists to prove that the platform actually served that purpose. We had been walking casually over the platform, now covered with grass, until Willie Folan cautioned us. Other buildings around the cenote had crumbled, and he guessed it was only a matter of time before the platform would be undermined and fall into the well. Buildings around the cenote are especially susceptible to undermining because, like all other sinkholes, the sacred well is expanding as its walls cave in; also, the south side of the well where the campsite was located is lower than surrounding land, causing an accumulation of water that hastens the destruction of buildings. Between the steam bath and the end of the sacbe was a mound of earth which supposedly covered the ruins of a structure long since destroyed by nature. Even on the other side of the well there was a mound that suggested the campsite section might not have been the only area of activity in ancient times. Piña Chan and Victor were eager to excavate the mounds if time permitted, and they used the current hiatus to make plans for this.

Archaeologists were not the only ones watching the campsite take shape. In fact the expedition was one of the biggest attractions in the area since a circus played at Pisté two years ago. The wives—

and occasionally the children—of laborers came to the site shortly after their husbands arrived in the mornings. Some huddled around the archaeologists' shed, which was adjacent to the chemical storage area. Others went to the far side of the cenote to get a panorama of the entire operation. The women would leave the site later in the morning and return at lunch with food for the men. Some even came back in the afternoon to complete the day's work as sidewalk foremen. They generally knew what we were doing but most of our activities must have been as mysterious to them as the well was to us.

The women left this afternoon as soon as the rain resumed. Still feeling weak, I did not hang around much longer. Scott stayed until the last minute before dinner and then returned that evening.

Saturday was the big day when pumping operations were to start. The engine had been run a few minutes on the previous day so there was no problem at the beginning. Fittings on the hoses had been checked several times and the topside manifold secured. The Mayas, meanwhile, had assembled several lengths of aluminum pipe for a discharge line that would empty the water in a shallow depression beyond the southwest side of the well.

By nine-thirty that morning the pump was sucking in the brown water of the cenote. When it came out of the pump, the manifold divided the water into the four hoses that flopped over the side of the raft. They ran for a few feet in the water and then began the long climb to the top, bypassing branches and ledges that jutted out along the route. The manifold on top took the water from the four hoses and directed it back into the one discharge pipe.

The two important questions were how much water were we actually pumping and how fast was the water level in the cenote declining. The two factors were not necessarily related. If the well were connected closely to the water table and if underground streams had easy access to the cenote, we could pump a million gallons an hour and still might not be able to drain the well. In the same way, if one dug a hole in the sand near a beach, he would almost have to dry up the ocean before he could drain the hole. Theoretically we might have to pump the entire peninsula dry in order to drain the well. An encouraging clue, however, was the stagnancy of the water. This meant that whatever water was feeding into the cenote underground was at least entering at a slow rate. But even if it were entering slowly at the moment, it might speed up as we decreased the pressure by pumping water out. A *dis*couraging factor was the constant level in the well. If the well were not affected by the water table, a big rain would raise the water level by several inches. Even after the current heavy rains, however, Folan and the other archaeologists could see no such increment.

"Well, all we can do is pump away and see what happens," Scott said.

Meanwhile, he alternately checked the outfall end of the discharge line, trying to get an idea of how much water we were

"The manifold divided the water into four hoses. . . ."
F. Kirk Johnson, Jr., on the left, with Scott.

pumping out, and the water level in the cenote, trying to determine how fast we could lower it. Since we had no pressure gauge, Scott had no sure way to tell how much water was being discharged. There was, however, a crude way to find out how much water was leaving the well: Scott had several stakes driven into the mud along the shallow edges of the water.

By midafternoon the water level had gone down nearly a foot according to the stake markers. The stakes had had little time to shift position so the measurement was probably accurate. As the water declined, a rim of mud began to be exposed at the westernmost edge. This was the area where years ago Thompson had

A workman cleans the first artifact that we found.

dumped the mud and silt he had gone through, and it was likely that in his many years of work a sizable deposit had built up under water. The archaeologists were very pleased that the water was going down so fast. They were convinced that Thompson had missed many artifacts in his excavations, and if the water continued to decline at a fast pace, they would have a chance to go through his tailings in about three days.

Scott, Folan and Segovia decided to take a look at the emerging area even though there was barely enough room to stand on it. They climbed into the metal cage which would eventually be used on the personnel lift but which was now being hoisted up and down by the crane. Beasom Painter directed the cage out over the water and then close to the craggy white cliff that forms the west side of the precipice. The cage snapped twigs and brushed against vines as it descended slowly toward the narrow spit of land. Scott waved his hand up to Beasom when the cage got to within three feet of the land. Beasom signaled to Howard Williams, and the cage stopped a couple of feet above the mud.

Segovia put one hand out and tried to hold on to the wall as he climbed down from the basket. His hand slipped and his legs plunged more than a foot into the mud. Scott reached out for the same wall and pushed the cage entrance toward the water. Then he jumped out into the shallow water.

When Folan climbed down, the three tried to walk around in the miniature swamp that the drainage was creating. But it proved nearly impossible to accomplish anything. If they walked in the mud, their legs sank beneath them, and if they walked in the water, they could not get close enough to the land to see what might be on it. Scott decided to wait until more water had been drained before considering excavating the land spit. As he waded through the water back to the cage, Scott tripped over a stone and fell face down in the water. He got up on his knees and then reached down to the stone he had fallen over. It was odd that a large stone would rest so far from the deep water. When his hand touched it, Scott noticed that the stone was carved. He called Segovia to help him lift it, and the two men managed to hoist it onto the floor of the cage.

The object was indeed carved although the design was unintelligible. But there the stone lay, covered with algae and dripping wet on the floor of the metal cage. It was hardly anything to get excited about, but it was the first artifact of an ancient culture that we had found. The find had taken place fast, only a few hours after actual operations had begun. Once the stone was dried off and some of the algae removed, the archaeologists could see more or less what it was. The stone did not contain a complete carving but was part of the kind of architectural ornament that often adorned buildings in certain sections of Yucatán and at Tula, a site about fifty miles north of Mexico City. Tula had been the capital of the Toltec people, and it was no coincidence that architecture there should be similar to that in Chichén Itzá.

We were all aware that for us to evaluate this and other future finds we must know much more about the people who inhabited the holy city of Chichén Itzá and about its mysterious conquerors from the west. Our archaeologists were always happy to instruct us on the history of Chichén, and later, with almost every find, we learned still more about the strange pattern of life in the city.

Chichén Itzá was undoubtedly an important northern city even during the classical period (A.D. 317 to 889) when Mayan civilization centered to the south. The earliest date glyphs found at Chichén correspond to the seventh century of the Christian era, and most archaeologists have assumed the city was founded a couple of centuries before then, about A.D. 450. Segovia thought the founding probably was closer to the year 0, basing his assumption on the belief that it would be difficult for a major city to spring forth in only two centuries. The building that later became the Temple of Kukulcán was begun during this early period and so was the Caracol.

Then suddenly, sometime between A.D. 900 and 1000 Chichén Itzá was invaded by peoples from the west. These were supposedly the Itzá or the Toltec or a combination of both. Archaeological evidence indicates there probably was more than one intrusion and that they were more or less peaceful. Regardless of the circumstances, the foreign influence in Chichén set it apart from other cities in Mayab.

Within the legends of the invasions is woven the story of the Feathered Serpent, Kukulcán. By the time Bishop Diego de Landa got the story, the Mayas themselves were probably confused about the order of events, and his writings on the subject reflect that confusion. Essentially, the bishop reported that Kukulcán reigned with the Itzá although he might not have come to Chichén with them. The Feathered Serpent was celibate, childless and a good statesman. We infer that these were rare qualities in Chichén during this time of invasion and turmoil. When Kukulcán left Chichén Itzá, he founded the city of Mayapán, which he refused to name after himself. On his return to Mexico, however, the Feathered Serpent stopped at what is now Champotón and erected a monument to himself several hundred feet off shore. (Archaeologists, by the way, believe they have found the remains of that monument.) There are many puzzling elements in De Landa's story, among them Kukulcán's reluctance to name a city after himself but his apparent eagerness to go to great effort to build a monument to his memory. According to the bishop, it seems that one group of conquerors invaded Chichén Itzá and were followed by a second group, which included the Feathered Serpent.

Historians have gained more knowledge of the mysterious invaders from sixteenth-century chronicles written in the Mayan language through the use of Roman characters. One chronicle presents a different order of events and says Chichén was a holy and peaceful city before the invaders spread vice, corruption and sickness.

There are various ways to bring the two histories into accord, one being to say that Kukulcán restored order after the Itzá destroyed it. That, however, does not take into account De Landa's statement that the Feathered Serpent founded Mayapán since in the other version the Itzá settled there. This would be the wrong sequence of events if the Itzá came first unless they somehow lingered around and settled there many years later. Also, there is good evidence that "Feathered Serpent" was a title given to certain rulers in Mexico, not necessarily the name of one man.

Legends of the Feathered Serpent abound throughout Meso-America. Some say he had a beard. If he had, he certainly would have stood out among others, who had little or no facial hair. Other legends predicted the return of the Feathered Serpent in a year corresponding to A.D. 1519. It is ironic that even if Quetzal-cóatl-Kukulcán never existed, the legendary man was responsible for possibly the single most important event in Mexican history.

In 1502 Maya traders had seen Columbus' ships from the island of Guanaja. The Indians, whose vessels were canoes that rarely exceeded forty feet in length, told the story of meeting bearded men who rode the seas in giant white ships. The story traveled along the coast until it reached the Aztecs, whose Toltec-influenced religion taught them about the second coming of the Feathered Serpent. Some legends said Quetzalcóatl had disappeared into the sea at Champotón; others said he was last seen at Veracruz. But if he returned, the Aztecs believed it would happen in one of the recurring years associated with the man-god's birth and disappearance. Several cyclical years had come and gone uneventfully. The last one corresponded to 1467 in the reign of Moctezuma I. The year would recur next in 1519.

In the spring of 1519 Hernán Cortés stepped ashore at Veracruz. The bearded leader and his party rode on animals never before seen in this hemisphere, toward the Aztec capital. They arrived in November. Thanks to the legend of Quetzalcóatl, Moctezuma II escorted Cortés across the causeways and made the Aztec noblemen kiss the ground on which he rode. The man who the noblemen thought was their savior was the conqueror.

Coincidentally, our expedition caravan had taken the same overland route from Mexico to Yucatán that many say Kukulcán traveled centuries before. From Mexico City we journeyed north through a mountain pass nearly ten thousand feet high, then down the lush slopes of the mountains to Veracruz, camping on the beach not far from where Cortés came ashore in 1519. We traveled on eastward along the coast, again across more mountains and finally to the vast swampland that forms much of the coast in the state of Tabasco. The twenty-one vehicles had to take three ferries before getting out of the swampland. Some legends say Kukulcán avoided this area by taking to the sea. If he did, our paths met again in Campeche. From there we pushed northeastward through a concrete arch that rises abruptly out of the jungle to mark the border between Campeche and Yucatán. It took us nearly a week to travel from Mexico to Yucatán in 1967. It must have taken Kukulcán years.

We had come to Chichén Itzá with a specific goal in mind; we had been lured here by the sacred well. But why would a Toltec king—if that is what Kukulcán was—pick Chichén Itzá? Why this particular city? After years of study, the great Maya scholar, J. Eric S. Thompson, concluded that the Feathered Serpent was ultimately attracted by one thing at Chichén, and that was the cult of sacrifice at the sacred well. If Thompson's conclusion is correct, the expedition had been lured to Chichén by the same cenote that had attracted Kukulcán.

Until recently the only connection between Chichén Itzá and the Toltec capital of Tollán was based on the legend of Quetzal-cóatl-Kukulcán. In fact, many archaeologists doubted the existence of Tollán even though the city had been mentioned by early chroniclers of the Aztecs. Scholars tended to discount observations made by Désiré Charnay about similarities between monuments he uncovered at Tula and those at Chichén Itzá. Admittedly it was not easy to envision several mounds of rubble at Tula as being anything more than the remains of a small and unimportant city. Sixty years after Charnay's explorations of 1880, a team of Mexican archaeologists became curious about the mounds at Tula and began excavating them. They were in for a surprise. Beneath the rubble lay the ruins of a magnificent city. But even more amazing was the discovery that a high percentage of what they found could just as easily have been found at Chichén Itzá. It almost seemed that the same architect had designed both cities. There were even statues of Chac Mool, the god of the sacred well, in a reclining position. Figures of the Feathered Serpent were found throughout the city. Charnay had failed completely in excavating the sacred well, but he predicted something that eluded scholars for decades: Tollán had indeed existed. It existed at

Tula, and at this site provided pellucid archaeological evidence linking the city of Quetzalcóatl with the hegira of Kukulcán to Chichén Itzá.

The stone that Scott tripped over in the water was an ornament that could be duplicated easily at Tula, and because it was found in an area that would soon be above water, Scott was determined to begin excavations on the mud bank. Segovia said that if the water continued to decline at this fast rate, there was no reason why preliminary work, such as clearing away the bush, could not start tomorrow.

Piña Chan had left the site but not before deciding with Victor on the archaeological techniques to be used. Ordinarily excavation of a site is a rigorously controlled undertaking from the standpoint of mapping and other field procedures. Archaeologists usually start with a scale map of the site and arbitrarily designate a datum point to serve as a geographical reference. The site is then marked off in quadrants so that, for example, an area in the site might be referred to as N3E4, meaning that quadrant which is three units north and four units east of the datum point. Mapping in this manner is known as making a grid. Archaeologists then select a spot away from the one they are to excavate to use as a control pit. By excavating the control pit, they can get a better idea of what is naturally found in the area and what is unique to the archaeological site. This method, efficient though it is in some undertakings, would be nearly useless in the cenote. Mapping a circle in quadrants would be possible, but the system would become complicated around the edges of the well. It would have been splendid if nature had given us a control pit in the form of another sinkhole of the same dimensions, but we were not this fortunate. Even though Chichén does have a smaller well nearby —once used as a source of drinking water but now functioning as a swimming hole—the idea of using it as a control was outlandish: it would be difficult enough to excavate the site itself without having to duplicate our efforts elsewhere. Piña and Victor decided to use a variation of the standard grid method. They selected the center of the well as a datum point, from which sixty radii were mapped. This gave us pie-shaped wedges three feet wide at the edge of the well. The wedges were then given numbers that would be used in cataloguing artifacts.

Overjoyed with the way pumping was going, all of us worked at top speed. Successful excavations seemed imminent. Scott talked with Segovia in the archaeologists' shed about the techniques he planned to use. In the well, expedition members set up more stakes to get comparative measurements of the water level. Inman and other Purex engineers began clearing off the filtration area which was nearly covered with tree limbs and other debris that had been hacked away as Mayas cleared the discharge area. Inman was annoyed at having to spend his time this way. He had intended to begin making a chemical analysis of the cenote water. Preliminary reports from the raft were inconclusive, but there was every reason to believe the water level was being lowered at a constant rate. Those of us on top could hear the water gushing into the bush behind the filtration area.

Then suddenly the well struck back at us. One minute we had been walking on drying mud, and the next we were walking on boiling rocks. Bubbles of water spurted through the porous limestone. Scott leaped to his feet, but like the rest of us he did not know what was happening. He yelled out in desperation for the pump to be cut off.

The command was too late. Just as the pump was being shut down, a wave of muddy water rolled down out of the bush behind the filtration area. Inman clutched one of the pipes leading to the first filter tank and hung on as the water bore down on him.

Then it ended as soon as it had begun. The big wave of water that had built up in the bush splashed violently on the muddy lower ledge and carried several inches of silt over the precipice. The men on the raft watched the water cascade down the cenote wall, splashing every few feet as it hit the protruding limestone shelves. On top, the ground continued to bubble several minutes after the wave passed. Inman, Bob Drake and Wayne Vanderlow wiped the water from their faces and stared blankly at the filtration equipment. The rushing water had left it littered again with tree limbs and debris.

67

Scott looked at Segovia and then turned toward Inman. The men called Folan over and then tried to figure out what had happened. The flood presumably resulted from the fact that the discharge area was too close to the cenote. At first it appeared that the discharge water was soaking easily into the ground. It was, but the ground could absorb only a limited amount of water. We were pumping thousands of gallons per hour. Inman figured that the new water caused pressure to build up within the porous rock. The water that had boiled up on the ground of the campsite area was not actually cenote water: engineers reasoned that the water in the ground had been there all along, undoubtedly augmented by the current rains. When pressure built up within the earth, this water was forced to the surface. The tiny holes in the rock were responsible for the boiling effect.

There was only one solution according to Scott. The discharge area had to be moved farther from camp. Even that, however, could not guarantee that we would not experience a repeat of the tidal wave. We might never be able to discharge water far enough to avoid pressure building up near the campsite. While Inman, Drake and Vanderlow began clearing off the filtration equipment once more, Scott hopped in the jeep-like Bronco. He and Folan took the road around the cenote to hunt for a deeper area in which to discharge water. A fifth of a mile southwest of the well they discovered a valley-like depression some two hundred feet across. Folan recognized it as another sinkhole that had dried up thousands of years ago.

Racing the approaching darkness, Maya laborers cut a path toward the old cenote while others laid twenty-foot sections of aluminum pipe. Axes, coas and machetes swinging, the workers cut the path faster than the others were able to lay pipe. In less than two hours, thirty-nine sections had been stretched from the filtration area to the beginning of a slope that led into the dried-up cenote. The pump was ordered restarted and the Purex engineers cautiously stepped away from the filter tanks. Scott told the Mayas the path could be widened on Monday. He was overwhelmed at how much they had done in such a short time this day.

Meanwhile Scott stomped through the wet bush to the end of

the new discharge line to check it for leaks at the joints and to estimate the amount of water coming out. There were virtually no leaks, but when Scott got to the end, he saw only a trickle of water pouring out of the last section of pipe. His hand went up to pull nervously on a stubble of a beard. It was the second setback in one day, a day that had begun with great hopes for success. From the trace of water, Scott realized that the one pump on the raft was not capable of pushing water from the cenote up the precipice and then nearly eight hundred feet into the bush as well. He would have to use a booster pump. That meant both loss of time and the unavailability of a spare pump in an emergency. But there was no other way. It was growing dark but it was still hot. Mosquitoes were thick in the air, and we felt miserable—physically and spiritually. After a day of furious work and many expectations, we found ourselves just about where we had been twenty-four hours earlier. We were tired and disappointed.

4

BY MONDAY members of the expedition were taking a more real-istic view of their situation. We could hardly justify disappoint-ment at not being able to crack the Mayas' time capsule in one week when it had remained largely unopened for more than fif-teen hundred years. The problems we were encountering were really minuscule compared with those faced by Charnay, Edward Thompson and even the National Geographic Society. Our suc-cess in pumping any water at all from the cenote was reason to cheer. We remembered Thompson's plan to use windmill pumps: it never would have worked, not with ten thousand windmills. Still we felt frustrated at not being able to accomplish more during the next two days while the booster pump was being connected.

Scott had spotted a likely place for the booster, if it were needed, soon after we had arrived the week before. That spot was directly behind the filtration area in a level section of the upper ledge. Since that area had already been cleared in making a path for the first short-lived discharge line, Scott decided to try op-erating the booster there; if something were wrong with the location, the pump could always be moved. The crane hoisted the pump over the filter tanks and onto the little clearing. Then another industrial engine was swung into position. Now expedition members worked at connecting the pump fittings and at hooking up the engine to the pump.

Meanwhile we continued to outfit the raft as a diving dock despite hopes that plan B might never go into effect. Working conditions on the raft were the worst in camp. The temperature soared close to 100 degrees and each day rain fell at least once. With no wind to clear the air in the cenote, workers were gasping

Now everything depended on the booster pump.

for breath as they would in a steam bath. Fumes from the engines made the situation nearly intolerable. I always thought of Harold Martin as being almost impervious to his surroundings, but even Harold began to feel the pressure of the tropics within the well. His body was regularly covered with sweat until the rain rinsed it off. Flies and mosquitoes bit into his back so often that he gave up trying to keep them away.

The work pace on the raft slowed down, but progress was still being made. Workers constructed a screen fence around the raft to keep artifacts from washing back into the well if they were missed at the screening tables. Folan had pointed out more than once that one of the big problems on the 1960 expedition was that the airlift discharge failed to hit the screening table. Airlifts were one of two devices that archaeologists and divers would use to gather artifacts from the mud. They could figuratively vacuum the mud by sucking it up through long hoses and then disgorging it onto the screening tables. The devices worked with air pressure while a similar apparatus known as a hydrolift did much the same thing by water pressure. We had both at our disposal. Expedition members were stacking the heavy hydrolift hoses in one corner of the raft near the fifty-horsepower hydrolift pump itself. Others filled two thirty-five-gallon gasoline tanks and lined up spare parts for a smaller thirty-five-horsepower hydrolift. Piled on the south side of the raft were fifty-foot sections of plastic hose. A small generator stood nearby. Jerry Kemler had run the umbilical cord to the southeast corner of the raft. It carried a telephone line for communications from the raft to the command shed on top. Bill McGehee was overseeing the storage of air tanks and the large air bank from which the individual tanks would be filled. Bill and Jeff Gill tested the high- and low-pressure compressors that stood near the air tanks. On the north side of the raft was equipment for hookah diving (air tubes to the surface),

In lowering the cage to the raft, the crane operator depended on hand signals since he couldn't see the site from his perch above.

and just beyond that was the centrifugal pump, the engine that powered it, a 275-gallon gasoline tank and fire extinguishers. Toward the center of the raft was a cleared area where the screening tables could be placed. Right now the area was occupied by two cots for the expedition members who tended the equipment at night. Despite all the equipment already on the raft, more would be brought down if Scott turned the operation into an underwater excavation. A diving locker would be erected to store wet suits, masks, fins and regulators, and of course the screening tables would have to be squeezed in somehow. There was no fear of overloading the raft, however; it could support one hundred tons. Nor was there any real chance that we would run out of space. The raft measured 32 by 36 feet for a total of 1152 square feet.

The girls had been busy with so much paper work that they hardly got a chance to see what was happening on the raft. When the rain stopped Monday afternoon they decided to take a look, and Scott gave them permission to take a sight-seeing swing in the personnel cage as soon as Howard Williams had a free moment at the crane. Our photographer, Chuck Irwin, said he wanted to take some pictures of the girls, so they put on their cleanest uniforms.

Finally their opportunity came. Dori and Ann along with Chuck's wife, Joyce, and Bill's wife, Sandy, climbed daintily into the cage. They asked Howard to hoist them up over the camp and then toward the jungle to the southwest so they could watch the Mayas widening the path for the pipeline. Next they wanted Howard to swing them directly out over the well so they could get a panorama of operations both topside and on the raft. Then the girls wanted to drop down near the west wall of the well to get a view of the area where the mud bank had emerged.

The girls locked the metal chain across the entrance of the cage. They were off. It was great sport from the beginning. Howard yanked the cage up fast just to give them a little scare, and the girls responded with polite little screams. Maya women on the other side of the well giggled as the girls were swung out over the trees. Howard took extra care in giving them a smooth ride until he finally lost sight of them over the side of the well. Now it was up to Beasom to guide Howard's actions with hand signals.

"Hey, Beasom, why don't you get a cup of coffee? We'll watch out for the girls."

Beasom recognized the voice behind him as Kirk's. He willingly obliged and stepped down from his perch atop the steam bath ruins. Kirk hopped up in his place, followed by our other photographer, Mike Freeman. They guided the cage around the well as the girls had wanted. The latter got a panorama of the dual operations and came within a few feet of a swampy western bank of the water where the Toltec ornament was found. Finally the girls signaled for Howard to bring them up. Kirk relayed the signal and the ascent began. The cage swung out toward the center of the cenote and then Howard began to hoist it up.

Suddenly Kirk's right hand changed position. Instead of motioning for Howard to raise the cage, he gave the signal that meant to lower it. The crane operator looked quizzically at Kirk but Kirk repeated the signal. The cage started dropping and the girls screamed. The Maya women who had been amused by the girls a few minutes ago were gasping.

Kirk grinned as he gave the signal for another four-foot drop. Howard complied. Joyce scrambled up the rigging of the cage while the other girls resigned themselves to the now inevitable dunking. The only ones really worried were the Maya women who had no way of knowing that they were witnessing nothing more than the latest of Kirk's practical jokes.

When the cage finally was brought back up, the girls stalked out dripping dirty water from the cenote, Chuck Irwin on hand to take pictures. Wet and dirty as they were, the girls had made history. They were the first women ever known to come out of the sacred well alive.

That evening at the hacienda we all got into a wild discussion about the nature of sacrifices. Some legends say that in post-Toltec times people were lowered into the well to receive messages from Chac and then brought out of the well to reveal the message to the priests. Actually very little was known about the sacrifices other

75

than that they did in fact occur. Who was sacrificed? What kind of ceremony was held? These were only two of the questions that archaeologists wished they could answer. Complicating the possible answers was the fact that the sacrifices, like other cultural aspects of Chichén Itzá, undoubtedly underwent many changes during the long and tumultuous history of the city.

Even though legends recorded the practice of retrieving victims from the well, they divulged the name of only one person who came out alive. He was Hunac Ceel, but some legends also refer to him as Cauich. His descent into the well of sacrifice marked the turning point of Chichén history after the course of events had been changed earlier by Kukulcán.

Toward the end of Toltec domination, Maya history becomes a maze of legends that can only partially be substantiated by archaeological evidence. Students generally agree that Chichén became one of three ruling cities along with Mayapán and Uxmal, the last possibility giving way to Izamal. If such a league existed, it was destroyed by the man named Hunac Ceel (or Cauich), the ruler or the son of the ruler of Mayapán.

The drama began when Hunac came to Chichén to witness the kind of ceremony in which persons were thrown into the well and then brought up, supposedly with a message from the gods. In one account of the incident, Hunac himself jumped into the cenote when none of the original human sacrifices survived the plunge. When Hunac was brought up, he had a prophecy that shook the foundations of Mayab. He said the gods told *him* to rule Chichén Itzá.

Legends are conflicting, but apparently Hunac Ceel held only a loose sovereignty over Chichén Itzá at this time. The man who presumably ruled in Hunac Ceel's stead was Chac Xib Chac. The two men were together at the wedding feast of the ruler of Izamal, Ah Ulil, when Hunac Ceel let the ruler of Chichén smell a cluster of plumeria blossoms. This flower was believed to be the flower of love, and Chac Xib Chac fell into Hunac Ceel's trap. He fell in love with Ah Ulil's bride. Since Chichén was the greater city, Ah Ulil could do nothing when Chac Xib Chac stole his bride, but later the cunning Hunac Ceel made overtures about a dual alliance to conquer Chichén Itzá. They were successful. And Chichén, once a city whose domain stretched for hundreds of miles, was sacked, burned and destroyed. Its Itzá inhabitants were sent retreating into the bush. The fall of Chichén Itzá had occurred because one man jumped in the well and another sniffed a flower.

Hunac Ceel had a brutal way of dealing with Izamal. Apparently in exchange for offering it protection, he took sacrificial victims from the city, thereby depleting its population and destroying it just as surely as, although more slowly than, Chichén was destroyed. Mayapán then dominated northern Yucatán for more than two hundred years.

The fall of Mayapán should be studied by all chiefs of state. It constitutes a classic example of self-induced political cancer. The descendants of Hunac Ceel, taking the name Cocom, held power by hiring Mexican mercenaries and extracting tribute from neighboring cities. The mercenaries were known as the *Ah Canul,* and their descendants, probably including our own local foreman, Avelino Canul, are scattered throughout Yucatán. This complete absorption was the end result of a Mayanization process that began soon after Hunac Ceel took power. The Ah Canul grew soft and became ineffective as a fighting team. This gave an aristocratic family named Tutul Xiu the chance it had been waiting for. A Tutul Xiu leader, Ah Uxpan, made his bid for power by appealing to two ethnic groups. He told the old Maya families that the Cocoms were selling Yucatecans as slaves to foreign traders, and he reminded those of Mexican ancestry that his own forebearers came from Tula. The bid for power culminated in a successful revolt in about A.D. 1450. Parallels to Mayapán's weakness and to the Xius' strategy are woefully common in Western history.

The Xius were unable to retain Mayapán's hegemony, and Yucatán fell into disunity. When the Spaniards came they found no pyramids being built, no ball courts in use, no magnificent temples being constructed and apparently no worship of Kukulcán. The most powerful of the old gods to survive was Chac, god of the sacred well.

Despite the state of decay and decline in which the Spanish

found the Mayas, some Spaniards recognized the true heights of Yucatecan culture and elected to fight on the side of the Mayas. That fight was slow but the outcome was certain. In 1541 the conquerors had subdued all the Maya cities except Tayasal, an island in Lake Petén deep in the jungle to the south. Tayasal had been the refuge of the Itzá when they were driven from Chichén. Spanish colonists talked about going after the stronghold but knew it would be difficult to move an army through the jungle of Chiapas, and that the land had little value anyway. It was not until 1697 that the Spanish decided to conquer the Itzá stronghold, and they accomplished the act with the imagination and glory attendant on swatting a fly. But with that act, Mayab was finally conquered by an alien culture, a culture which some of its members considered inferior to that of the vanquished.

"So even though Chichén fell into ruins, the Itzá held out for nearly two hundred years after the appearance of Columbus," Scott said near the end of the discussion at the hacienda.

"As a matter of fact," Folan said, "there are still families around here with the surname of Itzá. I hope I get to talk to some of them. I'd like to find out if they're descended from the Itzá here in Chichén."

We all hoped that the well of the Itzá would not be as defiant to excavation as its cultists were to conquest. Scott was interested in the Itzá's apparent attraction to water, and in the fact that here in Chichén it was water that sealed their sacred well and at Tayasal it was the water of Lake Petén that protected their stronghold.

Occupation of this city by the Itzá and so many other groups could add to the confusion in excavating the well, when and if we ever got to that stage. Resting at the bottom of the cenote were doubtless treasures from the classical Mayas, the Toltecs, the Itzá, the Mayapán rulers and from the people who lived in Chichén at the time of the conquest. Archaeologists pointed out that if these artifacts remained in position within the mud after they were sacrificed, it would be easy to pinpoint the period of origin. Such stratification, however, probably did not exist. Folan, who was on the 1960 expedition, did not rule out the possibility of finding relics in distinct strata but he said the odds were against it. It was also probable that much of the treasure we would find would not even be of Yucatecan origin since the Mayas would have had to import any metal or precious stones. Northern Yucatán was void of such riches. The problem to archaeologists could be compared with having to excavate London many centuries after an atomic attack. What conclusions could archaeologists of the future draw from finding ruins of an Egyptian obelisk near the ruins of a sign reading "Embankment Gardens"?

The people of Chichén Itzá had unwittingly created a time capsule like time capsules made and buried by people in the twentieth century. We put paper clips and phonograph records in our capsules, and the cenote was bound to have a similar assortment of common objects. But if the assortment made excavation difficult in some ways for archaeologists, it would also give them their first chance to see a cross-section of the objects that the Mayas considered precious enough to sacrifice to Chac. Just as those who open our time capsules will get a picture of twentieth-century life, we hoped to get a picture of the ancient Mayas from whatever lay at the bottom of the well.

Although archaeologists, especially in the last fifteen years, have added considerably to our knowledge of the Mayas, they have not been able to discover some very basic elements of their civilization. For instance, although more than 75 per cent of the Mayas' hieroglyphics can now be read, no one has ever found a piece of Maya furniture. The hieroglyphics, by the way, make pretty dull reading for the layman. They tell mainly about astronomy and deities, whereas even one piece of furniture would tell something about the people themselves. The Mayas imported metal, but not enough of it has been found for archaeologists to get a clear picture of the Mayas' commercial empire. From stories of the early Spanish we have assumed that the sacred cenote was the sinkhole into which countless virgins were sacrificed to appease the gods. Not enough skeletal material has been found to substantiate the stories, however. But more than anything else, archaeologists lack an insight into Mayan life before the conquest. We have pictures of battles painted on walls and effigies of gods carved in stone. But we have no pictures of the artists who painted the murals or of the men who worshiped the gods.

The booster pump was finally connected shortly after noon on Tuesday, and from the moment it was started it appeared that our problems were solved. The pump on the raft sucked in water like a whirpool and then rammed it up the fire hoses to the top of the precipice. Pressure was lost in the process, but once the water got to the ledge, the booster scooped it up and then spewed it out through the aluminum pipe. An immense pressure was built up at this stage to push the water through the twenty-nine sections. We could hear the water rumble through the sections as they pierced deeper and deeper into the bush. At the end of the pipe water gushed out with such a force that it broke saplings and dug large muddy trenches on its downhill route into the dried-up cenote.

A new series of markers was put up in the shallow area between the raft and the edge of the well. Even allowing for the errors of an imprecise measuring system, our progress was amazing. We were lowering the water by nearly two inches an hour.

As the water receded, we watched the mud bank on the west side which was again beginning to emerge. This time Scott said he was not going to make the mistake of exploring it too soon. By morning, he said, the water would have been lowered enough to make walking on the bank easy. Folan and Victor looked as though they wanted to jump down on the bank right now and scoop up a handful of mud. Folan was so happy that he nearly forgot about the sunburn he had acquired on his arms and balding head during the few hours each day that the sun had defeated the rain. We could tell he was in great pain, but he could not stay away from the site. He caked himself with sunburn lotion and sported a tam-o'-shanter on his head. It went almost unnoticed by the Mayas, who were now accustomed to seeing nearly anything at the campsite.

The pumping system was working well, but the aluminum pipe that had been connected in the rush operation still needed some attention. The sections hooked into each other perfectly but the uneven terrain and the constant water pressure inside caused some of the connections to loosen. Segovia and Avelino went out into the bush with some workers to see what they could do about leveling the ground under the pipe. The few leaks that occurred had been enough to let thousand of gallons of water escape from the pipe. The escaping water was quickly turning the earth into mud.

Segovia and the Maya work force plowed through the mud. The afternoon air was hot, wet and motionless. Flies and mosquitoes swarmed around the water trickling—or in some cases, streaming—from the pipe joints. The insects would have made a feast for the birds, but the day was too stifling for birds to be lured from their shady nests near the ground. Only the Mayas themselves seemed unconcerned about the wet jungle heat. They ran along ahead of Segovia like children on a field trip. Segovia could speak a fair amount of the Maya language, and he used it often in working with them. The job before them now was tedious. One group had to lift the pipe sections with water rushing through while the others rolled large stones beneath the sections in order to level them. It took a great amount of energy to hold the pipe high and steady for several minutes at a time while the rocks were placed beneath, but the Mayas were strong and made no protest. In fact they were amused at our attempt to remove the water from the sacred well. They said Chac would always see to it that the water returned. They reminded Segovia of Friday's disaster as proof of the point.

But even though they did not take the work seriously, they managed to level nearly all sections of the pipe. Some sections had yielded promptly to the leveling technique but a few proved nearly impossible to budge. At times the Mayas lost their footing in the slippery mud, and those standing close to the connection got drenched by geysers of cenote water. Rocks were sometimes hard to find, and at times the Mayas had to hold the pipes in position for as long as ten minutes.

At one point the cenote struck back at Segovia. A piercing spurt of water shot out from a pipe connection and hit him in the eye. Segovia reeled back with his hand in front of his face as a shield. He shook the water from his head and rubbed his eyes.

"That bastard Chac!" he shouted.

As soon as he said it, he realized he had made a big mistake. If Victor had sworn in Spanish, the Mayas would have laughed. But he had sworn in their own language, in fluent Maya.

Six workmen stared at him for a minute and then dropped a section of pipe. Two others tried to erase the blasphemy against Chac by making the sign of the cross. Victor tried to laugh it off, but he realized he could not. The Mayas resumed work after a few minutes, but there was no more joy in their labor. Every motion was made with utmost caution, almost as though they did not want to risk having to hear Chac's name taken again in vain. They looked often at Victor out of the corners of their eyes.

Chac has survived at least three conquests, and now we knew that the god of the sacred well was still alive despite centuries of Christianity. He was becoming our enemy just as surely as his home was our goal.

The Maya work force did not know precisely what it was helping the expedition do in the sense of technical accomplishments, but from what the laborers overheard they could tell that our objectives were nothing short of dissecting and dismantling the god's home, draining the holy water from it, sacking its treasure and enucleating the mysteries which the Mayas were trying to protect even in our own era. They worked for us, but they were not really on our side.

A couple of the Mayas who had been assigned to the filtration area crowded around Gordon late Tuesday afternoon. He was just finishing the preliminary chemical analysis of the cenote water and was hoping to have it completed for Scott and Folan to study before making plans to explore the mud bank. The Mayas watched with penetrating stares as Gordon and Bob Drake held up little vials of colored water and jotted figures in a notebook. The workers did not understand what the men were doing, and the engineers spoke no Spanish or Maya to explain it to them. The disapproval of the spectators needed no explanation.

The tests were important to the filtration experts because the

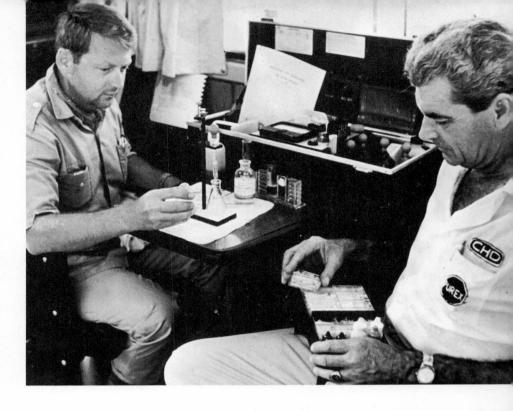

Bob Drake, here with Wayne Vanderlow, almost continually analyzed the cenote water, to the mystification of the Mayas.

chemicals with which they would treat the cenote would depend on what chemicals nature had already put in it. We also hoped the analysis would give substantial clues about the behavior of the water that was being pumped out.

I took a look at a chart that Drake was preparing, but it seemed as complex as a book on Maya history. Bob finally explained it to me, and I was amazed at the information he could deduce about the cenote merely from the chemicals that the water contained.

The Purex team measured relative acidity and alkalinity on a scale that ranged from total acidity of 0 to total alkalinity of 14. On September 20, the day after we arrived, the surface water registered 8.5 on this scale, meaning that the water was slightly alkaline. Soon after the pump was started, the surface water read 7.5, or almost neutral. Below the surface the water registered 6.8 at eighteen feet and 6.6 at thirty-six feet after we began pumping. These readings indicated acidity that could in time wreck any machinery it came in contact with. Inman was afraid that with continued pumping, the acid content of the water would increase still further. If it did, we would be in big trouble.

From the mere increase in acidity, engineers were able to tell something else important. They figured that the only way acid could be getting into the well was in the water seeping back into the cenote after we pumped it out. Inman theorized that this water picked up acid in the soil and carried it back into the well.

"There's still something else that this chart shows," he said. "Did you notice that increased acidity doesn't occur until halfway down in the cenote?" I nodded. "If our theory about the source of the acid is right, this means that acid particles are being carried into the well by underground streams. Everyone assumed this, but what they didn't know was how deep the streams were when they emptied in the well. Now we have some idea. They're all probably below eighteen feet."

Soon after the pump had begun discharging water, we noticed bubbles at the surface. At first we thought they contained hydrogen sulfide gas, but from the chart Inman was holding it was apparent that sulfides were absent at the surface and relatively scarce even at lower depths. Chemical analysis, however, pointed clearly to the culprit that was causing the bubbles. Inman singled it out as carbon dioxide, of which there were twelve parts in a million parts of water at the surface, 60 at eighteen feet and 52 at thirty-six feet. No one knew exactly what was causing the bubbles although presumably it had something to do with the pumping. Wayne Vanderlow said the water seeping back into the cenote might be pushing in pockets of air within the limestone caves. On the other hand, the gas might have been created when water, after picking up acid from the soil, came into contact with the alkaline limestone in the well.

My eye caught a section of the chart marked "turbidity scale" accompanied by a series of 7s and 8s.

"I suppose that means it's dark down there," I said.

That was an understatement. Water in the cenote registered seven or eight on the scale. Water in an average home swimming pool might register one.

Gordon was not much concerned about the presence or absence of the many minerals in the well since none was found in amounts large enough to harm our operations. I was interested to learn that cenote water contained only one one-thousandth of a part of iron in a million parts of water. That one entry in the chart clearly illustrated just how void of iron the Yucatán Peninsula is. It is almost inconceivable that the Mayas would have reached an iron age like that developed by Mediterranean cultures. Silica, however, registered three parts per million, an indication of the abundance of the mineral needed in firing pottery. Gordon was amazed when he first noticed the large quantity of nitrates in the cenote, but his amazement disappeared one evening when he saw thousands of bats fly out of their caves in the cenote walls. The excrement of so many bats would have been enough to start a small fertilizer plant, and a nitrate reading of 11.3 parts per million at the surface meant that a large part of this excrement found its way into the water.

All in all, the figures on the chart represented a succinct description of the well: dark and putrid.

I left Gordon and his colleagues at the filtration area and walked to the upper level from which Scott and the archaeologists were taking a last look at the emerging bank on the western edge of the water. Scott was anxious to start clearing the bank, but the workday was nearly over. Dozens of trees had to be cut down on the bank if excavations were going to be conducted in a systematic manner. In addition, thousands of rocks would have to be removed and trenches would have to be dug. Maya workers would be needed for the job, but Scott speculated that they might balk at going down into the home of their ancient god. The archaeologists said his doubt was justified. No one knew just how far they were willing to help us.

As the men were discussing the work schedule for the next day, a rain cloud sprang up in the north and darkness began to come on fast. The shadows of the bush were already creeping toward camp and bats began flying out of the cenote. At first a few "scout" bats erratically circled the rim of the well, quickly followed by swarms of others on the beginning of a nightly hunt for food. Scott and Folan walked over to the Mayas to tell them it was time to go home. With Folan translating for him, Scott mentioned to Avelino and several of the workers that it would be imperative to go down onto the bank tomorrow and clear it of trees and rocks. Avelino and the workers walked toward the precipice and looked down into the darkening pit through a cloud of bats. They looked down in silence and said nothing.

5

It was again hot and steamy the next day, even at eight-thirty in the morning when we arrived at the well for the daily meeting. As usual, I tried to pick out a shady place to stand, but even the shade was hot. As the meeting dragged on, it was apparent that feelings were as hot as the weather. Scott was upset because, as he put it, there was not the slightest indication of teamwork in our efforts. Jerry Kemler was angry because he could not find some of the tools he needed. Fred Wade was blamed because he was in charge of the tool shed. Fred was angry because many of us were not returning tools at the end of the day. The archaeologists were frustrated; they were anxious to begin excavations on the bank, but even if the bank were cleared, excavations would be handicapped because the cataloguists had not yet arrived from the National Institute. Jerry Griffin, an archaeologist from the University of Texas at El Paso, had come to the site to observe, but he was not interested in observing chaos. Purex engineers were eager to begin chlorination, but the automatic chlorinator had not yet arrived and no one could think of an alternate means of doing the job. Tempers that had been simmering during the two-week trip to the site, and the first hectic days of setting up camp, had been boiling over lately. (Recently I found myself mouthing off to Frank Taylor, the Ford engineer in charge of vehicle maintenance. Frank is about the pleasantest person one could know, and I cannot for the life of me explain why I got angry with him.) Scott was put out with nearly everyone and made a big point of saying that lack of co-operation could wreck the expedition.

One could not blame Scott for his attitude. Pablo Bush had left again along with Kirk and Piña Chan, leaving Scott with enormous responsibility at the site. Despite the pressure and the chaos he managed to keep his mind on the objective which some of us had all but forgotten. At the conclusion of this meeting he said we should all remember that we were here for one purpose and that all our actions should in some way benefit that purpose.

"We're bound to have more setbacks and more disappointments, and the confusion isn't going to end overnight. The only way to keep any sense of direction is to remember the goal. We're here for one purpose—to excavate the well."

Sweat was pouring down his face when he ended the meeting, but his words seemed to cool things off. They were also prophetic. We had hoped to clear the bank that day, but the job had to be postponed twenty-four hours. The Mayas were needed to widen the discharge path even farther, and the pump had to be stopped temporarily so we could replace a section of firehose that was leaking badly. Meanwhile, archaeologists kept eyeing the bank with obvious anticipation.

Edward Thompson had readily admitted that excavating the well was an obsession. Although Scott never mentioned his own emotions about the well, I am sure that it was just as much of an obsession with him. I wondered what Thompson would have thought if he could see our massive, hectic expedition, compared with his tiny team that worked the well for nearly seven years. He probably would have been amused, but he might also have been sympathetic, knowing as no one else could the hardships of achieving successful excavations.

88

Thompson had hired two Greek sponge divers as well as several men from Chichén Itzá as his expedition team in 1904. While we loaded one half million dollars of sophisticated equipment into twenty-one vehicles, Thompson struggled to buy and ship his supplies: his dredge, a winch, tackles, steel cables, rope, a stiff-leg derrick and a thirty-foot swinging boom. When Thompson

"Thompson's bank" was a muddy magnet for the archaeologists.

decided to work on a narrow strip of mud and rock on the western edge of the water, and as more and more buckets of silt were dumped on this spit of land, it built up into what Thompson called the "little beach." Much of the earth, the tailings from his screening efforts, rolled back or settled into the water. Most of it, however, did not settle very far under the surface. This was the earth that began to emerge when we started the pumps. It was odd that Thompson referred to the area as a beach; it was more on the order of a quicksand pit in the Everglades. We called it "Thompson's bank."

This narrow spit of mud and rocks changed very little between the time of Thompson's excavations and our own. He was amazed at the thick vegetation in the area, and now the jungle growth there was as dense as the bush that surrounded the well on top. Trees many feet tall also grew from the crevices in the cenote wall, and their roots dangled like snakes toward the bank. Rich green philodendrons flourished wherever they could find nourishment and wrapped themselves around the tree trunks, living up to the meaning of their name, "tree lovers."

Even though clearing had been postponed, Scott and several other expedition members made as many trips as possible to the bank, ostensibly to estimate how long it would take to clear it but primarily to show the Mayas how harmless the trip was. Scott did not even bother with the personnel cage on several trips. Instead, he straddled the metal ball on the end of the cable from the crane and rode cheerfully down. The metal ball disappeared under Scott's bulk, and it looked as though he were holding onto the cable with nothing but his hands. Actually, riding the ball was probably safer than being lifted down in the cage because more things conceivably could go wrong with the cable connections on the cage. The women and children who watched our every move from the north side of the well did not know this; a couple of days ago they had seen the four girls get dunked in the cenote, and now they thought they were witnessing an impromptu aerial act. It was an act, all right, an act designed to show the workers that going into the well was as easy as falling off a pyramid, so to speak.

When the big day finally arrived, the omens were bad. Instead of a blistering sun, the morning sky was filled with dark clouds. The air was heavy with moisture, and the stench of the well could even be sensed on top. It was hardly the day for a first trip into the home of a god who lived in water and demanded death. After the morning meeting the Mayas crowded around the personnel cage, speaking quickly and softly in their own language. I did not need a translator to figure out what they were talking about.

Scott cut short a conversation with Miguel to get to the cage. He walked fast but nonchalantly up to the Mayas. Folan was already there. Scott nodded to Avelino and then walked into the cage.

"Hey, Willie, how does this cable look to you?" he said.

Folan walked into the cage and looked up at the connection Scott was pointing to.

"Looks okay to me," Folan said.

"Of course it does," Scott said. "I wonder what Avelino thinks of it."

Scott told Folan to ask the foreman to step inside and give his opinion. Avelino walked into the cage. He knew as much about metal cables as he did about electroencephalography. Avelino called two other Mayas into the cage. They all looked at the cable and shrugged. Another Maya became curious and walked in the cage to get a better look. Scott smiled. The cage was full.

He raised his right hand as though he were pointing to the cable. Then he pointed straight up with his index finger and moved his hand in a circle. Howard Williams, watching the proceedings from the crane cab, got the signal.

Avelino was not afraid. He had been in the well many times during the 1960–61 expedition. The thoughts of his colleagues as they were hoisted over the trees and down into the cenote will never be known. I watched them stand motionless in the personnel cage, but it was debatable whether their immobility was a result of stoicism or terror. Scott took time to point out several good views of the campsite from the cage, but the only movement

I can recall from the Mayas came when one of them crossed himself.

Once the crane set the cage down, Scott began giving a long list of instructions on what had to be cut down and what did not. With their minds back on the job, the Mayas hardly had time to think about where they were. The bank had grown considerably wider during the night and had taken on a more secure atmosphere. When the other workers on top looked down and saw their friends calmly walking around in the depths of the well, they were less fearful about making the trip down. Still, at least one of us usually accompanied each cage-load of Mayas for the next week. It was to take a long time before they built up confidence.

Clearing Thompson's bank was a dirty, grimy job. I remember, a couple of days after the work began, seeing Jerry Griffin standing near the muddy little shore line. I took my eyes off him for a minute, and when I turned back, he was stuck waist-deep in mud and water. There was almost no breeze in the depths of the cenote, and the hot sun seemed to make the infested water boil into an unhealthy steam. When rain came, as it did nearly each afternoon, workers had to cling to the side of the well to keep dry, taking advantage of the cenote's convex structure for shelter. Some of us welcomed the rain and did not bother with finding shelter. Standing in the rain was the only way to rinse off the dirt which by midafternoon had worked its way into our pores.

Thompson mentioned no encounters with snakes in the well, although he got a terrific scare when one of his Greek divers dragged a slimy log across his back under water. Nevertheless, it was obvious that the cenote was an ideal breeding ground for reptiles and other animals. Iguanas played around the walls and lived in the upper crevices that were too small for a squadron of bats. Fish, most of them about eight inches long, flourished in the well, making themselves conspicuous by jumping out of the water to catch mosquitoes and other insects near the surface. Giant toads, at least a foot long, hopped awkwardly wherever there was enough land around the edges of the water. One day while the bank was being cleared a worker spotted a snake in the water, a snorkle-headed moccasin known as a kantil.

"Snakes persisted in being a problem. . . ."

We were well-equipped for any emergency involving snake bites. One of the firms that participated in the expedition, E. R. Squibb & Sons, supplied us with an immense range of medications, from aspirin to coral snake antivenom. A kantil injects its victim with a massive dose of poison, but we had more than enough medication to combat it.

The kantil that was spotted from the bank was a small specimen which was quickly killed. Other snakes, however, persisted in being a problem. Several days later expedition members discovered a coral snake in the campsite area, and two more *coralitas* turned up the next week. Although we could cope with a kantil bite, a coral snake bite was an entirely different matter. This snake injects quick-acting nerve poison, and unless the victim is bitten on an extremity, there is not much hope. Antivenom must be kept cool and administered promptly. Coral snakes fortunately do not bite often and actually have difficulty getting their mouths into position to inject poison. Their presence worried us more than the rattlesnakes.

Rattlers are not actually common in northern Yucatán, but we never forgot that four of them were found amidst the ruins on the day we arrived. This was the snake that formed the mythological body of Kukulcán, and that name should really be translated "quetzal snake" rather than Feathered Serpent. The quetzal is an exotic tropical bird with rich blue-green feathers. Both the quetzal and the rattlesnake were endowed with mystical meanings by many ancient inhabitants of Mexico and Central America. Quetzalcóatl was the Aztec name for this creature, the "quetzal snake," and Kukulcán is the Mayan translation. Modern Mayas are terrified of the same snake that their ancestors sanctified, and even though the expedition was equipped with an ample supply of antivenom, we, too, never walked through the bush without keeping an eye on the ground. As long as one is not bitten on the upper part of the torso, or has to wait too long for serum, a rattlesnake bite is rarely fatal.

Edward Thompson had worked in the cenote in an era when there were no antivenoms, and it was all to his credit that he did not let the hazards of animals or disease deter him. In fact, Thompson had a rather romantic notion about the well and its inhabitants.

"This little beach is like a scene from the time when the world was young," he wrote.

Now that scene was being changed. The clumps of trees and tangled vines yielded quickly to the axes, coas and machetes of the Maya workers. I thought their diligence was remarkable considering their fear of the bank only a short time ago. During the next couple of days we saw the bank change from a lush spit of land into a quickly enlarging, desolate mud flat. Segovia, Folan and Griffin followed close behind the Mayas to stake out the area in segments three meters wide that would be used to map out excavations.

While most of us were preoccupied with starting these excavations, there was also another important job at hand. The water had to be chlorinated. The bank was relatively unimportant since all it could possibly contain was the leftovers from Thompson's excavations more than a half century ago. The situation Scott feared most was the prospect of finding it impossible to drain the well, with the bank yielding nothing of value and the water left unclarified. In that case we would have to start from scratch in order to clarify the water for a full-scale diving operation.

"I'd like to hedge against that possibility by chlorinating as soon as possible," Scott said at the Thursday morning meeting.

Then he explained that this was not as easy as it sounded. The automatic chlorinators, he said, had arrived at the site, but since we were using both pumps for drainage, there was no pump to circulate the water through the chlorinators. The filtration system was set up so that the pump on the raft could bring water to it. This water would go through the filter tanks and be chlorinated at the end of the cycle. It would then be dumped back into the cenote. But if we were to use the pump on the raft now for filtration and chlorination, we would not be able to continue draining water from the well.

"If we weren't making some headway in drainage, I'd say go ahead and shut off the pumps and begin filtering with just one," Scott said. "But if we did that now, we'd be taking a big chance. For one thing, we'd lose the bank."

Segovia winced at the idea.

It was actually difficult to assess our progress in drainage. The filtration team had predicted that the water level would decline at an uneven rate, but even they were surprised at how uneven it was. Sometimes we could lower the water by about one and a half inches an hour, and then the rate would go up to two inches. At one time we hit a peak of four inches an hour, only to see a quick decrease to about one half inch an hour. Inman guessed that we already had changed the water in the cenote two or three

95

times. This accounted for the increased clarity in the water without any chemical treatment. The water we were pumping into the abandoned cenote evidently was being filtered naturally as it passed through limestone en route back to the sacred well.

Scott had gotten together with Inman and Drake the night before at the hacienda to discuss alternative ways of chlorinating. Inman disclosed at the morning meeting the plan they had chosen. It was a pretty tricky scheme, but the idea was to mix chlorine and water by hand in the cenote itself. Inman explained that we would lower a one-ton tank of compressed chlorine into the cenote, attach a plastic tube to the nozzle and let the gas spurt out into the discharge of a small water pump. Scott said we would be working from a raft which CEDAM had built for the 1960 expedition and which had been left at the campsite.

The raft was lowered into the cenote that morning, and it floated for all of thirty seconds. It was basically nothing more than a wooden deck atop two metal pontoons, both of which had corroded so badly that they began to take water as soon as the raft was lowered into the well. The crane hoisted it back up so that Jeff Gill and Jerry Kemler could begin welding the holes. More than just a few holes were involved it turned out; there were hundreds. Jerry could not spend all day at the job, but Jeff kept at it until late in the afternoon, sweating in a shower of sparks. By the afternoon break he looked exhausted. He flipped back his welder's mask and walked over to the command shed for a glass of tea, and then we realized that more was wrong with him than mere exhaustion. By welding for such a long time, Jeff had nearly blinded himself. His eyes were fiery red and swollen.

Jeff was lucky. Had he continued welding much longer, he might have lost his sight permanently.

Jerry took up the job where Jeff left off, but after estimating the work remaining on the raft he said it would be impossible to finish before the middle of the following morning. Inman was disappointed. He had hoped to begin the experiment in chlorination that afternoon.

Shortly before noon on Friday Jerry pronounced the raft ready. Cables were laboriously attached to the bulky raft, and the crane

A child's skull—
one of many—suggested
a grim history hidden
beneath the originally
turbid, green water
of the cenote below.

The sound of these copper "bells of death" was the last heard by the sacrificial victims who wore them centuries ago.

The enlargement here shows the remarkable detail in the much-prized ring woven of gold threads.

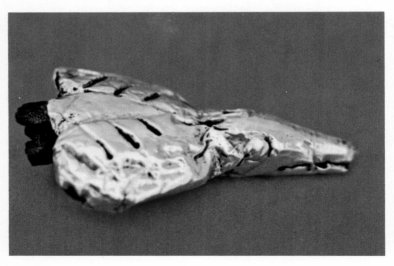

Though gold was not native to the region, it abounded in artifacts recovered, like the effigy above, probably of a god, and the representation of a serpent head below.

The eventual clarification of the water permitted this dramatic
nighttime display of well and camp.

Some of the invaluable Tepeu ceramic paintings showed rich details
of daily life and dress—earplugs, sandals, costume detail,
and a Maya merchant's black-painted face.

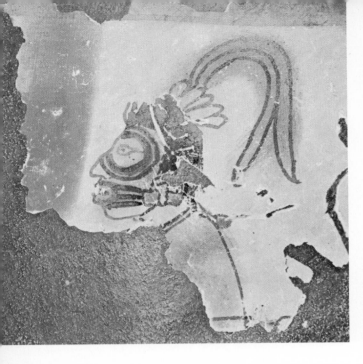

More Tepeu
ceramic paintings,
these of warriors,
the one below wearing
a jaguar helmet.

once again lowered it into the water. This time it worked 100 per cent better—that is to say the raft stayed afloat for sixty seconds rather than thirty.

Bill McGehee spotted a series of large holes that the welders evidently had missed. The raft was hoisted back topside for a quick repair job at the places Bill pointed out. An hour later the holes had been sealed.

Somewhat miraculously the raft floated when it was lowered for the third time into the well. McGehee went down to install an outboard engine to the raft while Inman and Scott prepared to lower the tank of chlorine and the water pump. Howard operated the crane as though he were handling nitroglycerine, easing the tank up and over the campsite and then gently down into the well. If it were to rupture, gas would shoot out and it would take off like a jet. At the raft expedition members were waiting to ease it by hand to a soft landing.

The descent of the tank might have gone on for forty more feet. As soon as the weight of the tank shifted from the crane cable to the raft, a discouraging sound was heard, a gurgle. The raft was sinking again. The metal pontoons could barely support themselves and the wooden deck, let alone a one-ton tank of chlorine. The men on the raft waved frantically at Beasom, who signaled Howard to pull the tank back up.

Inman was disgusted. Another day had almost been wasted. To salvage the few hours that remained, Scott suggested trying the same chlorination plan on the big raft. It was designed to support up to one hundred tons so there was no fear that it would not support the tank. It did, however, have the disadvantage of immobility. Working from the big raft, we would not be able to move around the well as we would have been able to do on the outboard-powered CEDAM raft. Inman still figured this plan would be better than nothing: the chlorine would eventually diffuse in the well, but the diffusion would take longer since we were putting it into the water at only one spot.

The big raft hardly budged as the one-ton tank settled on its deck. The plan was basically the same as it would have been on the CEDAM raft. With the valve on the tank open, the chlorine,

97

which was actually a liquid under pressure in the tank, would flow out into a plastic tube. At the same time, it would be changing into a colorless gas. The tube would direct the gas into the discharge of the water pump, and the chlorine-enriched water would then flow into the cenote. We would have to rely on the currents—natural ones as well as those the pump was creating—to circulate the chlorine. Inman said the experiment would be hazardous because mixing chlorine with water is a delicate operation. The automatic chlorinator was a device made by Wallace & Tiernan to do the mixing in precise, controlled proportions whereas

"The experiment would be hazardous . . ."
A catastrophe was only seconds away.

doing the job "by hand" required guesswork. Moreover, chlorine is a deadly gas. Home swimming pools contain only a minute amount. When inhaled, chlorine destroys lung tissue, making breathing at first painful and later impossible. The effect within the lungs is similar to that of pneumonia. In both cases the lungs fill with water.

Those with the best view of the experiment were Jerry Griffin and nineteen Maya workers who watched from Thompson's bank. As usual, the Mayas were not sure what was going on, and Griffin had only a vague idea since our plans had changed several times during the last few days.

When the chlorine tank was in position on the raft, the crane lowered Inman, Drake and Vanderlow. They hooked up the tubing and directed it into the discharge of the pump. Bill McGehee had some trouble getting the small pump started, but it soon began doing the desired job. It simply sucked in water from the well and then dumped it back in. According to the plan, the chlorine would mix with the water as it was returning to the cenote. The crane made the last trip to the top before chlorination began, taking Vanderlow, Drake and several others. Six men were left on the raft to oversee the operation—Frank Taylor, Harold Martin, Austin, Bill, Inman and Scott.

Inman had brought down a bottle of ammonia which he now opened as a safety device. If any chlorine escaped, it was vital to detect it immediately. In the presence of ammonia, chlorine becomes visible as a smoky gas.

Gordon turned the valve on the tank, but too much chlorine started gushing through the tube. It was difficult to regulate the flow of the gas. Within a few minutes, however, he achieved what looked like a safe amount. Scott felt the plastic tube. It was cold. Inman had explained that when chlorine—or any other element—changes from a liquid to a gas, cooling takes place. It is essentially the same cooling process that causes swimmers to feel cold when they first come out of the water, and tree shade to be cooler than the shade of something that is not giving off water. The process is, of course, evaporation, and under controlled conditions, man uses it for refrigeration or air-conditioning. But this

99

evaporation can be dangerous when it is extreme and uncontrolled.

Frost appeared on the plastic tubing within minutes after the chlorine began passing through it. The air began to smell heavy with the sterile odor of the element, but Inman said this did not indicate danger.

A second later the icing of the tube got out of control. The plastic snapped, and the gas gushed out into the air. The men standing close to the rupture reeled back when the first cloud of chlorine reached them. One of them turned off the pump, but the jet of deadly gas kept them from getting at the valve on the tank. The plastic was brittle. Another piece broke off and the gas spurted out even faster.

There was now enough ammonia in the air so that they could see the danger which before had only been felt.

Chlorine was engulfing the raft. Scott jumped into the water and started swimming. He had breathed in so much of the gas that he was having real difficulty. He tried to swim under water but found it nearly impossible to hold his breath. Chlorine had already gotten to his lungs.

Griffin and the Mayas saw the turmoil on the raft. The workers had no idea what was happening, but Griffin sensed the panic. A gentle wind within the well began spreading the gas to the bank where they were standing. Chlorine, made visible by ammonia, rolled toward them like a deadly fog.

Scott was now within wading distance of the south end of the bank. He stood up in the middle of a cloud of chlorine. His lungs were empty from the underwater swim, and he could not help taking a deep breath. He buckled over from the pain and staggered toward the bank.

The Mayas had seen what the fog did to Scott. They reached for the walls and started climbing as the gas rolled on toward them. The ancestors of some had undoubtedly reached for the same walls to escape death from drowning many centuries ago.

Scott reached land but he was still doubled over with pain. The men on the raft could hardly be seen in the cloud of gas that spewed from the tank.

The men on top had seen the emergency. Someone thought of air tanks: if the men below had diving rigs they could save themselves by breathing from the tanks even in the midst of chlorine. One rig was thrown over the side to those on the bank, but it was obvious that this would not work. There was a danger of hitting the men and of breaking the rig. A ruptured air tank would only add to the catastrophe.

By now Howard Williams had reached the controls of the crane, and he had never operated it so fast. He slung the cage over the precipice, hardly waiting for Beasom to give the signals. He had dropped so many loads on the raft that he knew its position almost by touch. His instinct paid off. The cage landed directly on the raft.

The men crawled toward the metal cage. But Inman went in the other direction, back into the middle of the dense chlorine that spewed from the tank. He groped along until he reached the tank itself. His hand touched the cool surface and ran along it to the end. Unable to breathe and barely able to stand, he reached the cold valve. He tried to turn it but bits of ice had made it stiff. He gave it a frantic blow with his palm and it yielded. With another turn it was closed.

He crawled back to the cage and climbed in. Howard yanked it up and pulled the men away from danger. A few seconds later they were on top, sprawled on the ground or on their knees, gasping painfully for air.

Howard swung the cage back to the bank. Beasom could hardly see through the enveloping gas to give signals. But even before the cage landed on the mud, the Mayas lunged for it. They hung on any way they could, from the cable, from the connecting lines and from the bottom of the cage itself. Eleven managed to scramble up in the device built to hold a half-dozen at most. Howard brought up the cage like a giant Yo-yo.

He set them down on top and then let the cage fly out again over the precipice and down to the bank. He was operating the crane so fast that the metal cable grew hot spinning around the winch. Seven Mayas leaped for the cage when it touched down on the bank for the second time. Within seconds they were on top.

Most of them staggered around coughing; one elderly worker collapsed as soon as he stepped out.

Howard dropped the cage on the bank for the third time. Scott, Griffin and the last Maya dragged themselves aboard and were whisked to the top. Howard deposited them in the middle of the campsite. Then he decided to move the cage so it would not be in the way. He had lifted it about ten feet when the crane engine gave a chug and stopped. He tried to restart it but could not.

We tried not to think about the fact that if this had occurred five minutes earlier two dozen men would probably have been dead by now. The crane had run out of gas.

Inman limped back to his room. He coughed and vomited throughout the night. Three Mayas were rushed to the hospital in Valladolid. One of them, the old man, nearly died. Jeff kept him alive at least three times by mouth-to-mouth resuscitation before they reached the medical center.

If the old man or the others had breathed in much more gas, we would have been taking them to the morgue instead of a hospital. A few minutes' delay in rescue would have jeopardized even more men. If it had not been for Gordon's courage, the chlorine would have spurted out for hours until it filled the well.

But except for those who were taken to the hospital, the next day everyone showed up for the Saturday morning meeting. I had talked with Scott the night before and he had felt certain that none of the Mayas would be at work. He said he could hardly blame them.

To our amazement, the Mayas showed up. Some were even early.

Scott was surprised, but not so much that he abandoned his customary unemotional attitude at the meeting. Still coughing, he thanked everyone on the expedition and singled out a few for special credit.

"We learned about chlorination yesterday. We learned how not to do it," he said.

With Folan translating, he told the Mayas that the expedition would take care of any medical expenses resulting from the accident and assured them that the same method of chlorination would not be attempted again.

With one of his rare smiles, Scott announced that we would work only until noon. He suggested that we get plenty of rest that afternoon and have a good, stiff drink in the evening. From the number of nodding heads, I had little doubt that everyone would take his suggestion.

"One other thing," he said. "You know . . . we proved one thing yesterday. We proved we could work as a team."

Harold, Scott and Kirk survey the cenote after the chlorine experiment. Their expressions tell the story.

6

We had nothing but high expectations during the next few days. They began with anticipation of a good breakfast at the hacienda, now that the staff had learned our preferences, and we sometimes got it. Not that it was like ordering a toasted English and coffee before catching the eight-fourteen, of course.

Austin spoke in a low voice as he put in his order.

"Huevos rancheros, jugo de tomate, frijoles fritos y café," he said in recently acquired Spanish.

Austin spoke softly because he wanted to remain as inconspicuous as possible in case Scott walked into the dining room. There was just a slim chance that Scott had not heard about last night's incident, and Austin saw no reason to provoke any questions. The rest of us could not help glancing over at Austin's table where he tried to disappear behind an order of eggs. It had been four days since the chlorine catastrophe, and it was good to have something—or somebody—to laugh at. Here was our chance. Scott walked in. It was the expedition leader's custom to intone a general "Good morning" and then begin his daily fight with the waitress over whether he would be brought three or four glasses of orange juice. This morning his greeting was different.

"Good morning, Austin," Scott said as he walked in.

His nephew sank a little lower in his chair and mumbled a greeting.

"Have a good night last night?" Scott asked.

Austin nodded.

Scott had been especially sensitive about good relations with local officials so no one knew how he would react to last night's incident. Apparently Scott thought it was pretty serious.

Austin had been in the habit of riding his Vespa motorscooter to the campsite each evening after dinner at the hacienda. Since the road around the ruins was full of muddy potholes and ruts, he habitually took a shortcut across the wide expanse of lawn that workmen take great pains to keep neat. In wet weather like this, the tires on the scooter dug up the turf like a tractor. There was, of course, a sign in front of the lawn that read *"No Hay Paso,"* but Austin was unaware that it meant "No Passage." It was not until the guards by the gate told him that he realized the Vespa had to stay on the road. Still, late at night when he was exhausted after a day's work, it was a temptation to defy the guards' orders and sail back to camp across the smooth grass.

The guards could take the defiance only so long. And they might not have taken it that long if they had not known that Austin was the nephew of the boss. Finally, last night, minutes after they saw the scooter plowing up the lawn in the moonlight, they decided to act. Four of the guards got out their rifles, fixed bayonets and marched into camp. They seized the scooter and impounded it, taking the vehicle to the gatehouse and making it clear that it was to remain there. As Scott rushed through breakfast he mentioned casually that he had heard about the scooter incident. Breakfast had been a tense twenty minutes for Austin. A couple of years ago he had been fined five dollars for pushing Dori Dowd off a pier during an argument, and he expected to pay a slightly higher penalty this time.

He usually drove one of the trucks to the well after breakfast, but this morning he elected to ride in the back of the pickup truck that his uncle was driving. The truck rumbled down the highway and then turned off at the gatehouse where the Vespa was parked in plain view of the road. A couple of guards were looking it over. Scott leaned his head out of the cab and shouted back to Austin, "Why don't you see if they want to buy a used scooter?"

In the back of the truck Austin stared at the others.

"He's got to be kidding," he finally said.

Well, one never could be sure about Scott. It *was* an imaginative solution: sell the scooter to the guards. Austin brooded about it, but it was a long time before he concluded that Scott was joking, and longer before he got the scooter back.

It was during the morning meeting on the same day that I realized our recently established teamwork was now making a regular work routine possible. There was an air of efficiency around camp. It took Scott only several minutes to make the job assignments, and there were only a few questions. Later, after the meeting, Scott asked me to help him with an official report for the National Institute of Anthropology and History. It was then that I got a clear picture of the order which had been established.

Scott and I sat in the command shed. Shouting over the roar of trucks and motors, he listed the items he wanted mentioned in the report. One of the main things, he said, was to give the institute a precise idea of how the expedition was organized.

The hierarchy was a troika consisting of Scott, Pablo Bush and Dr. Román Piña Chan. In the background was Kirk Johnson, who rarely had a hand in actual operations (he was not at the site often enough), but who had done no less than put up the working capital for the entire expedition. Harold Martin acted as a liaison between Kirk and the administrative team. The office staff was headed by Dori, and Frank Taylor was in charge of maintaining our vehicles and industrial engines. Gordon Inman headed the team responsible for clarifying the water, and Bill McGehee was chief diver. Victor Segovia was chief archaeologist in Piña Chan's absence. The Maya laborers were under the rather personal control of Avelino who, I soon found out, had selected the work force almost exclusively from his kinfolk.

Archaeologists were no longer waiting for something to happen. The bank was being excavated and artifacts were being brought to the surface. The institute had sent a cataloguist, a man named Otto Schondube, whose appearance startled everyone because he looked exactly like Abraham Lincoln. It was one thing to see the bones of men who were sacrificed a millennium ago, but it was quite another to see the sixteenth President of the United States walking around camp.

Scott's report also gave a good picture of the separate operations at the well. Beyond duties connected with maintaining living conditions at the campsite, operations fell into three categories. We were continuing to follow plan A by pumping water from the well. This allowed us to begin excavations of Thompson's bank, a job that was requiring more and more work each day. Finally, we were also making preparations for plan B in case drainage was impossible. These preparations were difficult since it was often impossible to spare manpower needed in the excavations below. Removal of debris was a continuous job and almost a thankless one for the divers because, while laborers were finding valuable artifacts on the bank, the divers were bringing up nothing but rocks and limbs. Gordon Inman wanted to resume chemical treatment now that the automatic chlorinator had arrived, but the best he could do was to get Scott to stop pumping a few hours each night so the pump could be used for chlorination. Scott's report noted a reduction in algae as a result of this treatment, but actually the reduction was small according to most topside observers and almost nonexistent according to the divers.

Scott and I had to move away from the command shed before he finished with the report since the men working on the winch for the personnel lift had to use a corner of the shed. Scott said not to mention anything about the personnel lift. He had hoped to have it working a few days after we arrived. It was now several weeks since that time, and for a half-dozen reasons the lift was still inoperable.

"Let's take a ride down and have a look at the bank," Scott said.

I signaled to Howard to bring up the cage, and Scott told him to swing us around the southwest quadrant of the well, keeping the cage about fifteen feet from the water level. Although it always made me a little dizzy, I could never keep from looking straight up as the metal cage lifted off the ground. Howard's instant-vertigo machine rose out of the jungle and over the trees, then into the hot blue sky that had not yet filled with rain. A breeze cooled us slightly as the cage swung out over the water and then began a slow descent. Beasom signaled by clenching his fist when we reached fifteen feet, and Howard brought the descent to a halt. We were several feet away from the beginning of the bank, about halfway between the raft and the area where excavations had begun.

As the cage began an arc around the crescent-shaped bank,

"The mud was brought
to screening tables that stood precariously in the slime. . . ."

I saw several huge toads hop laboriously around the southern section. The chlorine might have had some effect on them, but it certainly had not killed them. The chemical had very likely killed off many insects, however, which were the toads' food supply. I also saw the results of the clearing and defoliation efforts which left the bank barren and the cliffs above it white. The Mayas, swinging their efficient coas and machetes, had peeled a slice of jungle off the limestone walls. The breeze had stopped by this time since little wind ever reaches into the depths of the well. The exhaust fumes from the machinery on the raft hung over the water like a cloud. Although the chlorine and fumes had apparently killed most of the insects immediately around the water, there were swarms of gnats and flies where we were, a few feet above the water. Sweat began pouring down our bodies as we neared the excavation site. Freshly turned earth usually has a distinct—almost pleasant—odor, but this was not the case on the bank, where mud smelled of decay and death.

Segovia, Folan and Jerry Griffin were working knee-deep in the mud. They had put up stakes to mark off three-meter sections, but the stakes appeared to be slipping out of place. Maya laborers were working methodically to remove rocks from the bank and to turn over the soft earth according to the archaeologists' direction. Then slowly, working with a trowel or their hands, the archaeologists sifted through the freshly turned ground. After they removed large objects, the mud was brought to two screening tables that stood precariously in the slime. A small pump brought water out of the cenote to the tables where archaeologists let it splash over the soil. The earth was quickly dissolved by the water, but solid objects were left on the screen. Scott and I saw Folan hunched over one of the tables sorting through a batch of these solid objects with the help of several Mayas. Every few minutes Folan or one of his helpers would take something off the screen and put it into a bucket.

"Hey, Scotty," Folan yelled to us, "take this up for us."

He was holding the bucket in his hand. It was half full and had to be taken topside to Otto. Scott waved to Beasom, who gave Howard the signal to lower the cage several more feet.

The copal, which was once burned as sweet incense to Chac,
now smelled of the decay that had enclosed it in the mud of the well.

When we got within reach of the bank, Scott stretched out his
hand and took the bucket from Willie. I looked in it and saw
a variety of objects—bones, small round bells, bits of gold and
globs of copal, incense of the ancient Mayas. It was a temptation
to poke around in the bucket to see what else it contained, but
archaeologists are very sensitive about anyone else handling artifacts, especially before they are catalogued. The bucket smelled
of decay and Scott held it carefully at arm's length. It still
dripped with mud from the bank.

"I never thought pay dirt would be so slimy," Scott said as we neared the top.

Otto was busy at work at the archaeologists' shed. On a table in front of him were the artifacts already found during the two days that excavations had been under way on the bank. He had just finished cataloguing all of them and was now separating those that had to be shipped quickly to Mexico City for preservation and the ones that could be stored at the gatehouse. Jeff and Beasom had seen us bring the bucket up from the bank. They walked quickly over to the shed to watch Otto unload it. Dori and Ann followed a few steps behind them, and within a few minutes several other expedition members had crowded around the shed. Only a few of them had seen any of the artifacts found over the weekend because Otto had taken them out of the buckets one by one as they were examined and catalogued.

We crowded around the table to see relics that had not been touched by sunlight for a thousand years. We peered at the

Pay dirt—or at least, pay mud.

exotic shapes of metalwork and the twisted shapes of bones. The globs of white copal that lay on the table might have burned sweetly when offered to Chac, but now they smelled of the decay that had enclosed them in the mud of the well. These objects on the table, the grotesque and the beautiful, were part of one of the unique treasures of the world, the sacrificial treasure of the Mayas. A small part of the time capsule had been opened, and its contents were being extracted.

Otto was swamped with questions as the crowd grew in the archaeologists' shed. His English was good but not polished enough to handle all the inquiries. Instead, he pointed to one artifact after another, describing it as simply as possible.

Scott and I peered over his shoulder. There were many pieces of gold—a crushed bell, not more than two inches long, topped with the effigy of a god; a fragment of another bell which apparently had been crushed in a similar manner; five or six strips of gold leaf, and four laminated discs.

"These are projectile points," Otto said, pointing to two small and delicately carved pieces of flint.

" 'These are projectile points,' Otto said. . . ."

Someone called them arrowheads in asking a question, but Otto made the distinction. Archaeologists did not yet know the function of the points, and since archery as we know it was unknown in ancient Mayab, the word arrowhead did not apply. I examined them myself and was surprised by their fragility. The points were so thin that one of them was translucent. It seemed that they would have easily broken if used to kill any animal larger than a rabbit. A man would almost have to co-operate with his assailant in order to be killed by such a delicate weapon.

"Dientes perforados," Otto said for the benefit of two Mexican divers, Luís Concha and Hernán Gutiérrez, who had also joined the crowd in the shed. "Perforated teeth," he translated for the rest of us.

The teeth he held in his hand were small and dull, the normally jagged edges having been worn away either by a lifetime of eating tough food or by a millennium of attrition in the cenote. Otto explained that ancient Mayas perforated the teeth so they could be strung into necklaces. Looking somewhat less macabre were the jade and stone beads that Otto pointed to next. Fragments of jade plaques, two or three bones and several small copper bells rounded out the array of artifacts.

While several expedition members were still asking questions, Otto began to unload the bucket we had just brought him. Another projectile point lay on top. He lifted it out gently and put it to one side. Next came several jade beads, similar to the ones we had just seen on the table. After taking out three large pieces of copal, Otto reached deep into the bucket and withdrew a human skull, the cranium of a sacrificial victim. We were silent as he turned the skull from one side to the other. It had not belonged to a sacrificed warrior or a woman. It was the skull of a child, a boy or girl not more than five years old at the time its death was declared necessary to propitiate Chac.

Scott and I left the archaeologists' shed to find his brother, Sam, who had just returned from Texas, where he had gone to find a pressure gauge for the discharge line. Scott was in a hurry to have the gauge attached so he could determine how much water we were pumping from the well. We found Sam near the

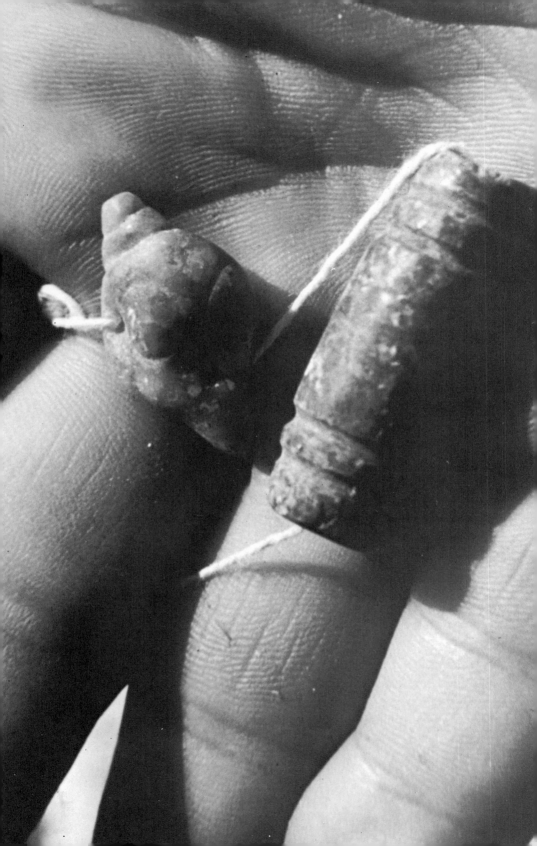

Jade beads, like those once worn by the young victims.

Jerry Griffin holds a suspiciously small skull.

winch for the personnel lift; among other things, Sam was in charge of getting the lift to work. Scott asked him where the gauge was.

"This is it over here," Sam said. He walked a few steps and picked up a piece of wood that looked like half of a pair of stilts. Scott looked incredulous.

Sam had tried to buy a gauge for the eight-inch pipe last week in Yucatán, but he could not find one. We had expected him to return from Texas with the type of pressure gauge customarily used for measuring water flow in a pipe. Instead, he had come back with this wooden gadget. Sam grinned and challenged Scott to watch him put the device to work at the end of the discharge line. Scott nodded dubiously.

Lack of a gauge had been one of our big problems. Before Scott could make any decision about how long to continue pumping, he first had to know how much water was seeping back into the cenote, and to know that, he had first to determine the amount of water being pumped out. The centrifugal pump on the raft, boosted by the topside pump, was capable of moving 120,000 gallons an hour. But since the pipe that ran from one pump to the other had to climb vertically up the cliff of the well, it was inconceivable that we were discharging at maximum capacity. Some speculated that the pumps were running at only 50 per cent of capacity, but no one actually knew.

Scott asked Inman to go along on the hike through the bush to the end of the discharge line. Gordon had said earlier that he wanted to talk about some new problems that had developed over chemical treatment. Since they might be related to the pumping operation, Scott thought this would also be a good time to discuss them.

We followed the aluminum pipe from the booster pump into the bush. It was cooler under the shade of the scrub jungle, but mosquitoes and gnats swarmed around the trickles of water that spouted from several pipe joints. Considering the uneven terrain and the speed with which the pipe had been assembled, the discharge line was remarkably free of leaks. Scott figured that leakage would amount to only a small fraction of 1 per cent of the water being discharged through the line. The pipe had been supplied to the expedition by the W. R. Ames Company, an international manufacturer of irrigation equipment, and it was of a type particularly adaptable to our needs. The thirty-foot sections were lightweight and could easily be carried through the bush. Assembling was accomplished simply by joining the ends of two sections. Springlike devices on the ends linked them easily and water pressure made the joints tight.

"The Mayas say the water will always go back in the well regardless how much we pump," Scott reminded us. "They think Chac is more powerful than our equipment."

Two weeks ago some of the expedition members were inclined to agree with the Mayas, but now it appeared that Chac was losing out. We could hear the water rumbling through the pipe with a force Chac had not been able to overcome, at least not yet.

"I suppose you've heard the stories about how Chac is going to get his revenge," Sam said as we walked farther down the line.

Scott raised his eyebrows.

"The rumor circulating among the workers has it that three men must die because of what we're doing to the well," Sam explained.

"Why three?" Scott asked.

Sam said he did not know, and Inman's short chuckle apparently indicated his opinion of Maya rumors. Scott also laughed. I knew that he had risked death dozens of times during his career as a treasure hunter, and that superstitions bothered him less than the gnats around his face.

The earth was muddy near the end of the discharge line, and our feet sank deep into the soil as we neared the gushing water that flowed down an incline into the dried-up sinkhole. The water was gushing out at a rate of somewhere between one and two thousand gallons a minute.

"Where's that wooden thing you've got?" Scott had to shout to make himself heard over the roar of the water.

Sam brought up the measuring device, which resembled a capital H with one of the vertical sides removed. Essentially it was a yardstick with a short peg attached perpendicular to it. Sam laid the yardstick portion on top of the pipe so that the perpendicular peg dangled in the outflowing stream. In this position the water caught the peg and moved the entire device forward. It moved, of course, only to the point at which the flow bent downward and no longer touched the peg. Sam looked at the yardstick and noted that there were about twenty-four inches between the end of the pipe and the downward bend in the water spout.

"We're dealing with constants," he said. "That downward bend is different for each volume of water flowing through an eight-inch pipe."

He pulled a chart out of his shirt pocket, unfolded it and ran his finger down one side of the paper to the number of inches that corresponded to the distance the water had pushed out the piece of wood. Sam then correlated this figure with the diameter of the pipe.

"Eighty-five thousand gallons an hour," he shouted.

That was the answer. We were taking eighty-five thousand gallons of water from the well each hour. Gordon winced and Scott shook his head. We were pumping at only 70 per cent of capacity.

Sam repeated the measuring procedure, further explaining the wooden gauge.

"Eighty-five thousand gallons of water flowing out of an eight-inch pipe will always bend down at exactly the same distance from the mouth of the pipe," he said. "If we had a ten-inch pipe, the water would start falling closer to the mouth. If the diameter were smaller, the water would gush out farther before bending down."

The second and third checks gave more or less the same answer although there appeared to be some fluctuation in the rate. It varied between eighty-two thousand and eighty-six thousand gallons an hour. This variance led Scott to think that there might be something wrong with the fittings on the pump connections. He said he would have them checked the first thing that afternoon.

Meanwhile we took a closer look at the old cenote where the discharge water was being dumped. The sinkhole was obviously not filling up with water, but this was actually a mixed blessing. At least there was no danger of having the old cenote fill up and overflow, but Scott was disappointed at the fast rate at which it was absorbing the discharge water. He theorized that because the sinkhole was so deep, the water was seeping quickly into the underground streams and flowing back to the sacred well.

"Sam, why don't you and Folan scout around for another drainage area. Maybe this one's actually too deep," Scott said.

The ideal would be an area large enough to hold the water we were pumping out but not so deep that the water would seep into the underground network of streams.

Gordon was especially worried about this problem of seepage since it was affecting the critical acid-alkali balance, picking up acid from the soil as it passed into the underground streams and carrying this acid back to the well. If much more acid built up in the cenote, he said, the water would become so corrosive that the pump would probably break down in a matter of weeks.

"Of course, it's true that this water is losing some impurities as it passes through the soil," Gordon continued, "but from my point

Wayne Vanderlow (left) and Gordon Inman mix up a new batch of chemicals . . . to counteract the last batch of chemicals.

of view the increased acidity is too high a price to pay for slightly clearer water at this stage of the game." Scott said he agreed.

Gordon was worried about acidity for another reason. In order to get the maximum benefit from chlorine, he had to introduce cyanuric acid into the well, thereby adding to the corrosiveness. To counteract the acid the filtration team had to dump more soda ash into the well, but this was a tedious job. To be effective soda ash had to be spread around evenly, not just dumped in one spot, and, of course, the only means we had to spread it was the CEDAM raft, which was currently undergoing a new round of repairs. Gordon had used the raft yesterday morning before it began listing, but a sudden and heavy rain ruined his efforts. The two bags of soda ash on the raft solidified and became hot as soon as the rain came into contact with the alkali compound.

As we walked back along the pipeline, the discussion centered on the cause of the well's filling up nearly as fast as we could

Austin watches some hand-spreading of chemicals from the CEDAM raft, for once floating instead of sinking.

pump it out. It could be refilling in one of two ways or, more likely, in a combination of the two. Either the same water was finding its way back to the well, or the underground streams were pouring new water into it nearly as quickly as we could pump the old water out.

"I guess from our standpoint it would be better to have re-circulating water in spite of the acid problem," Scott said. "I don't think we'd ever have any hope of controlling the in-flow if the cenote is filling up constantly with new water. On the other hand, if it's refilling with the drainage water, we have a chance of controlling it by shifting the discharge line. The objective is to find a place that can hold the water the longest."

Folan had come up from the bank while we were in the bush. He and Otto were poring over another bucket of objects which had been caught in the screening tables. Scott and Sam talked with Willie for a few minutes about finding a new discharge while I watched Otto sort out the relics and make entries in his catalogue.

"*Número treinta y nueve, disco pequeño, oro laminado, S1.*" Number thirty-nine, a small disc of laminated gold. "S1" referred to the section on the bank in which it was found. "*Punta de proyectil*"—another projectile point; "*cascabel de oro*"—a gold bell, and "*cuenta pequeña, rectangular*"—a small rectangular bead, in this case of jade.

Sam and Willie agreed to spend their lunch hour looking for a new depression to hold the discharge water, but Sam first wanted to assign some of the Mayas to work on the personnel lift. There were two things that hampered the lift. First, the winch had been difficult to control although this problem appeared to have been solved. Beyond that, the H-frame did not extend far enough out over the ledge. Since the frame was implanted in concrete and was therefore impossible to move, Sam planned to lower some Mayas over the side and let them hack away at the protruding rock that was getting in the way of the lift.

Scott, Folan and Sam continued to talk about a new drainage site, but I was too absorbed with watching Otto sort out the new pieces of treasure to hear much of what they said. Suddenly, however, I was aware that the conversation had stopped abruptly. I turned around and saw the three men staring at the entrance to the campsite.

When I looked in that direction, my jaw sagged. The man walking into camp was one of the strangest men I had ever seen. He stood about five-foot-nine and wore no shirt or shoes. His body was dark brown from the sun. His nose was a massive beak. His hair was shoulder-length and it was tied in back, American colonial style. He didn't really walk, he bounced, and his hair bobbed up and down with each step.

Whoever he was, he seemed to know most of the Mexicans at camp. They greeted him with waves and smiles while the Americans greeted him with silence and stares. I had not noticed at first but walking behind him was Pablo Bush, who motioned to the man when they came near the archaeologists' shed.

"Norman, I want you to meet a friend of mine," Pablo said. "This is Gitano—'Gypsy' in English."

Scott grinned and put out his hand. "I've heard your name," he said.

Gypsy nodded as though he understood what Scott had said.

I had heard of Gypsy too. Gypsy was one of Mexico's most famous divers. In this part of the country he was *the* most famous. He lived on Cozumel and made his living showing visitors to that island a world beneath the ocean. He had done a lot of work with CEDAM, and it was in that connection that I had heard his name.

Don Pablo said Gypsy would be around camp for several days and would put his talents at our service.

"Tell Gypsy that we're honored to have him here and that his talents will certainly be needed. We have a lot of diving work to do in the next few days," Scott said.

Gitano laughed and bounced away for a look at the well. Judging by his laughter, I figured he got a kick out of seeing the formidable home of Chac humbled by tons of modern machinery. The next time I looked he was being lifted down into the cenote.

Don Pablo had just come back from overseeing repairs on his

house in Cozumel and was interested in the artifacts that Otto was sorting. He spent several minutes examining them before walking around the camp for a look at the rest of our operations.

"Why don't we have lunch at the hacienda, Norman?" he said before leaving.

"Thanks, but I want to take a look at the pump fittings on the raft. We found out this morning that we're only pumping at about seventy per cent of capacity."

Scott was in the habit of skipping lunch. At best he would stuff a sandwich in his mouth while doing two or three other things. He went off with Sam to talk to the Mayas who were going to chip some of the cliff away, and I decided to head back to the hacienda myself. I was thirsty and hungry.

The hacienda was the nearest thing to a home we had on the expedition, and it had been home to earlier explorers at Chichén Itzá. Before that, it stood as a witness to the violent history of Yucatán. I had missed a ride to the hacienda and it was a long walk from the camp. The road was hot and the ubiquitous gnats swarmed around my face as I walked up the sacbe past the Temple of Kukulcán and then onto the main road. Twenty minutes later I was at the entrance to the hacienda, and indeed it felt like home.

The limestone walls of the ancient building blurred before me as heat rose from the ground around it. Sixteenth-century Spaniards had pillaged the ruins and removed limestone blocks with which they built the hacienda. Its role for nearly three centuries was that of a plantation house that oversaw hundreds of acres of impoverished land. The plantation was destroyed and the hacienda burned during the bloody uprising of 1847, when Mayas regained control of the Yucatán Peninsula. When Edward Thompson saw it at the turn of the century, it was just another ruin, "shapeless heaps of toppled walls and jungle tangle," as he put it. Still, he dreamed of repairing the building and setting up a productive farm. Thompson accomplished only the former objective. He was in the midst of restoration when his troubles began with the Mexican government, which was outraged by his decision to send to the United States the objects he found in the well. There was a law suit, and an enterprising Mexican, Fernando Barbachano, saw an opportunity to acquire Thompson's land, which encompassed nearly all of Chichén Itzá. After litigation and negotiation, Barbachano found himself the owner of the oldest city of continuous occupancy in the Western Hemisphere. He died between the 1960 and 1967 expeditions, and his descendants inherited the property, now part of a tourist empire that stretches from Cozumel to Mexico City. The hacienda is fully restored now and has the look of a building that has been home to many people. Despite the modern touches and the thousands of guests who have stayed there, the hacienda still looks as immutable as the Temple of Kukulcán. In fact, the building blocks of both structures had been dug from the earth many centuries ago. In a very real sense the hacienda has risen from the earth that surrounds it.

I climbed wearily up the stone steps and sank into a chair on the veranda. A boy brought me a rum and tonic, and I asked him to tell the kitchen that I would be ready for lunch as soon as it could be put on the table. Then I sat back, took a couple of swallows and looked out at the gardens in front of the hacienda. Just visible beyond an ancient tree was the Gate of Sadness which formed another entrance to the hacienda enclosure. Its slightly Byzantine form would have been inconspicuous in Eastern Europe, but here the stone archway stood out as a reminder of Moorish influence in Spanish architecture. It was at this gate that Mayas divided their booty after attacking Spanish homes during the rebellion of 1847. It became known as the Gate of Sadness because the booty included women and children. Now I saw a little girl playing under the gate with one of the dozen dogs that guard the hacienda. I was thinking about the irony of the scene, but my head kept nodding and my eyes closed. I was exhausted and simply could not stay awake.

"Hey, Don, how about some lunch?"

The voice was Don Pablo's. I had no idea how long I had been asleep. He chuckled. "I'll meet you in the dining room in five minutes," he said. "The food's already on the table."

7

DON PABLO was excited about the treasure that was coming up from Thompson's bank.

"This expedition is going to be a great victory for CEDAM," he said as we began our lunch at the hacienda.

He was proud of CEDAM's role in the expedition, but I was embarrassed to admit that I really did not know very much about the organization. I had found out, however, that CEDAM is politically powerful, an attribute one would not usually associate with a diving club without taking into account the unfathomable politics of Mexico. Don Pablo briefed me on the organization which he founded and which he personally controlled.

The club had its beginning in 1948 when the Frogmen Club of Mexico was organized. Although the frogmen were devoted to diving mainly as a sport and recreation, some of the members wanted to broaden the aims of the group. In 1958 it became CEDAM, an organization devoted not only to sports but to science. In 1966 the scope was broadened even further with the creation of CEDAM International.

"CEDAM places the sport of diving and the talents of its members at the service of country, science and humanity," Don Pablo said.

Don Pablo himself had grown up in Mexico City, working his way up from a workman in an automobile shop to owner of several car dealerships. He was also one of Mexico's best-known sportsmen and hunters. One of several books he has written deals with his hunting adventures in Africa and Mexico.

"But you know," he said, "I don't hunt any more."

I asked him why not.

"Several years ago on a safari in Africa, I shot a monkey out of a tree," he said. "When I went over to look at it, I saw a face that was more human than I'd expected. It was like a child. I've never killed an animal since."

I asked him what he thought about the prophecy of death that was being bruited about camp by the Mayas. Don Pablo said most contemporary Mayas put a great deal of stock in *brujería,* or witchcraft, and that the prophecy must be understood in light of the ignorance that breeds this witchcraft.

"But what if some of the local people take matters into their own hands in order to make the prophecy come true?"

Don Pablo was silent for a few seconds and then burst out in an enormous laugh. I could not tell whether he thought I was a fool even to think about such things or whether, just possibly, he was laughing to cover up his own apprehension.

"Speaking of witchcraft, did you get a chance to talk to the woman who came here to see the doctor today?" Don Pablo asked.

I explained that I had been with Scott all morning and had little chance to speak to anyone else. Don Pablo said he had heard about her just before he drove to the hacienda for lunch. The woman came from one of the remote villages about twenty miles from here. She had stepped on a nail or spike, and since there was no doctor in her village, she walked here to see the physician at the campsite.

"The point is," Don Pablo said, "that the woman stepped on the nail nearly two weeks ago. The men in her village tried to heal it with *brujería* but the wound got no better. Finally she defied her husband and started out with her son to walk to

Valladolid. They got lost on the way but met someone who told her we had a doctor at camp so they headed here instead."

The expedition doctor, Sol Heinemann, had seen to it that we would have ready access to medication and treatment but he visited the site only from time to time. He was not here at the moment. Don Pablo said someone volunteered to drive the woman to Mérida but that her son, who was about fifteen years old, was afraid to go with her.

There was an interesting point in the incident that helped allay some of my fears about the prophecy: witchcraft seemed to be harmful only in a passive sense, in the way that it blinded people to the modern world around them. The woman might easily die, but the men in her village did not actively plan her death; instead, she found herself hopelessly trapped in the world of *brujería* and could not free herself until gangrene had become the real threat to her life.

"I hope this expedition goes on into next year because I'd like to take you deeper into the jungle," Don Pablo said. "Life there hasn't changed appreciably in more than nine hundred years, and the last real change that occurred was when the Toltecs invaded Mayab."

"Hope" was a sour note in what Don Pablo said. I had been led to think that if we were successful enough, the expedition would automatically continue into the next year. Don Pablo looked as though he did not want to dwell on the subject, but he did indicate that the expedition had run into some kind of financial difficulty. It was doubtful, he said, that we would be able to work past December 5. If that were true, we had less than two months in which to continue excavations.

"That's why I'm so excited about the discoveries on Thompson's bank. We're finding a lot of artifacts at a fast rate, and that's important since we're working against time," he said.

Nearly everyone has his own idea about the origins of Maya civilization, but Don Pablo's was unique. He believed the ancient Mayas had many contacts from beyond the sea and that these contacts occurred so long ago that specific traces had been erased or so interwoven with other sources as to be indistinguishable.

This idea differs from the thought of many students who believe the Mayas were influenced by one specific cultural group—the Phoenicians, the Egyptians, the Vikings or, as some even believe, the Hebrews. The fashionable opinion now among archaeologist-anthropologists is to credit the Mayas with everything and to discount the theory of foreign influence.

Don Pablo was also obviously enthusiastic about the discoveries on the bank because they might give him the shreds of evidence he wanted to bolster his theory.

One thing bothered him about our current progress. It was Scott.

"As soon as I came back from Cozumel and saw him at the site, I noticed how exhausted he looked," Don Pablo said.

It was true. Scott had been awake until two in the morning last night and then got up before dawn to catch up on paper work. At the site he had to oversee each operation and be every-where at once.

When we returned to the well after lunch, Scott was coming back from the bush with Willie Folan. They had found a new discharge area some eight hundred feet west of the well and just to the south of the airstrip. It was a shallow depression that might, ages ago, have been a sinkhole. The depression was larger than the old sinkhole we were using now, and they hoped shallow enough to keep the water from seeping down into underground streams.

Scott told Willie to round up a Maya work force to blaze a new trail through the bush this afternoon.

When expedition members arrived at the well, even if they had been away only an hour or so, they invariably went to the ledge and looked at the water. I was no exception; I went to the ledge and peered down to see how much progress had been made, how much more of the bank was exposed and how much clearer the water was becoming. What caught my eye this time were rain-bow streaks across the surface of the water—oil.

I asked around camp how the oil got there, but it took a little time before finally one of the Mayas was willing to tell me. Jeff and Austin had changed the oil in the pump engine before stopping for lunch. Beasom Painter had not realized that they were taking up two buckets of oil when he decided to give them a dunking. Jeff and Austin were halfway out of the well when Beasom gave Howard the signal to lower the cage. The divers shouted up for him to stop, but Beasom could not hear them over the roar of the topside engines. A few seconds later the cage was under water, and the two buckets of dirty oil were emptying into the cenote. By the time Beasom realized what had happened, it was too late to do anything about it.

What started out as a practical joke ended as a minor catastrophe. We had no means of removing oil from the water. Since it was on the surface, the oil would never reach the intake line to the filtration system. The only way to get it out was by hand; we would have to scoop it off the surface, bucket by bucket, a process that would not only take many days to accomplish but which would divert our manpower from more important jobs. Beasom, of course, felt rotten about the whole thing.

The same Maya who told me about the oil (he was Avelino's cousin, I think) told me two more coral snakes had been found behind the campers. He theorized that the garbage which we were throwing out attracted small animals. These, in turn, attracted the deadly *coralitas* which fed on the small animals. As he told me about the snakes I could see fear in his eyes. Like other inhabitants of Mayab, he was unreasonably afraid of snakes. The Maya pointed toward the archaeologists' shed where two jars stood at one end of the sorting table. I walked over and saw the two live coral snakes, both small and lethal, but both ringed with beautiful colors—as though nature were trying to disguise the fact that the coral snake is the most poisonous serpent in North America. I assumed that Jeff, a zoology student, was responsible for keeping the snakes. If the Mayas had had their way, the *coralitas* would have been killed.

Snakes were the only thing that Mayas feared in the bush, and they had developed a sharp eye for anything moving in the undergrowth. There was no evidence of timidity in the way they lunged into the task of cutting another trail for the discharge line, and as I stood there at the archaeologists' shed I could already hear the swish of the machetes and the sharp cracks of the coas. If two snakes had been found on the edge of camp, many more would probably turn up as we cleared a path eight hundred feet long into the bush.

I glanced over at Otto, still working hard on the latest package delivered to him from the bank.

"*Cuenta tubular, dos perforaciones, material—jade.*" In English the catalogue entry would read: "tubular bead, two perforations, material—jade." Below that entry Otto listed offerings of copal and copper bells.

I could hear the workers hacking the trail in the bush, but Scott's voice rose above all the noise. He wanted to supervise the start of the work, and I could hear him shouting orders to Folan, who translated them into Spanish for Avelino. The foreman translated the orders into Maya for the fifteen men who were stomping over the muddy jungle floor and hacking down the tough trees that stood in their way.

Scott emerged several minutes later to look for Jack Kiefer. He wanted Jack to oversee the construction of wooden ramps from Thompson's bank to the big raft. Apart from the other almost unbearable working conditions on the bank, archaeologists were having trouble with the screening process. The small pump that brought the water from the cenote to the tables was constantly breaking down. Scott thought he could avoid using the small pump altogether by moving the screening operation to the big raft. The idea had many advantages. It was easier to set up tables on a wood surface than in the mud, and getting the tables off the bank would give workers more room to work in. Scott said Jack would be in charge of building the ramps, but he wanted to go down to the raft with him right now to make sure the distances were measured correctly.

Scott also wanted to check on the oil, which by now had spread over some 80 per cent of the well. With all our equipment, he thought that there must be a way to remove the oil without having to do it by hand.

To Scott and Jack on the raft, it was obvious that the raft would have to be moved closer to the bank in order to make the ramp idea feasible. The raft was now fifty feet away from the main work area on the bank, and Scott said it would have to be brought within twenty feet. Moving it would not be easy, and Scott went back topside to check with Jerry Kemler on lengthening the umbilical cord and shifting the firehoses.

On top Scott was greeted with the news that the new trail had been completed. Again, it seemed spectacular that fifteen Mayas could blaze an eight-hundred-foot trail and lay thirty sections of pipe in less than an hour. Scott gave the order to turn the pumps back on. Within seconds we heard the water gushing up the hoses, into the manifold, up to the booster and then out into the jungle where—we hoped—it would remain.

Before he could confer with Kemler, Scott spotted Piña Chan, who had said earlier that he needed to talk with the expedition leader a few minutes. It had begun to rain, but like other expedition members, Piña and Scott had become reconciled to discomfort. They stood in the rain and chatted as calmly as though they were standing at a bar in a Holiday Inn.

Piña Chan had decided that a limited amount of recovery could begin in the well itself. Chlorination and filtration had extended the visibility in the water to three or four feet, making it possible for divers to see what they were doing under water. As long as they worked carefully, Piña said, he saw no reason why they could not begin to bring up some of the less fragile artifacts.

By less fragile objects, Piña meant large pieces of ceramics, copal, carved stone, cast metals and possibly bones that were obviously not part of an articulated skeleton. Right now the divers were leaving everything alone at the bottom of the well except a few items they spotted while clearing away the boulders and limbs. Piña agreed that there was hardly any point in not bringing these up since it was unlikely they could be found again easily. The type of objects which archaeologists wanted the divers to leave alone included gold leaf, delicate pottery, cloth, wood (although the odds were a million to one against our finding man-made objects of wood) and bones found joined or in clusters. No articulated skeleton of a sacrificial victim had ever been found, although finding one was vital to reconstructing the rite of sacrifice.

When Scott went back to the raft he told Bill McGehee of Piña's decision. The news was a big morale boost to McGehee and the other divers. Bringing up nothing but massive chunks of limestone was not the most rewarding experience, although the divers even had this job worked out to a precise routine. In addition to the personnel lift, we had a large square bucket that looked something like a sandbox. This was used primarily to lift rocks and debris from the well. The crane put the bucket directly into the water and lowered it to the bottom where divers could fill it. When it was full, one of the divers pulled on a rope attached to a small block of floating Styrofoam. When Beasom saw the block bob up and down in the water, he would give the crane operator a signal to lift the bucket. Divers also had signals for the bucket to be moved to the right or left and closer to or farther from the bank. The system worked well, but the divers were more than eager to forget the rocks and bring up the treasure that lay under them.

Jeff and Austin were working under water at the moment, but when they came up Bill would tell them about the decision. In addition, Bill suggested it might be a good idea for Piña or Victor to have a talk with the diving team tonight at the hacienda. Bill also said he could give diving instruction to the archaeologists any time they were ready.

Until this point in the expedition not much had been said about teaching the archaeologists how to SCUBA dive, but it was a crucial step in the success of the venture. In fact, the 1960 expedition might have lasted much longer if Mexican archaeologists had been trained to dive. Since they were not, there was no way to resolve a controversy that arose over whether the airlifts were breaking artifacts as the mud was vacuumed from the bottom and disgorged at the screening tables. Scott had several ways to eliminate such a controversy this time. He planned to train archaeologists to dive so they could see the objects *before* as well as after the airlift handled them. He was convinced that the airlift, while very powerful, did not break artifacts because water cushioned them throughout the operation. Clarification of the water would further aid archaeologists in determining the harm-lessness of the device. Moreover, if the water were clear and if archaeologists were in it, they could single out any particularly fragile object if there was the slightest doubt about whether it should go through the airlift.

Jeff had surfaced and come to the raft while Bill and Scott were talking. Bill excused himself and reached for a back pack. It was his turn to join Austin in the grimy work at the bottom of the cenote. The surface of the water looked as though the *Torrey Canyon* had sailed through earlier that day, and Bill spent no time swimming through the oil. He somersaulted off the raft and plunged head first into deep water. Seconds later, bubbles broke the surface where he had descended.

The sight of the oil disgusted Scott. Part of the filtration team was on the raft, and he asked them again if they had any ideas about clearing it up. Inman was at a loss for suggestions, but a visiting businessman connected with Purex, Harvey Campbell, was experienced in the problem. He ruled out the possibility of burning off the oil but thought we might be able to rig up a device that would skim it off the surface. Campbell suggested that a barrel be submerged in the well just a fraction of an inch below the surface of the water. This, he said, would cause the surface water to pour into the barrel. A small water pump could be used to empty the barrel, but it would have to pump the water out as fast as it was coming in. Scott thought the plan might work and told Inman and Campbell to get whatever materials they needed to put the device in operation.

Below the oily surface Bill was finding his way to the area where Austin was working. The afternoon sun pierced the first ten feet of water with a dim green light. Bill reached for the line that was attached to the signal buoy and followed it down. The light turned greenish brown as he descended further, and finally he was in a world of near blackness.

He reached the end of the buoy line and swam toward a hazy shape which he thought was the wooden basket. When he came nearer, he realized it was nothing but the white limestone on the south wall of the cenote. He reversed himself, swam cautiously back to the buoy line and then headed to the right. About ten feet away he spotted the dim outline of Austin's body. The young diver was carrying a large chunk of rock toward the wooden basket, which Bill could now see in the distance as his eyes adjusted to the dark. Bill swam to Austin and made his presence known by a tap on the shoulder. Austin smiled through his mask and proceeded to dump the rock into the basket.

The two divers began scanning the area for other debris that could be taken up in the same load. The area they were swimming in was directly below the altar from which sacrifices were believed to have been made; most of the archaeologists thought it was going to be the most fertile area for treasure. This section of the bottom was generally free of large tree limbs but it was dotted with boulders, many of them so large that the crane would have to remove them one at a time. When the divers looked straight up they could see a faint glow of light, but when they looked horizontally, visibility seemed to be much worse. When Bill stretched out his arm, he could barely see his finger tips. The well was so dark that in order to search the bottom, he and Austin swam with their bellies scraping against the jagged stones that protruded from the mud.

Austin spotted a cluster of rocks that looked challenging, several small ones resting on top and between three boulders directly in the altar area. The divers went back to bring the basket closer. The plan was to get the basket adjacent to the cluster so the smaller rocks could be toppled in. The smaller ones weighed between one and two hundred pounds, but a man has no trouble moving that weight under water. After removing the rocks on top, Austin thought there was a chance, however slim, of shoving one of the boulders into the basket. But even if that were impossible, the large rocks would at least be in position to be hauled up individually by the crane.

It took about ten minutes to put the smaller stones into the basket. While Bill was trying to get them evenly distributed, Austin looked over the next target, the three large stones, at least one of which had carvings. Two of them looked as though they weighed several hundred pounds and the third might have weighed a ton. Austin picked the one to the right end of the cluster to work on first. It had a straight side that sank into the mud, but he also noticed a small crevice near the bottom of the stone that could be used for leverage if he could get himself into the proper position.

Austin had no way of knowing how far down in the mud the boulder extended, but he wrestled his body down beside one of the other rocks so he could work his hand into the crevice. He finally succeeded. With both hands now firmly inside the opening, he strained to push upward. But as he shoved, his feet slid farther into the slime. He tried again, but his legs only sank deeper in the mud under the rock.

The boulder moved. The movement was sudden and in the opposite direction from what Austin had expected. It was only when he tried to move to the other side of the rock that he realized what had happened.

He was trapped, pinned in the soft mud from the thighs down. He tried to grab hold of the boulder and pull himself up but the motion only caused the rock to slip once more.

Now he was pinned in the mud from the waist down.

Austin could see Bill circling the area not more than ten yards away, but Bill did not see him. If Austin took his hands off the boulder, he knew he would slip down farther, but he had to signal Bill. Hanging on with one hand, he raised the other and waved slowly. A sudden movement might make the rock slip again. Bill did not see the signal at first but as he headed toward the rocks he saw Austin's hand barely sticking out above the boulder.

The chief diver realized the emergency. Bill did not know exactly how much air Austin had left, but he remembered seeing him change tanks about an hour ago. Thus Austin would be out of air any minute.

Austin breathed slowly. He controlled each breath, spaced them as far apart as possible. Bill could see the fear in his face. Bill jackknifed his body and headed for the surface. He hit the top and swam for the CEDAM raft where Scott was talking with Gordon Inman.

"Austin's trapped."

Scott stopped in midsentence.

"Not much air left. Give me another tank," Bill shouted.

Scott jumped from one raft to the other, grabbed a fresh tank and heaved it over the side. Bill took it and dived for the bottom.

Scott gave the order to start filling all air tanks. He signaled Beasom to raise the basket and then ran for the intercom. Scott gave instructions for the basket to be lowered to the big raft and remain there until he ordered otherwise. Topside personnel were told to get a car ready for ambulance duty.

On top, a carload of gear was thrown out of a vehicle, and one of the cots that night watchmen slept on was readied as a stretcher. Jerry Griffin assembled a supply of first-aid equipment.

In the water, Bill could still see bubbles from Austin's air supply as he plunged down toward the bottom. Once there, he could see Austin was trying something dangerous, desperately trying to twist his body free while still hanging onto the boulder with his hands.

Bill had to make a fast decision: give Austin the new air tank or try to pull him free? Bill made his choice; he set the fresh tank on the bottom and reached for Austin.

Austin waved him away. He was afraid any movement on that side of the rock might cause it to slip again.

Bill went to the other side. Maybe there was a chance he could pull the boulder away or at least move it in the opposite direction so Austin could squirm free. On the first attempt Bill managed to budge the stone but Austin had no time to slip out of the trap before the boulder settled again.

Bill decided to take another chance. He swam to the other side of the rock and grabbed Austin under the arms. He wanted to pull back as hard as he could, but there was no leverage. He could not get any leverage by standing in the mud and he could not risk bracing himself against the boulder.

On the raft, diver tenders worked quickly and silently to fill every air tank in sight. The crane operator lowered the basket to the raft, and Scott repeated his orders for it to stay there. The expedition leader put on a diving rig himself and jumped over the side.

Scott swam to the spot where he thought he had seen bubbles coming to the surface and plunged down.

Under the water Bill pondered the seriousness of the problem. It might take hours to get Austin free. The crane might have to be used to move the boulder. He decided to give Austin the fresh tank.

While Bill was reaching for the tank, Austin felt his hands slipping away from the rock. He was exhausted. He sank deeper into the mud. As he sank, he realized something about the trap. When Bill lifted up the new air tank, ready to exchange it, Austin waved him away again. He had just discovered his own escape route.

Scott was not more than twenty feet away from the divers, but he could not see them. He had misjudged the location of the bubbles and his descent had taken him too far toward the center of the well. He groped around the rocks; it was nearly four o'clock and visibility had diminished to less than eighteen inches in the area where he swam. He doubled back and headed more toward the west, then made a series of wide circles, each taking him farther from the altar area. Finally he reached the south wall of the cenote and followed it to the east in another desperate attempt to find the divers.

Scott reached a part of the altar area where the bottom appeared to have been recently disturbed. He saw a cluster of three rocks and noticed a wide hole beside one of them. He reached his hands into the mud but found nothing but small stones. Bill and Austin must be still farther to the east, he figured. The minutes dragged on. To Scott it seemed he must have been searching for a half hour. Darkness was enveloping the well. Gripped with fear and frustration, Scott decided to surface. Maybe he could still see air bubbles at the top.

His head broke the oily surface of the water a half minute later. Harold Martin yelled to him. Scott looked in the direction of the small raft. The emergency was over.

Austin was stretched out on the small raft. Bill was huddled over him, doctoring his leg. Scott swam closer to the raft, pulled himself onto it and walked over to Bill. He gave the chief diver a pat on the back and then looked at Austin. His leg was badly bruised, and one knee cap had been slashed on the side by a jagged rock. But on the whole his injuries were minor.

Neither of the divers could explain exactly how Austin had gotten free. Bill said that after Austin had waved him away, he had watched anxiously as Austin sank deeper into the mud. Austin explained that it had occurred to him that he might slip out from under the rock by first getting down deeper.

"I had to try something," Austin said.

The near-catastrophe had exhausted us all, but when we assembled on top for a ride back to the hacienda, we were met with more disappointments.

Sam walked over to the command shed where we were standing and told Scott that the new attempt at fixing the personnel lift had failed. Maya laborers had hacked at the cenote wall all afternoon, Sam said, but they managed to chip off only a fraction of the obstacle that stood in the way of the lift. He said the only way to get the lift in operation was to extend the H-frame farther out over the precipice, a job that would require extensive welding.

"In that case, we'll probably have to wait a few days," Harold said.

When Scott asked why, Harold explained that Jerry Kemler was sick in his camper and that Jeff's eyes had not recovered enough for him to do any welding. A few minutes later Scott found out that Kiefer was also running a high fever. Luckily, however, he had managed to finish taking the measurements for the ramps.

Although these were the only illnesses so far, some of the divers were having a rough time combating ear infection. The small amount of chlorine that had gone into solution might have killed some bacteria, but there was still enough around to make ear infection a constant hazard. Daily swabbings with alcohol were prescribed, but some divers had to work with throbbing earaches. Dysentery was also a problem, not nearly the major problem it had been in 1960, but it was nearly impossible for a diver to work with even slight stomach cramps or loss of energy.

The Mayas were virtually immune to dysentery, but some of them were still suffering from the after-effects of chlorine inhalation that made it painful to breathe. Doctors had assured them that the pain would stop within a few more days, but the Mayas were skeptical about taking the word of a doctor.

We were waiting at the command shed when Gordon Inman walked up. He had still more bad news. The worst was that one of the two automatic chlorinators had been damaged and was not operating. It would be a least a week, maybe more, before a new one could be sent from Mexico City. In addition, the device that Harvey Campbell had rigged up to skim the oil off the water did not work because no one could figure out a way to keep the barrel exactly a fraction of an inch below the water.

Scott was not worried so much about the oil as he was about the chlorinator. We could devote only short periods of time to chlorinating in the first place, and now, with only one chlorinator, there was little chance of getting enough of the chemical in the water to do any good at all. Scott raised his eyebrows and sighed.

We were just getting ready to hop in the truck when an excited little man came running down the back road from the airstrip. He ran past the guards at the gate and yelled out for the expedition leader in broken English.

Scott climbed wearily out of the truck cab and identified himself. The visitor unleashed a whirlwind of Spanish that Scott had no hope of understanding. Folan came up and listened to the man, whose excitement now bordered on hysteria. He and Folan spoke in Spanish for a few minutes, their hands going as fast as their tongues. Finally Folan turned to Scott with one of his more succinct translations.

"He says we've flooded the airport."

Scott did not say anything. He walked slowly back to the command shed, picked up the intercom to the raft and gave the order to stop the pumps. He told Harold to find Avelino. Scott wanted both of them to go with Folan to take a look at the airstrip. We also had to find another discharge area, and we did not have time to look very far. If the pumps were shut off for more than a few hours, Thompson's bank, with its carefully dug trenches and section markers, would disappear under the rising water. Scott wasted no words. He said simply that the problem had to be solved or we might as well pack up and go home. He told Harold he would be back at the site after dinner.

No one spoke much on the ride to the hacienda. The dusk was speckled with fireflies, which would become food for the bats already swarming up from the cenote. It had begun to mist, but luckily we found a tarpaulin in the back of the truck. Huddled under it, we bounced along the sacbe, around the Temple of Kukulcán and then to the main road that led to the hacienda. There was pain on Austin's face each time the truck hit a bump, but he said nothing. No one had to speak to express the gloom that we all felt.

Chief archaeologist Román Piña Chan
was enthusiastic about the finds from Thompson's bank.

Some of the workers at the hacienda had formed a band, and we heard their music as we walked up the steps. They were playing *Peregrina*, a song that was commissioned nearly a half-century ago by the reformist governor of Yucatán, Filipe Carrillo Puerto, for the American lady with whom he had fallen in love. Carrillo was killed before they were married, but Yucatán never forgot him or the song. It was Pablo Bush's favorite, and I guessed that Don Pablo was already at the hacienda.

I found him on the back veranda, listening to the music and talking with Gypsy. At the other end of the veranda I noticed a boy crouched in a chair and staring out into the rain. He was the child of the woman who had walked to camp in search of a doctor. The night was hot and sticky, but the boy looked cold.

"You should talk to him," Don Pablo said. "You'll be able to learn more about Mayab in five minutes of conversation with him than in four years with history books."

I promised I would talk to him, but later. Right now I was hungry. I joined the others in the dining room, ate quickly and then returned to the veranda, where I saw Piña Chan, Victor and Otto talking excitedly. I joined them.

In the crush of disappointments and setbacks I had all but forgotten the excavations. While some of us were concerned with the technical problems, it seems the others were beginning to solve the problems that had faced archaeologists for more than a century.

"We've found between fifty and sixty human bones on the bank, but almost none of them belongs to anyone over ten years old," Piña told me.

Thompson had also found skeletal remains of children, and that led some archaeologists to believe the early Spaniards had been wrong in their stories about the sacrificing of virgin maidens into the well. It now appeared that we might be able to debunk the stories of virgins altogether. If we did, students might have to rearrange their entire outlook on the Mayan character, so often described as nonviolent and intellectual. Although Nazi Germany showed that these two characteristics are hardly mutually exclusive, people have the idea that the ancient Mayas stood out as

141

"The bones and skulls were of children. . . ."

pacifists among their warlike neighbors, sacrificing an occasional young woman but on the whole devoting most of their time to astronomy and pyramid building. If the skeletal material found so far represented a pattern in sacrifices, archaeologists would have to make room in their concept of meek intellectuals for a child-slaughtering cult.

"Thompson's bank is considerably richer in artifacts that we imagined," Victor said.

The expertise of Victor Segovia brought forth
some startling conclusions about the sacrificial victims.

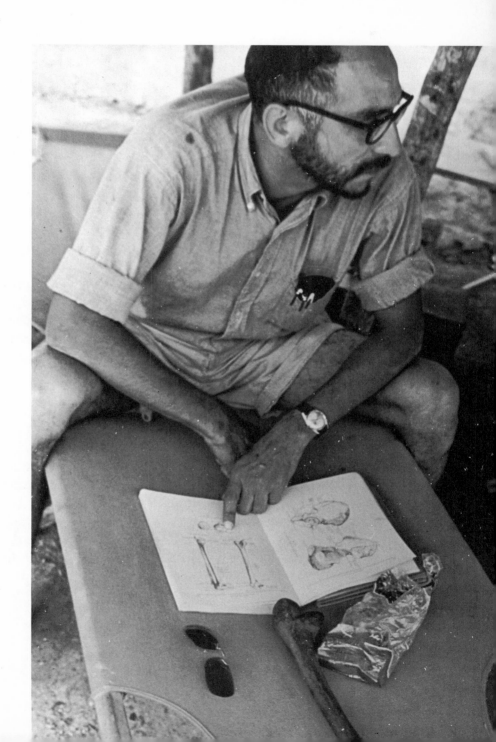

Otto handed me his catalogue and I ran my finger down the column headed *"material."* From the mud of Thompson's bank had come gold, copper, jade, ceramics, bone, carved stones, obsidian, copal and even one object of an unusual alloy of gold and copper. I was holding in my hand no less than the first pages of an index to the sacrificial treasure of the Mayas.

I wanted to talk more to the archaeologists, but we were interrupted by Harold and Folan. By the mud caked on their shoes I could tell that they had come from the airstrip. Their report was not nearly so bad as we had expected. There was a good four inches of water on the west end of the runway, but they said it started to recede as soon as our pumps were shut off. The runway was long enough so that the one or two planes that came to Chichén each day could still safely land and take off. Moreover, Harold said that by a slight change in the position of the discharge line, the flooding could be halted. He said the change had already been made and the pumps restarted. Meanwhile, water in the cenote had risen only two inches.

Folan was looking for Scott but could not find him. Finally he spotted Dori, who said Scott was in his room and could not be disturbed, even for good news. He was suffering from complete exhaustion and running a high temperature. We agreed to wait until morning to give Scott the news. It was obvious that more than anything else he needed a full night's sleep. In the morning we could tell him that at least one problem had been licked and that from the archaeologists' point of view there were more than just a few seeds of hope scattered through an expedition that occasionally looked barren.

I wanted to hear more from Piña and Victor, but they were already heading back to their quarters. Expedition members usually sat on the veranda and talked several hours after dinner, but tonight everyone was exhausted. I ordered a rum and tonic and asked the musicians to play their favorite song. Then to the melody of *Peregrina* and to the rhythm of rain, I fell asleep in my chair on the veranda.

It had been a very long day.

8

THE SEEDS of hope took root during the next few days. Scott recovered quickly and was back at the site after missing only a half day's work. Jack Kiefer and Jerry Kemler took only a day longer to recover and get back on the job. The airstrip drained and the water in the cenote continued, however slowly, to decline. The device to get rid of the oil was finally made to work by fastening it to the side of the big raft, and nearly all the oil had been skimmed off within forty-eight hours. Otto's catalogue grew so fast that Piña sent for two students to help both with cataloguing and with actual excavations on the bank. Howard Williams was relieved by Al Datz, an expert crane operator from Florida. Visitors from Mexico City and elsewhere came to the site to see the hemisphere's largest expedition in operation and to get a glimpse of the cataloguing table in the archaeologists' shed. There were no velvet-lined glass cabinets in which to display ornaments nor any sophisticated lighting effects. But there in the archaeologists' shed, spread out on a rough wooden table, were the beginnings of a primitive treasure that had not been seen in a thousand years. With that collection growing each day, and with operations going smoothly for the first time in weeks, we had every reason to be hopeful. Our lagging ambition was now completely renewed.

During these productive days I took Don Pablo's suggestion and talked to the boy who had walked into camp with his mother. Predictably, the woman's leg had to be amputated at the knee, and the only problem now was that she did not want to go back to her village in the jungle. She was still at the clinic in Mérida and from what I heard she wanted to remain in that city. It was a sad situation; she hardly had the education to get a job there, and the loss of a limb would make finding employment even more difficult. I did not know just how primitive life must have been in the village until I talked with the boy. His name was Nuncio Canul, and he spoke Spanish as a second language to his native Maya.

When Nuncio asked where I lived, I told him Florida, but the name of the state did not mean anything to him. He wanted to know how far it was from Mayab. I took a rough guess and said about thirteen hundred kilometers.

The boy laughed. "Nothing can be that far away," he said as though I had been trying to put something over on him.

I insisted that the figure I gave could not be too far off, but he only continued to laugh. Finally he looked serious and asked, "Do you see the same moon in Florida?"

When I admitted that in Florida we see the same moon that people see in Yucatán, he had me in his trap. Since the same moon is visible in both places, he reasoned, Florida could never be so far away.

About the only subject of which we had a common knowledge was popular music. Nuncio spent nearly each evening listening to one of the two transistor radios in his village. In fact, he had experienced electricity in only three forms before he came to Chichén. He had seen electric lights on the planes overhead, he had listened to the radio, and about three years ago, when he was eleven, a man had brought a flashlight into the village. I did not understand exactly how, but the flashlight had been used in religious rites until the batteries played out. Transistor radio batteries were available at a nearby village, but no one could get batteries for the flashlight, which he said currently stands alongside a statue of St. Joseph in a hut that serves as a church. Last year a visiting priest offered to get batteries, but the old ones had corroded so badly that the flashlight was now useless, a relic to be revered by those who remembered its light in the wilderness of a jungle. Now the radios and the planes were the only sources of electricity, and Nuncio was a devoted radio fan.

The favorite station in the village (and the only one that could be tuned in with constant clarity) was Radio Belize from British Honduras. That station had what we would call unorthodox programing. It interspersed classical music among the popular songs so that it is not at all unusual to hear the Beatles' "I Want to Hold Your Hand" followed by a Prokofiev symphony. The programing technique evidently resulted from the government's desire to disperse culture among people who would be considered primitive by any standard. Nuncio listened to the station nearly every evening and had a deep interest in what songs were popular in England and the United States (both of which he considered closer than Florida).

"How is Mozart's Turkish March doing in the United States?" he asked.

"What do you mean, 'how is it doing?'" I replied.

"I mean on the *desfile de éxitos,* the hit parade," he said.

Then I realized what he was thinking. He was so used to hearing classical music and rock and roll at the same time that he never drew a distinction between the two. Should I tell him the difference and perhaps shatter an illusion, however harmless it may be? I thought for a minute and decided I might as well set him straight on the subject.

Very slowly and very seriously I said, "Nuncio, there's something you should know. Mozart is not on the hit parade. He's been dead for more than a hundred and fifty years."

The boy looked up and grinned.

"You know," he said, "I thought there was something different about his music."

Otto at his cataloguing, assisted by Ann and Dori.

It was all down hill from there. Later I showed him a map of the Caribbean and convinced him that Florida was indeed as far as I had told him. I asked one of the local residents to take him through the power station at Chichén, and Nuncio was awed by the two small turbines housed in an oil-splattered garage. I began explaining the difference between popular and classical music but discovered I could not. (Maybe Radio Belize has the right idea after all.) Before Nuncio left to join his mother in Mérida, I told him she had had her leg amputated. If he was concerned, he did not show it. But I suppose he felt lucky that she was still alive.

Most expedition members were not even aware that Nuncio and his mother had come to Chichén, but this was hardly surprising in view of the enormous efforts being made at the site. One group of people was working day and night to make sure the water level in the cenote kept going down; another sweated out the hours on Thompson's bank in what must have been one of the muddiest excavation sites in history; a third group hauled up tons of debris from the bottom, while a fourth, Otto and his newly acquired assistants, catalogued the results of the excavations.

Kirk Johnson arrived in Chichén to check on our progress, but he did not seem particularly pleased. Ann Campbell had joined him in the States and they had both flown back to the site with their two pet skunks. Ann's was named Posey and was completely descented. Kirk's was called Stink, a larger and more rambunctious animal which, as its name implied, was less thoroughly deodorized. "His" and "hers" skunks might seem slightly outlandish, but one of our photographers, Mike Freeman, had gone one better. Mike had a completely domesticated, highly intelligent, well-mannered tarantula. Charley, as he called it, looked as fierce and as ugly as any tarantula could, but in the hand of his loving master, Charley became docile and even tractable. Mike taught him to walk on a string leash and to perch on his shoulder. Contrary to popular belief, tarantulas are not particularly dangerous. The Yucatán variety, if Charley was a representative example, do not bite at all.

Everyone was in good spirits during those days. We felt sure we were on the verge of making archaeological history, and we were enjoying ourselves for the first time since our journey to Chichén began nearly two months ago.

Then suddenly I noticed an attitude among several expedition leaders that I could not readily describe. It was only after our morning meeting one day that I realized what it was. Our renewed ambition had changed to urgency.

The urgency was apparent as Willie Folan paused only briefly after the meeting to rattle off a translation of Scott's instructions to Avelino. He usually took time to joke with the foreman, but

"The crane was working fast. . . ." Al Datz at the controls.

not now. Folan turned quickly from Avelino and walked directly to the archaeologists' shed, where he greeted Segovia and Griffin with a quick *"buenos días."* Willie started talking to the archaeology students from Mexico City, but the conversation was interrupted by Beasom Painter, who yelled out that the crane was ready to lower the first group to the bank.

Folan, Segovia and one of the students, a Japanese girl, sprinted to the basket and squeezed in with a half-dozen Maya workers.

As Griffin called out that he would be down in the next load, the crane began hoisting the basket into the air. The crane raised it straight up, fifty feet or more, then swung the basket high over the ledge of the well. As it disappeared from Al Datz's sight, Beasom's eyes took over. Peering at the basket over the ledge, he gave Datz hand signals that guided the basket to a landing spot on the bank. Even the soft landing made a squish in the watery black soil. As the group hopped out and started to wade through the mud, the basket disappeared over their heads. The crane was working fast. Painter and Datz shared the sense of urgency that I had noticed earlier in Folan.

I should have guessed what was wrong, but I had been out of touch with Scott for the last forty-eight hours and had not attended a meeting he had held with Kirk and Victor the night before. As I looked at the workers being unloaded on the bank, I became aware of a strange sound, silence. The pumps had been shut off. That was what was wrong. This was the last day of work on Thompson's bank.

It had been a difficult decision for expedition leaders, but they realized—perhaps as we all had in the backs of our minds—that the expedition could never be a complete success without getting at the heart of the treasure, the relics that lay at the bottom of the well. We had all been so excited at finding Thompson's leftovers on the bank that we had let our vision stray from the target. We had also pretended not to notice that the water level was declining at an increasingly slower rate each day. The water table of the Yucatán Peninsula had finally caught up with our pumps, and that brought Scott to the point where a decision had to be made. We could either let the pumps continue to hold water level low enough to permit excavation of the bank, or we could forget about the bank and use the pumps to filter the cenote for a full-scale underwater excavation of the entire well. We could not do both. We could not filter the water while we excavated the bank because two pumps were needed to keep the water level down. In a sense, plan A had failed: we could not drain the sacred well dry. The rate of decline in the cenote had dropped to an inch a day, and it was apparent that we would soon reach a point at which the water level would cease to decline at all. Then, Scott reasoned, we would have wasted at least a week more and have nothing to show for it other than a few more relics from Thompson's bank. The decision he reached with Kirk and the archaeologists involved considerable risk. If clarification of the water proved impossible, then we not only would lose out in excavating the bottom of the well but we would lose priceless time in resuming excavations on the bank. It was a choice between going after a small treasure that was a sure thing or going after a big treasure that we might or might not be able to reach. The decision, I learned, had come after five hours of debate. The archaeologists generally wanted us to continue work on the bank while Kirk wanted to go after richer pay dirt in the well. Ours was a commercial expedition, and that counted a lot in making the final decision. However successful the excavations on the bank might be from the archaeological point of view, the expedition would be a failure if we did not go after the whole prize.

I went down with the last load of workers, and as we neared the bank I thought I noticed that the water had already started to rise. Although the increase was actually imperceptible at this point, we all realized that within twenty-four hours Thompson's bank would disappear into the same brown water from which we had raised it.

Folan and Segovia decided to concentrate on a newly cleared area, and if they felt any despair over losing the bank, they did not show it. Segovia carefully told the Maya laborers that instead of opening new trenches, they were to build a rock wall about two feet high from one end of the bank to the other. No one knew how effective this retaining wall would be, but archaeologists wanted to make every effort to prevent the loosened soil from falling into the deep parts of the well once the water rose. The best they could hope for was that once we were working on the bottom of the well, some effort might be made to return to the bank.

A second wheelbarrow of silt had just been pushed up one of the ramps to the screening tables when it began to rain. The long afternoon rains we encountered early in the expedition were no longer with us, but the short autumn thunderstorms were equally as menacing. They could come in the morning as easily as in the evening. When the downpour began, we stopped work and ran to the cenote wall for cover, looking for overhanging strata of limestone to huddle beneath. Most vegetation had been cleared from the bank itself, but there was still rich growth on the walls. Giant philodendrons and ropelike vines dripped with water. The morning was hot and rain fell in steamy trickles down the wall and onto our heads. We watched it fall on the loose soil and form little streams that flowed toward the rising water in the cenote.

Gnats began to swarm around our faces, and the wind carried the rain under the overhanging ledges. Folan put his hand up to the tam-o'-shanter on his head and felt a soggy piece of cloth.

Now there was furious activity before Thompson's bank disappeared forever.

Meanwhile, the debris came out of the well. . . .

Disgusted, he took it off and wrung it out. He said that since we could not get any wetter away from the well, we might as well be working.

Most of the Mayas did not bother stopping for the rain, and as two of them loaded another wheelbarrow, Yoko, the Japanese girl, looked in and saw a yellow object half hidden by a short tree limb. She stopped the wheelbarrow on the ramp and carefully reached under the limb. She brought out a small piece of gold leaf. Although the rain was already washing it off, she took the gold to the raft and put it in a pail of water. After a few minutes she carefully raised it from the water and brought it back to the bank for us to look at.

The gold had been pounded as thin as the page of a book and then embossed. Since it was crumpled, we could not see enough of the embossed portion to make out the design. It had probably been used for one of two purposes—either as part of a sacrificial costume or as a covering for an object, such as a sacrificial knife carved from hard wood but made to look gold by covering it with leaf. Perhaps the leaf became loosened as the wood rotted away in the water, or maybe it had been crumpled by Thompson's dredge. Like the other pieces of leaf we had found, this one would have to be examined at the National Institute, where archaeologists were trained in unfolding such delicate pieces of metal. Once unfolded, the design would be visible and perhaps give a clue as to the actual function of the object.

As more and more gold found its way from the bank to the cataloguing table, we became increasingly aware of the ancient Mayas' expertise in every phase of goldwork except casting. This was an immense achievement considering that the Yucatán Peninsula is void of metals and that all gold had to be imported. Unless they were lucky enough to import pure nuggets, Mayas usually traded their goods for cast gold. Maya goldsmiths then pounded these cast objects into leaf. There is probably no more expensive way to make gold leaf, but the ancient Mayas had little choice, and they were only too willing to expend such elaborate efforts in producing objects worthy of sacrifice to Chac.

Archaeologists, by the way, have devised a clever way to trace

"The piece of gold leaf
that Yoko found had
a few bits of copal
within the folds. . . ."

the source of pre-Columbian gold. The technique is based on the fact that virtually all gold has impurities; in ancient Meso-America these consisted chiefly of silver and copper. To the detective archaeologists the important point is that the quantity and proportion of these impurities changed rather consistently from one area to the other. Samuel Lothrop, who analyzed metals brought up by Thompson, concluded that it was unlikely for hammered gold discs in the well to have come from Mexico because they contained only 3 per cent silver, and sometimes even less, as an impurity. If they had come from Mexico, Lothrop pointed out, the gold in the discs would undoubtedly have contained a much higher percentage of both silver and copper impurities. On the other hand, the silver content of cenote discs exactly matched that of gold found in the Coclé region of Panama, which is nearly two thousand miles away by the ocean route of Maya traders. By the same technique, he concluded that nearly all the cast gold that Thompson dredged from the well came from Panama. People there were great exporters of gold just as the Aztecs were the great importers. Even the ancient people on Mexico's Pacific coast, themselves excellent goldsmiths, are known to have imported gold from Panama.

Regardless how much scientific data is accumulated on gold of the Mayas, we are still a long way from understanding their reverence for the metal. The Mayas called it *takin*, which means "excrement of the sun." Imagine walking into a jewelry store and saying something like, "What do you have in moderately priced wedding rings made of solar feces?"

Since Mayas had virtually no silver before the Spanish conquest, they also called this metal *takin* when the Spaniards showed it to them. Although it is probable that Maya traders, who were in contact with silver-hoarding Aztecs, had seen a few pieces of this metal before the conquest, no one seems to know what word they used for it. Since some students believe the Aztecs' language,

This piece of copal is incised with the figure of a leaf.

Nahuatl, was the lingua franca of pre-Columbian tradesmen in Mexico, Maya traders might have used the Nahuatl word in the same way that English-speaking people still resort to the lingua franca of a less distant era in such words as repoussé or mise en couleur. When Spaniards introduced silver to Yucatán, Mayas called it "white gold" or *sac takin* while gold itself became known as *kankan takin,* meaning "yellow excrement of the sun."

The piece of gold leaf that Yoko found had a few bits of copal within the folds, which suggested that the metal had been used in a sacrificial rite. And perhaps it was crumpled for a reason we had not thought of earlier: maybe the object which it covered had been ceremonially "killed." This was a ritual that entailed breaking or mutilating an object before it was thrown into the well in the same manner that a human victim was killed. So many ceramic vessels that we found had been chipped on the rim that it was apparent that these vessels had been "killed" in the same way.

The rain eventually stopped, but none of us on the bank could dry off. Water was still dripping from the ledges and vines, and the atmosphere was almost unbearably humid. If our faces were not covered with sweat, they were splashed with water from the screening tables. I cannot recall hearing anyone complain however. In fact Folan observed that he had it pretty good compared with the 1960 expedition. Seven years ago he had exactly one Maya helping him sort through all the material disgorged by the airlift, and Folan's wife did the cataloguing. He said work often started at dawn and continued until late evening when he had to rely on a couple of small light bulbs by which to see.

There was much more than gold in the wheelbarrow of silt that had yielded the piece of leaf. Copal seemed to be everywhere in the well, and we were bringing up bushels of it from the bank alone. Some of the copal was stuck to fragments of sacrificial vessels that once held it, but we still had not discovered a complete copal offering in an unbroken vessel. The wheelbarrow of silt had hidden nearly a dozen bones, some of them so tiny that they obviously came from infants scarcely old enough to walk. Victor, an expert on bones, quickly separated the human from animal bones, which were also surprisingly numerous on the bank. Sixty years ago Thompson thought he had found the remains of a fight to the death when he discovered jaguar and deer bones side by side in the well. In view of the vast quantity of animal bones, however, we speculated on the possibility that creatures of the jungle had also been sacrificed to Chac.

Throughout the morning water splashed on the screening tables, and our hands sifted through the grimy silt. We were alert for the shiny bits of metal, but more often we found flint and jade. A dozen flint projectile points had turned up, and two more were spotted soon after it stopped raining. Now we theorized that the needle-sharp points may have had a part in the ritual sacrifices to Chac. We were well aware that Mayas drew blood from sacrificial victims and that devout men often drew blood from their ears or penises as an offering to the gods. Perhaps the delicate arrowheads that we were finding were used in these bloodletting ceremonies that apparently flourished after the arrival of Kukulcán.

We had fewer doubts about the purpose of the many small copper bells that were hidden in the mud of Thompson's bank. Archaeologists have long known that the bells were associated with Ah Puch, the god of death, so it was hardly surprising that more than two dozen of them had already turned up on the bank. Victor was sure that there must be hundreds, maybe thousands, more at the bottom of the well. These were, after all, the bells that rang for the victims who were sacrificed. The tinny jingle of the copper bells was the last sound some of the victims ever heard.

Copper was known as *mazcab* to the ancient Maya. The etymology of the word is confusing, but it seems to mean "red stuff that grows in the earth." While most of the gold in the cenote apparently came from Central America, virtually all the copper was imported from Mexico, especially the states of Chiapas, Michoacán and Guerrero. There the copper was cast into little round bells and stones were inserted for clappers. Although the copper had now turned black with age, many bells still had the clappers inside. Nearly all had their original shape while the one gold bell that had turned up so far had been crushed, apparently with

The copper "bells of death."

a single blow, and the clapper had been removed. We guessed that the gold bell had been ritually killed while the copper ones might have been left intact because they alone, being the bells of death, were permitted to ring in the netherworld.

Along with the copper and gold, one bell of *tumbaga* had

been discovered. This is an alloy which the ancient Maya would have described as a mixture of solar excrement and red stuff from the earth. Otto was particularly pleased at the discovery of *tumbaga* since the alloy had been considered relatively rare in this area. *Tumbaga,* which is nearly as yellow as pure gold, was a useful alloy to early civilizations because it had a lower melting point than either component metal. In the best alloy proportions, *tumbaga* will melt at 878 degrees Fahrenheit, more than two hundred degrees lower than the melting point of copper.

The last morning on the bank had been three hours of on-again-off-again rain, and ironically it was one of the most profitable mornings in terms of artifacts uncovered. Before lunch we gathered up two pails of relics to take to Otto. They included four pieces of gold leaf, all of which would have to be left in water to prevent air from damaging the metal. Otto's reaction to the large number of relics was something between a smile and a sigh; he was glad to see so many objects come up, but they meant a good eight hours' work in sorting, identifying and cataloguing.

Before we sat down to eat under the archaeologists' shed, we looked down from the ledge at the bank. The water was creeping over it at a faster pace than we had realized, and it was doubtful that the workers could finish the retaining wall before the bank would sink below the surface altogether.

As we unwrapped our sandwiches from the hacienda, I noticed a dozen wives of the workers walking down the sacbe with food for their husbands. Several Maya couples joined us at the archaeologists' shed, giving us a first-hand comparison that I had always been curious to see—an Oriental alongside a Maya. Yoko probably thought I was staring at her for other reasons, but actually I was intrigued with comparing her to the descendants of the pyramid builders. Mayas, almost more than any other American Indian group, are said to resemble Orientals, but as Yoko chatted with two of the wives, their differences became apparent.

It is undeniable that contemporary Mayas look vaguely oriental, but the similarities seem to have been overemphasized. Yoko, like many other women from East Asia, had small, delicate features, a long, slender neck and tiny hands. Her stature was small but well proportioned, the antithesis of buxomness. The Maya women seemed short and big-boned by comparison. An unkindly observer would call them dumpy. Their necks seemed shorter, and their muumuu-like dresses, *huipiles,* accentuated their stockiness. Naturally, the one brief comparison between Yoko and the Maya women could not begin to serve as a comparison between Orientals and Mayas, or even between twentieth-century females in southern Japan and their counterparts in northern Yucatán. The comparison, however, interested me because anthropologists had somehow led me to think there was something uncannily similar about the two groups. It was also interesting because I realized how much clothes make the man, or in this case the woman. I tried to picture the Maya women in Japanese dress and Yoko in a *huipil.* With that imaginary picture in mind, I found it even more difficult to pinpoint their physical differences.

The comparison also illustrated something about the amorous preferences of the ancient Maya. Yoko would have been considered beautiful in eastern Asia (as well as in many other parts of the world), and the two Maya women would also have been considered sexually appealing to men to Yucatán. Since appealing women are the first to be selected for marriage, culture groups breed selectively for beauty without fully realizing the long-term results.

The point is that physical characteristics of the Mayas have changed very little from the arrival of Kukulcán in Chichén Itzá to the arrival of our expedition in the same town. The major factor of change has been intermarriage with Europeans, which has been far less frequent than in most other parts of Mexico. Visitors to Mayab should not be surprised at all to see living faces that greatly resemble the faces depicted in paintings and carvings from many centuries ago. It would be remarkable if they did not resemble each other, and they will continue to do so as long as Maya women, like the ones talking to Yoko, and their male counterparts are considered appealing. In order for Yucatán to develop a population with small, broad-faced, short-necked people, selective breeding for this particular type must have been going on for a very long time, at least as long as it has taken

Western man to develop a population with a high percentage of slender, fair-skinned, slightly bosomy women a few inches shorter than his own tall self.

It is a fascinating process.

The difference between Yoko and the Maya women does not detract in the slightest from the probability that aboriginal Americans came to this hemisphere via a land bridge from Asia, and neither do their many similarities necessarily prove such a theory. Even as our expedition was in progress, archaeologists at Harvard and Columbia universities were evaluating data which indicated man was already in South America by 12,000 B.C., far earlier than previously supposed. Since 12,000 B.C. there has been ample time for scores of migrations as well as for development of unique traits among those who stayed in Asia and those who migrated. By itself, anatomical comparison of contemporary populations is insufficient to prove or disprove common ancestry.

Yoko and the Maya women shared a taste for tea, which was now brewed at the hacienda and brought to us at the well in five-gallon containers at lunch time. We were all thirsty after the morning on the bank, and the three or four containers of tea were quickly drained during lunch.

Kirk and Ann walked up to the archaeologists' shed and showed us their new acquisition, a coati-mundi. The little animal poked an enormous nose out of Ann's straw handbag and sniffed the sandwiches on the table. Before she was able to stop him, the coati bounded out of the bag and hopped on the table where he began tearing apart every sandwich in sight. I cannot explain why coati-mundis are funny, but I suppose it is because of their utterly ridiculous appearance. They walk like ducks, have fur like raccoons and behave themselves in somewhat the manner of a four-year-old brat. The nose goes into everything, and if it sniffs anything interesting, the claws tear it apart. Ann thought her new pet was about the cutest thing she had ever seen, with the possible exception of her pet skunk.

She had one problem with the coati however. She had no idea how to get it into the United States. Bringing foreign animals into the country is often a long tangle of red tape, a barrier that neither she nor Kirk had any patience with. The skunks were properly documented and could be whisked through customs with little effort. Getting the documents for the coati-mundi, however, might take weeks. Kirk hit on a scheme which we allowed would have a good chance of success. He would put the coati in one of the skunk cages, on the theory that the cages were covered and he had never known a customs inspector to lift the cover to examine the contents. There is a natural reluctance on the part of everyone, customs agents included, to go poking around in a skunk cage. Kirk said inspectors usually would just look at the documents and wave the animal through, then wait until they thought Kirk was out of earshot to snicker. Ann was genuinely fond of the animal, and we hoped Kirk's plan would work. In any event, *sic transit coati-mundi*.

Ann spent part of her lunch hour talking to Otto, whom she would soon be assisting. Folan and I talked with McGehee and a couple of the other divers who had walked over for an extra glass of tea.

The divers were already having great luck in bringing up large ceramics, and Bill said he had located a spot near the raft where several complete pieces lay buried in about three feet of mud. It was mysterious that such a high percentage of complete ceramics should be found in one place, but as it turned out, the answer to the mystery was deceptively simple. Bill himself discovered the explanation about two weeks later.

Pottery can look pretty dull when it exists in hundreds of little brown fragments, but archaeologists can often tell more from these little pieces than from some of the most lavish gold artifacts. Sylvanus Morley, the man who directed most of the restoration work at Chichén for the Carnegie Institution, said, "Of all the imperishable remains of former cultures which man has left behind him, his pottery best reflects his cultural progress. . . ." Archaeologists do not always agree with each other. Victor von

A young woman from Chichén Itzá inspects a fine example of decorated ceramics made by her ancestors.

Hagen, an archaeologist who has studied many pre-Columbian civilizations, has no patience for preoccupation with ceramics. The Mayas, he said, "who raised stone temple-cities and out of the coas of the jungle built a concourse of roads, have now been reduced to being only a sequence of pottery." At this point in our expedition it was difficult to envision being preoccupied with pottery. Few good pieces had been found.

What we did not know was that in only a few days we would pull from the mud some of the most exquisite Mayan pottery ever discovered.

Lunch hours, whether on Madison Avenue or in the Yucatán jungle, are inevitably too short. And on this day, with water continuing to envelop Thompson's bank, we cut ours even shorter. It was this same urgency to get what we could from the bank that took our minds off the enormous gamble that Scott had taken in the first place. Anything not dug up on the bank today might never be uncovered. With that in mind, we left the archaeologists' shed and returned to a much smaller bank than the one we had left. The workmen who were building the retaining wall never went topside for lunch. They had worked through the noon hour on the wall and had eaten only a few sandwiches that were sent down.

Two important finds were made during the last hours on the bank. One of the laborers working on the retaining wall had poked his hand in the mud to bring up a rock. Instead, he found an almost complete copal offering in a shallow three-legged bowl. It was virtually perfect except for a few chips around the rim. The copal itself had a design etched into it, but it was too badly eroded for us to tell what the design represented. The offering, apparently from the Mayapán era, also had blue paint, the color of sacrifice. Although expedition members on the bank were enthusiastic about finding the first complete copal offering, we learned later in the afternoon that divers were finding offerings in nearly as good condition at the bottom of the well.

Thousands of small copal fragments had turned up both on the bank and in the well itself, but it was not until now that someone suggested putting a match to a piece of the incense. I had always

An important find—"an almost complete copal offering
in a shallow three-legged bowl."

been curious about the odor of the substance, but somehow I had
considered the contents of the well too sacred to tamper with.
Victor assured us that the National Institute would not mind if we
burned one of the many small fragments. He reached down in a
bucket by one of the screening tables and pulled out a piece that
was about the size of a large marble. Copal, by the way, looks
like soft plaster; depending on age and quality, the samples in the
well ranged in color from white to gray and to a yellowish gray.
The piece Victor selected was of the yellowish type. From the
bank, we walked over the ramp and got under the sheltered area

of the raft. Victor put the incense on a piece of wood, and we stared at it for several minutes. All of us had seen hundreds of similar pieces during the last few weeks, but we were awed by the prospect of putting a match to anything a thousand years old.

Yoko held the wood on which the copal rested, and Victor struck the match. As soon as the fire reached the incense, black smoke began streaming up. Seconds later the air in the tarpaulin-covered shelter was thick with copal smoke. It burned strongly with a pinelike aroma. The thousand years beneath tons of stagnant water had not weakened the odor that accompanied the sacrifices to Chac. In fact I cannot recall ever having smelled a stronger incense. Anyone who likes the currently fashionable Eastern incenses would probably be disappointed in copal, but those who like the odor of cedar chests would think copal is terrific.

The fragrance of copal is strangely out of place in a tropical climate, smelling as it does of pine or cedar. It might, however, have been this very strangeness that led the Mayas to consider it holy. Copal is actually the Spanish word for the substance; the Mayas call it *pom*, and the tree from whose resin it is derived is also called *pom*. Roman Catholic churches deep within the interior of Mayab are known to burn copal at the altar instead of the traditional Christian incense. In general, however, copal is relatively rare today in northern Yucatán, most of it now coming from the Mexican state of Chiapas or from Guatemala.

We thought the odor of copal on the raft was marvelous, especially since the most prevalent aromas had been stagnant water, chlorine and exhaust fumes.

The second important find that day on the bank was also discovered by one of the laborers. A Maya who was working alone with a trowel on the far side walked proudly over to the archaeologists and opened his hand. He held a gold bell, crushed but still shiny. In place of a handle the bell had a splendid cast effigy of a bird. Like another gold bell we had found, this one also had the clapper removed or, more probably, ripped out in a ceremonial killing of the sacrificed ornament.

From its distinctive style, archaeologists reasoned that the bell had come from Panama, probably from the Veraguas area. Gold-smiths there had apparently cast the bell by the lost-wax process similar to the method of the Aztecs. A Spanish priest, who watched the Aztecs cast gold shortly after the Conquest began, managed to describe the process in no fewer than ninety-two steps without really explaining how it was done. Pre-Columbian craftsmen apparently used wax to make a mold of charcoal and clay that had ducts into which gold was poured. When it hardened, the gold underwent a complex polishing, first with alum and then with mud and salt.

After Indians in Panama polished the bell we had just found, they probably sold it to a merchant; he, in turn, dealt with the Maya traders who started sailing as far south as Panama about A.D. 900, possibly even earlier. The trader loaded the bell onto his big canoe, that might have measured more than forty feet in length. Hugging the dangerous coast line, the canoe headed back to its home port, perhaps Nito on the Gulf of Honduras. In Nito, the bell may have been sold to another merchant, who resold it to a trader heading even farther north. If the trader traveled inland along the *sacbeob,* the bell reached the winding Usumacinta River, where it was carried by boat to the Mayas' busiest port city, Xicalango, on the Gulf of Mexico. More probably, the bell continued to be carried north by sea from Nito to a port on the east coast of Yucatán near Tulúm. From there it would have been a relatively short journey over the sacbe to Chichén Itzá. When the merchant unveiled his prize from Panama, it must have caused a great stir in the holy city. Only a few persons in Chichén had enough cacao beans to exchange for it, but when a price was agreed on, the bell was sold to a new owner who decided it was worthy of sacrifice to Chac.

Gold, copal, copper, quetzal feathers, *tumbaga* and ceramics were all items of trade with the Mayas, who had developed the hemisphere's most advanced combination of highway and sea communications. As a larger variety of treasure was brought from the well, we got a clearer picture of how far the trade routes extended. To appreciate the Mayas' commercial empire, consider that they had no written contracts and used cacao beans for money.

Beans might not seem like a very practical currency, but they actually had several unique advantages. Inflation could not exist because cacao beans were edible: whenever there was an over-supply of money, Mayas could afford the luxury of making more chocolate, and when they did this, beans were automatically out of circulation. Counterfeiting was also difficult for only God can make a tree, or cacao beans. The nearest the ancient Maya came to counterfeiting was the practice of hollowing out the beans, using or selling the contents and then refilling the shells with clay or avocado rind. The surprise that we experience when we are stuck with a counterfeit bill could not compare with the disgust of a Maya who sat down to make a refreshing bowl of chocolate and found himself grinding up clay.

Most archaeologists believe that the market in Chichén was the largest in Mayab. It was here that residents traded their cacao beans for gold bells from Central America, copper from Mexico, quetzal feathers and jade from Guatemala, copal from the lowlands and pottery from dozens of sources. In plentiful years it was also a buyer's market for corn, beans, fabrics, shells, salt, skins and animals. De Landa was interested enough in economics to record some sample prices at the time of the conquest. Rabbits went for ten cacao beans, pumpkins for four and slaves for a hundred. The good bishop also recorded for posterity the price of prostitutes—eight to ten beans.

The Mayas of north Yucatán, without native metals or precious stones, probably devoted most of their artistic talents to architecture and weaving. If wall murals are any guide, Mayas in many areas could easily have excelled all other aboriginal American groups in the weaving of cloth and feathers. It is sadly ironic that of the Mayas' many works of art, only fabrics have disappeared. Their stelae have been worn down by the elements, but many are still remarkably clear; wall paintings and polychrome pottery are alive today with the same vitality they possessed a millennium ago; many jade carvings and gold discs exist only in fragments, but they still give clues about the lives of those who fashioned them; ceramic figurines have been difficult to find, but even these tell us much about life in ancient Mayab. Maya fabrics, which were among the most beautiful in the world, have rotted from existence. The few tiny shreds brought from the well in 1961 were the only pieces of ancient Maya cloth ever found, and these were fragile and had lost even the vestiges of pattern. There was nothing to make us believe we would find better pieces of fabric, but there was always hope.

As the water reached the first stone of the wall, it was dramatically clear that all our hopes now were pinned on the success of clarifying the water. Not more than a hour remained for us to work the bank. More workmen had been brought down during the afternoon to assure completion of the retaining wall while others continued to cart wheelbarrows of silt from the narrow spit of land to the screening tables on the raft. The afternoon was hot, and the water from the tables was refreshing when it splashed on us. Several loads of mud yielded more copper bells, bones and dozens of jade beads. As the bank diminished, the finds became fewer, and after only a few minutes there would be none at all.

From the raft we could see Jack Kiefer, who apparently had made a complete recovery from his illness. Jack was standing close to Kemler near the H-frame. Jerry, also recovered, was again trying to figure out a way to get the personnel lift operating.

Yoko suddenly looked up from the screening table to the ledge. "Jack's coming down," she shouted.

There was nothing particularly unusual about Kiefer's decision to come to the raft except that he had not bothered to wait for the crane. Formwise, it was not much of a dive. He just stepped off the platform and kept going, feet first. Unfortunately he picked an area of the well that was cluttered with rocks and tree trunks, many of them only a few feet below the surface. Moreover, the water level still was below normal.

That made it about an eighty-foot leap, long enough for us to get a good look at the bored expression on his face as he waited to hit the water. When he finally did, the noise from the splash echoed around the walls of the cenote and the impact sent a water spout in the air. Afraid that he had struck a rock under water, we held our breaths probably as long as Jack did. I glanced at Yoko and learned how big an Oriental's eyes can get. It seemed like minutes, but it was only seconds before Jack bobbed to the surface and leisurely swam to the raft. He was greeted with applause from all but Scott, who was less than enthusiastic about the risk Jack had taken.

"Glad you're feeling better," Scott said.

Jack must have been feeling great at that moment. After all, he was one of the few men who have ever leaped into the well and lived to tell about it, and he was the first to dive in after the water was lowered.

At the rate the water was rising now, however, it would soon be back to normal. The workmen put the last stones in place for the wall, which was already going under water in several places. It had started to grow dark as the last wheelbarrows of silt reached the raft, but we screened them as carefully as though they had been the first. By five o'clock we had three more buckets of artifacts and bones for Otto to catalogue.

After we returned to the top, I looked over Otto's shoulder as he catalogued some of the relics discovered this morning. We had more than a dozen projectile points, and one beautiful obsidian blade had been discovered by one of the divers.

Some of the pilgrims who came to Chichén were not as wealthy as the man who bought the gold bell from Veraguas. They could not afford jade so they sacrificed beads made of common stone. There were many, however, who could afford jade. We had found three fragments of jade plaques, thirteen small beads, twenty-one plain beads, two very large ones, seven tubular beads, three bags of fragments from jade ornaments, one bag of nondescript fragments, one fragment with a carved human face, one plain plaque, one earring, one perforated disc and two earplug covers.

We had nearly three dozen copper bells, four gold ones, five pieces of gold leaf, sixteen laminated rings, one gold disc, one fragment of a gold plaque and two unidentified gold fragments.

Human remains included more than a dozen perforated human teeth, nearly a dozen infantile jaw bones, one adult jaw bone, two shin bones, two infant skulls and countless smaller bones and bone fragments.

172

Archaeologists knew there would be some spare time while we were clarifying the water, and they were eager to use this time to study some of the treasure we had already found. Scott ordered the hydrolifts and airlifts tested, and this meant even more free time for the archaeologists because divers would be occupied with the equipment for the next few days during which time not too much material could be brought from the well. Scott's hope was to have the lifts working by the time the water was clarified.

The chips were down now on the gamble since we had now lost Thompson's bank. If the water failed to clear up, we would be right back where we started almost four weeks ago. Before we left for the hacienda, Scott walked over to Inman and Drake, who were standing near the filtration equipment. The entire success of the expedition now depended on their ability to clarify the water. The three men walked down to the platform in front of the filtration tanks and peered over the side of the well. There was not much to see. The murky water had risen over the retaining wall, and the shadows of the evening had enveloped the cenote. A few of the hungrier bats were circling near the top. The big aluminum pipe rumbled near the platform as it dumped clear water from the filtration tanks back into the well.

As we rode back to the hacienda, Scott told me he had no choice but to take the gamble and was convinced that the risk was attractive. We had to remember that the bank had been built up from silt that Thompson had dredged from the bottom and carefully screened. It was only after he had gone through the mud that he piled it in an area that later became the bank. For the first time in history we had brought the bank to the surface, but impressive though our finds had been, they were only what Thompson had missed.

"So far," Scott said, "we only have the leftovers."

9

WE THOUGHT the pace would slacken after the pumps were shut off, but we were mistaken. Scott doubled the workloads, and maybe that was a good thing since we needed something to take our minds off the loss of Thompson's bank. Only the heat slowed us down as we approached the start of what we expected to be another stifling week.

On Monday I saw Jerry Kemler propped on a perch far out over the edge of the well, dripping with sweat as he tried to weld an extension on the personnel lift. In the archaeologists' shed Yoko and Otto tried to take notes, but their notebooks became soggy and the ink blurred from their sweaty hands on the pages. Men who worked on the raft constantly gasped for breath but often got nothing more than a lungful of exhaust fumes from the big pump. Scott came down from the command shed to station himself on the raft where he could oversee the testing of the airlifts and construction of wooden ducts that would direct the flow of the water from the screening tables back to the cenote. Because the raft would be subject to extra strain during diving operations, Scott decided to beef up the wooden guard rail that encircled it. He would ordinarily have allotted two or three days for the jobs, but now he tried to get it all done on Monday. We worked furiously in the heat, and two five-gallon containers of tea that had been lowered to the raft early in the morning were drained by midafternoon. We, ourselves, were drained of energy and tired almost to the point of immobility.

Suddenly, with an unreasonable quickness, Yucatán turned cold at night. Sunday night had been hot and muggy, but twenty-four hours later the weather was cool and dry. Had anyone told us even a week ago that we would be sleeping under blankets, I would have laughed. But now it seemed that a single wool blanket was hardly enough. As the week progressed, we noticed that it began growing cold as soon as the first shadow of evening

"Scott doubled the workloads. . . ."

blotted out the sun but quickly warmed up again the instant the
sun reappeared the next morning. We were not sure what it was in
Yucatán that caused this unique climate, but it probably had something to do with the rocky soil which, like sand of the desert,
heats up quickly but fails to retain warmth. Chilly nights and
warm days are known as Indian summer, but "Mayan summer"
might be more appropriate for this extreme type of weather.

Conditions in the well were growing steadily worse for the
divers. On Tuesday morning I watched Jeff Gill fold his arms

"Jerry Kemler . . . tried to weld an extension on the personnel lift."

and rub his shoulders with his hands as he prepared for more work on the airlifts. His tanned body was a pattern of goose pimples, and like the other divers he now relied on a wet suit for warmth. The cavernous walls of the cenote shielded the bottom from the morning sun. Only eighteen hours ago the air in the well had been hot and steamy, but now it was frigid and damp. Jeff zipped up his wet suit and reached for a rig, into which he dropped a tank containing seventy-two cubic inches of compressed air that would, with controlled breathing, last about one hour. The two-stage regulator hissed as Jeff adjusted it. Still shivering, he grabbed a mask and fins and hobbled across the raft to a gap in the wooden guard rail. He glanced at the cold water and put on the mask, fitting it as tightly as possible over his mustache. Jeff jerked forward, causing the rubber hoses from the regulator to flip over his head. He fitted the mouthpiece between his teeth and jumped into the cold water of the cenote.

The water that had been slimy and putrid now was dark and sterile and smelled of chlorine and oil. Jeff spent as little time on the surface as he could although most of the oil had been skimmed off. All of it would have been removed except that rain had spread the oil and caused it to emulsify. The divers reconciled themselves to a thin, spotty film of oil residue that would have gone all but unnoticed by anyone who did not have to be in it eight hours a day. Those of us who had grown beards had never thought there would be oil in the well. Beards virtually strained the water, and washing them at night with cold water did not really get them clean. Scott had little trouble with the billy goat tuft on his chin, but Kiefer had a rough time with the dark brown growth that enveloped his face. Austin had also decided to join the bearded set, leaving only Jerry and Bill clean-shaven among the divers. Chlorine, of course, had another effect on beards: it bleached them in streaks.

Jeff sank slowly to the bottom of the cenote where visibility was less than four feet. Although visibility had not increased nearly as fast as we hoped, there had been at least one dramatic change in the well. It was dead. Only two weeks ago fish broke the surface every few minutes as they jumped for insects, snakes

"Most archaeologists considered the devices too rough in handling artifacts. . . ."

crawled around the tree trunks near the edge of the water, and frogs hopped on Thompson's bank. Now there was no life except for the bats that emerged each evening, and even the bat population was getting smaller, presumably because their supply of insect food around the cenote had nearly vanished.

Once on the floor of the well, Jeff dodged rocks and moved slowly, exploring what he could as he waited for Bill and Austin to join him. There had been some trouble with one of the airlift nozzles, and the three divers planned to inspect it. Jeff noticed that vertical visibility was slightly more than four feet, and he could just see the pale green air bubbles that he emitted rise steadily to the surface. He swam under the raft, where there was a current created by the intake from the big pump and the discharge line that was dumping back into the well nearly one hundred thousand gallons of filtered, chlorinated water each hour. Finally a black figure glided through the gray water a few feet away. Another figure appeared on Jeff's right. Now that Bill and Austin were down, work could begin on the airlift. Scott had scheduled the hydrolift for testing this week, but there was a chance of delay because divers would have to find a test site far enough away so that the work area would not be muddied.

It turned out that the problem with the airlift was minor. A rock that had got stuck in the intake section was easily removed, allowing divers to accomplish a great deal during the day on Tuesday.

That evening at the hacienda Scott discussed the problems of recovery with Piña, Victor and Folan. It seemed that the airlifts were going to prove more successful than the hydrolifts for vacuuming the bottom of the cenote. They were lighter and more easily wielded. While the hydrolift is basically nothing more than a water pump with a long nozzle, an airlift operates by forcing air under the water and letting it return to the surface through a hose several inches in diameter. Through an opening in the nozzle water is also forced to the surface by the rising air.

The mechanics of the devices were academic to the archaeologists, who were much more concerned about whether or not artifacts would be damaged, regardless of which type of lift was

179

used. Disagreement over the effectiveness of airlifts put an end to the 1960–61 expedition of the National Geographic Society and caused hard feelings between the society and CEDAM. Most archaeologists considered the devices too rough in handling artifacts, although Folan said he saw no evidence of this. Folan, easily one of the most knowledgeable men in the world on the sacred well, had other doubts about the airlifts however. The archaeologist pointed out in one of his reports that the device makes it difficult to work stratigraphically. He did not argue that stratigraphy existed in the well but merely said that if it did exist, no one would know it if airlifts were used. To divers who had already been to the bottom it was difficult to believe that artifacts had settled in chronologically detectable levels: they had found a Coca-Cola bottle buried under rocks in five feet of mud, and part of a carved jade pendant resting on the surface. That, however, still was not proof that strata did not exist since the bottom had been disturbed many times in history.

The argument over airlifts had never been settled after the 1960–61 expedition, nor was it concluded Tuesday night at the hacienda. Piña, who was calling the shots, said we could start using the airlifts with extreme caution. But he made it clear that as soon as there was evidence that they were breaking artifacts, we would have to stop.

The next morning Scott helped Kiefer and Harold Martin work on fortifying the guard rails around the raft. When Bill McGehee came to the surface for a fresh tank of air, Scott recruited him for help in fastening the rails beneath the waterline. Scott could have used a dozen more divers that week since there was still more urgent work to be done. A couple of the firehoses that stretched from the big pump to the filtration units were scraping on rocks under water. Since the hoses vibrated as water surged through them, the abrasive rocks could in time rip the hoses. They had to be moved. Scott also realized that at least one diver would have to be spared within a day or two to teach the archaeologists how to dive.

It was obvious that we were short on manpower. Accordingly, I expected the expedition leader to set a fast pace, but I hardly realized how fast it would be. Nor did I realize that Scott himself would try to handle more jobs that he ordinarily would have assigned to others. One minute he was working in the cold water and the next he was in the hot sun that was already scorching the raft by ten o'clock each morning. Orders came as fast as he could speak. More and more we realized that Scott considered it a personal challenge to excavate the sacred well.

I noticed by Thursday that the water was definitely getting clearer, but the process was disappointingly slow. Inman, Drake and Wade gazed into the well periodically from the platform near the filtration tanks, and their faces hardly expressed optimism. After the bank was flooded, visibility had been about two feet, and now it was four, maybe five, feet. The increase was an accomplishment for the filtration experts, but it was far from the successful clarification that would let divers excavate the well like a swimming pool.

Several problems were solving themselves. Acidity ceased to be much of a worry because the natural alkalinity of the well prevented it from reaching a dangerous level. Moreover, since pumping had stopped, we were not bringing acid from the soil into the well. Although hundreds of pounds of cyanuric acid were being added to the water to improve chlorination, this also represented only a relatively small amount compared to the total alkalinity of the well.

There was one serious problem which it seemed would never be solved. Although we had killed all life in the cenote, filters were not taking the material out fast enough. Apparently the mud kicked up by the divers and the airlifts was frustrating that function of the filters. There were several ways to cut down on the mud that was being stirred up but none seemed particularly appealing. Although he hated to take any more men off their other jobs, Scott ordered a wooden chute built for the muddy discharge water from the screening tables. Until now, water from the tables splashed directly back off the raft and into the well, carrying in dirt as fast as the filters could remove it. The big wooden chute would catch the muddy water and hopefully direct its settling to the bottom.

Scott helped in construction of the chute, and by late Friday it was ready to be lowered into the water. He climbed back on the raft after the chute was put in position, wiped the water from his face with the back of his arm and reached for the telephone on the raft. Beasom Painter answered in the command shed and heard Scott tell him to lower the basket. Beasom walked back to the center of the campsite where a half-dozen Mayas were unloading a basket of rocks that had been cleared from the area where the airlifts were working. Beasom told the Mayas to hurry, and as soon as the basket was emptied, he gave Al Datz the signal to lower it.

Scott was spending so much time in the water that his eyes were beginning to sting from the chlorine. He blinked hard several times as he stepped into the basket. Before he signaled Beasom to hoist away, Bill put two excellent Mayapán era pots and several fragments of thin orange ware into the basket. Scott nodded impatiently and then waved toward Beasom. The basket rose slowly out of the well.

Inman and Wade were huddled down near the outfall line when the expedition leader walked up to them. They had just repaired the elbow fitting that directed the rushing water downward after it passed through the filters. Scott nodded slightly as he approached them, but he looked over the filtration units before speaking. The four firehoses gurgled and shook from the water forced through them. These were the hoses that were moved earlier in the week. They were connected at the filtration platform to a manifold that channeled them into one eight-inch pipe. Before the pipe reached the first filtration tank, it passed an inlet where cyanuric acid entered the stream. Beyond that, there were four cut-off valves, each leading to a filtration tank in which the water was forced through a two-hundred-square-foot grid of diatomaceous earth. The earth absorbed the impurities as the water passed through the grid, and clear water from each tank was channeled back into a single outfall line. Before plunging off the cliff, the water passed through the automatic chlorinators that mixed it with the deadly gas. From there it rumbled along the outfall line that bent down at the elbow joint over the edge. The shiny aluminum shook

182

as the water roared down seventy-five feet into the well. In the midst of a muddy well, clean water bubbled to the surface like a fierce spring. Scott peered down at it from the platform as Inman and Wade finished tightening the joint.

Gordon's right hand and arm were red from handling cyanuric acid. Wade looked exhausted, hardly the demeanor Scott hoped to find. The expedition leader had come up to ask the filtration team a crucial question. Why wasn't the water getting any clearer? One look at Inman and Wade told Scott that the men were working as hard as anyone could expect them to. Before he got to the big question he asked if they needed more manpower. Wade said he could use another man to backwash the filters at night, and Scott promised him Kiefer.

The answer to the big question was one that Scott had expected: the water was not getting clearer at a faster rate because too much mud was being kicked up. He told the filtration team that he expected the chute to correct that situation, but Wade was unconvinced that the makeshift device would be adequate. Although Scott did not mention it, the problem of clarification was linked to money. Even if the Purex personnel could clarify the water in two weeks, the expedition would be in trouble because there would hardly be enough time afterward to accomplish adequate excavations. Money to keep the expedition going would run out before Christmas. Gordon said mud was also being kicked up by the fins that divers used. Scott raised his eyebrows.

"You're not suggesting that we work without fins, are you?" he asked.

Gordon said that he was not a diver, and Scott explained that without fins a diver uses much more energy to propel himself in the water. The conversation ended there, without a direct response from Scott on Inman's point.

The expedition leader walked from the filtration area to the command shed. It was nearly time to go back to the hacienda, and he reminded everyone in sight that we would all be working on Saturday, possibly a full day. Harold, who had seen him talking with Wade, asked what the story was on the clarification problem.

"Says it's going great," Scott said. "Should be cleared up in a day or so."

Harold said it was a little ironic that at this point the entire expedition depended on eight hundred square feet of filters and a couple of tons of chemicals.

"I hope those boys know what they're doing," he said.

Scott was gathering some papers he wanted to take back to the hacienda. "By the way," he said to Harold, "tell the divers not to use fins any more."

When I thought about that decision later in the evening at the hacienda, I realized what I had known for some time, that Scott would go to almost any limit to make the expedition a success. I was convinced that if given enough time, he could make it a tremendous success, but as money runs out, so does time. While we were listening to the music on the veranda of the hacienda after dinner, I had wanted to ask Scott what he really thought our chances of success were, but he looked too exhausted for that question. We spoke for some time about specific problems, and then he said, "You know what the hardest part of this expedition is?"

I looked blank.

"It's passing the gatehouse each morning and seeing the rusty old dredge that Thompson used," he said.

Scott said that seeing it each day was a constant reminder of the success, however limited, that Thompson had with a fraction of our equipment, personnel and funds.

Thompson's success can be measured by the number of years that elapsed before anyone else thought he could equal the American's accomplishment. Obviously, if someone had thought he could excavate the sacred well, the Mexican government would have let him try. No one had stepped forward with a workable plan until more than a decade after Thompson fled Mexico when the resident inspector of ruins in Yucatán, Manuel Cicerol Sansores, tried to promote an expedition. Unfortunately he could not drum up enough money or even enthusiasm. In 1935 Cicerol suggested a diving bell, but again his proposal never passed the idea stage. In 1954 another Mexican archaeologist, Jorge Acosta, drafted a plan, but it too was never put into effect. In the same year, almost going unnoticed, the aforementioned Mexican engineer, Edgar Espejo Evie, modestly suggested that the cenote could be excavated by pumping it dry or, alternatively, clarifying the water. Although his method of clarification was faulty in the original proposal, we are indebted to Espejo for giving us the prototype of the plan in the same way that we are indebted to Thompson for giving us the incentive. The National Geographic Society had been on the right track in 1960, and its attempt gave Scott a chance to evaluate the effectiveness of Espejo's forgotten plan.

Now it was Scott's turn. He had had to convince hundreds of people, from American businessmen to Mexican bureaucrats, that he could do it. It was hardly surprising then that he disliked seeing Thompson's crude equipment with which, up to this point, he had achieved more success than we had. Neither was it surprising that Scott was working us hard. He certainly drove himself just as hard.

We talked for nearly an hour on the veranda, the flow of conversation being interrupted repeatedly by Scott's harping on when I was going to learn to dive. I evaded the question thoroughly, and he laughed at each evasion. Finally we both grew tired of the game. I walked over to the bar for another rum, and Scott met with Dori in the main room of the hacienda to go over the upcoming payroll.

The next morning at breakfast I could see his bloodshot eyes from across the dining room. It was clear that he had been up all night, and I supposed that he spent the time going over budgets for the coming weeks. Since clarification was taking longer than anticipated, Scott had to find extra funds to keep the excavations going. If these extra funds were not available, he had no choice but to cut costs any way he could. From the look on his face, I judged that he had not found many ways last night.

There was no morning meeting that Saturday in an effort to save time, job assignments having been given out the day before. By ten o'clock Scott was ready to return to the hacienda to make arrangements for the payroll. Dori and I accompanied him. It was ironic that accumulating enough cash for a payroll was a

major operation. We were in the midst of conducting the largest
archaeological expedition ever undertaken in the Western Hemisphere, yet we found it extremely difficult to put our hands on the
few hundred dollars needed for the bi-weekly payrolls. It was
Scott's policy to pay 10 per cent of our salaries in cash and the
remainder by a check drawn on the company's bank in Florida.
There were frequent complaints that the cash was insufficient,
but we were actually lucky Scott could come up with as much
as he did.

Arrangements for the cash were made through the manager of
the hacienda who, with elaborate security precautions, had the
money secretly delivered from Mérida and stashed away in her own
room, probably under the mattress.

Scott asked me to drive the red pickup truck, and the three of
us bounced up the sacbe toward the hacienda. Scott said he wondered why it was so hot today, but both Dori and I thought it felt
cool. I was still wearing the sweater I had put on before breakfast,
but I noticed that Scott's face was wet with perspiration.

When we arrived at the hacienda, the clerk told us that the
manager, Señorita Lupita, was not in. That meant that she *was* in
but that she did not want to be disturbed.

"Tell her we're here for the payroll," Scott said impatiently.
The clerk spoke little English and pretended to speak even less.

"The money," Dori said.

"Money?"

Scott paused and then said very slowly, *"Pesos."*

The clerk smiled and led us to the manager's room. We saw
Lupita carrying a large brown box and looking very nervous. She
gestured for us to come in, and thirty minutes later Dori was
counting pesos.

Scott, meanwhile, said he was going back to his room for a nap,
and I volunteered to help Dori with the counting. From the historical point of view, I might mention that our payrolls were
probably the largest amount of cash ever seen in Chichén Itzá
since cacao beans were being exchanged for gold ornaments in
the ancient market.

When Dori and I finished the count, we gave Lupita a check

186

and then went back for Scott. The door to his room was open, and we found him stretched out on the bed. All efforts to wake him failed. One touch of his forehead told Dori that he was running a high fever. We rushed to the only phone in Chichén and called Mérida for a doctor.

The doctor who saw him that afternoon told us simply that Scott was a very sick man and would not be able to work for at least a week.

Harold Martin, who took over the leadership of the expedition, spent most of the day Sunday conferring with Segovia, Bill McGehee and the filtration team. There was nothing he could do but to continue the expedition in the same direction Scott had pointed it. Our energies would be directed toward two goals in the coming week: clarifying the water and recovering what material we could through the airlifts.

The only pleasant memory I have of the next week was of Gypsy, who came back from Cozumel to work with us for a few days. Considering himself somewhat impervious to the cold, Gypsy resorted to a wet suit with the greatest disdain. He made himself useful to the first person who would ask for his help. One minute I saw him diving into the water and a half hour later I would see him helping the archaeologists with the cataloguing.

That was a job that went along steadily despite the confusion that plagued the rest of the expedition. The list of sacrificial treasure grew each hour, and now that the airlifts were in operation it was all Otto, Yoko and Ann could do to keep up. Scott received reports on our progress twice a day and on Tuesday evening met with his section leaders for the first time. He was cheered by the quantity of artifacts being brought to the surface but was quick to point out that the rate could be tripled if the water were clear.

Bill, meanwhile, solved the mystery of the broken pots. We recalled that several weeks ago he discovered a place to the east of the altar area, almost under the raft, that was virtually piled with broken pots. Pots from other areas also had been broken, but in them the break appeared deliberate, nothing more than a chip from the lip of the vessel. The pots from the area under the raft looked as though they had been torn apart. Archaeologists might have assumed that this type of breakage was another form of ritual killing, but Bill determined that nearly all the severely damaged pots were found in association with very old tree limbs and that the vast majority of these vessels had handles, or at least the vestiges of handles. He theorized that the pots had been lowered into the well but had got caught on limbs and could not be withdrawn. Archaeologists bolstered this theory by determining that most of these vessels were of the Mayapán era, during which residents might have considered the well less holy and accordingly drank its water.

Folan liked Bill's theory and it was proved many times during the expedition. In several other areas where there were obviously

Bill gives Victor one of the oldest skeletal remains found in the well.

old limbs, there were also more broken ceramics of the Mayapán era but fewer complete pots from earlier periods. We already had more pottery than we were able to put into the storeroom at the gatehouse. Our only disappointment was that the ceramics were rarely painted.

By Wednesday afternoon Bill and Austin were removing some large rocks to clear an area for the second airlift. Bill was groping at one large rock when he felt distinct carvings on it. It was after three in the afternoon and therefore the visibility was nil in the cenote. Bill put his face several inches from the carving and saw a face staring back at him. The carved chunk of limestone required more than an hour's work to dislodge, and divers were reluctant to attempt bringing it up by the basket. Instead, the crane dropped a metal line that was tied around the rock.

As Al Datz turned the controls, the metal line was reeled up. The object broke the surface of the water and a few seconds later we saw a three-foot-high carved jaguar swinging through the air. Once on the ground, the cat was immediately the object of curiosity by everyone at camp. It sat on its haunches, and midway down its spine was a ring carved into the stone. The statue was in excellent condition, much of the red paint still visible around the mouth, in which some of the delicately carved teeth were still intact. One ear had got lopped off somewhere along the centuries, but there was surprisingly little erosion on the beast. Still clearly visible were the embossed circles which the artist used as stylized spots. Segovia recognized the style as Mayapán and identified the statue as a standard-bearer. A flag, probably made of bright feathers or fabric, was propped up through the ring on the spine to display the colors of a god or possibly of one of the ruling families, such as the Tutul Xiu, who warred with each other during the era.

The next morning the divers found another jaguar standard-bearer in the same area. This one was slightly smaller, but the paint on it was in better condition. Although the statues were not mates, archaeologists presumed they had been used together, either at the cenote or in the temple area of Chichén. The latter was probably the case, but it was difficult to explain how they got to the bottom of the sacred well.

"The cat was immediately the object of curiosity by everyone at camp."
"Gypsy" on the left, with Don Pablo.

It was not an easy matter to ascertain the origin of large carvings or statues found in the cenote, for two reasons. First, many buildings around it were of secondary construction, meaning that Mayas had used stones from other buildings to build them. Some of the supporting stones of the building at the end of the sacbe, for instance, were carved. There was no over-all pattern to them, however, since the stones were taken at random from many other structures. Secondly, it is known that vandals took materials from the temple area and dumped it into the cenote.

190

The jaguar, by the way, took on special importance in Mayan culture after the Toltec intrusion. The Toltecs had two warrior cults, the jaguar and the eagle. It is interesting that in so many different cultures animals are used as military symbols, almost as an admission that war is animalistic.

"The jaguar . . . took on special importance in Mayan culture. . . ."

Kirk had got word of a story about Thompson finding a gold statue of a jaguar only to have it slip irretrievably from his hands back into the well. Thinking it might build up a little incentive, Kirk posted notice of a five-hundred-dollar bonus for anyone who found the gold jaguar. He was mixing a bullshot in the office-Cortez when he asked me if I believed the story. I waited until he had carefully mixed the beef boullion with the vodka before telling him that I thought it was the safest offer he had ever made. Kirk took a gulp of the drink, grinned and then imparted some of his own philosophy. "Always bet on the one that got away to stay away," he said. "Take it from a man who's been married three times."

Kirk ordinarily left the everyday task of the expedition up to Scott, but now that the expedition leader was ill, Kirk took a more direct hand in the operation. I must admit that I was impressed by his ability. With one hand holding a bottle of beer and the other pointing to this or that piece of machinery, he was able to make complex decisions with ease and accuracy. Even the archaeologists, to whom he had been something of an embodiment of commercialism, developed a respect for his ability. And not to be ignored, of course, was Kirk's willingness to share the cases of beer which he brought to the cenote each day that he was at the site.

Scott had assigned me to make out the next official report on the expedition for the National Institute of Anthropology and History. I had it ready Thursday evening, and went to Scott's room to present it to him after dinner. Seeing the bleak outlook in the cold verbiage of the report was hardly good medicine for the expedition leader, but I had no choice but to give him the facts as they were. Scott was still running a fever, but it was not as high as it had been earlier in the week. The doctor said he had a severe virus infection, aggravated by a relapse of the exhaustion that had overcome him several weeks earlier. Although the report made no projections, Scott was able to crystallize his own analysis of the future as he read the document. If the water did not clear up within a few days, the expedition would fail and we would have to pack up and go home. On Thursday the visibility was

The well cleared to the point that photographer Charles Irwin captured this eerie shot of divers, from the bottom looking up.

Three excellent examples of ceramic heads
taken from the well; the one at bottom right
is an effigy of the strange "diving god."

At left is the curious stag-horn turkey; above, another gold god effigy.

The "decorated porpoise"—symbolic or merely whimsical?—
that charmed our treasure hunters.

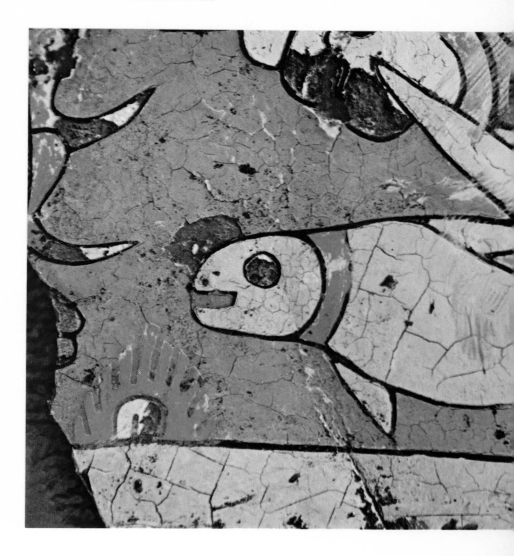

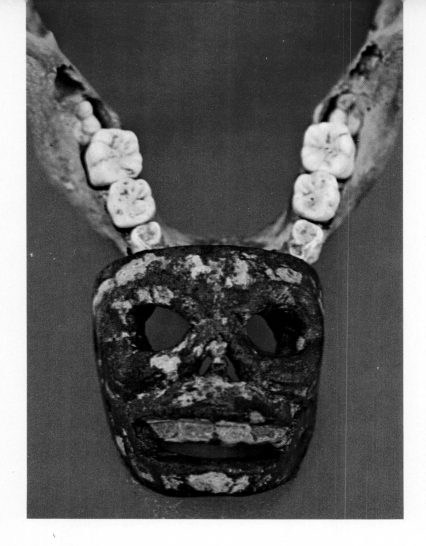

The death mask and jawbone, above, symbolize the cenote's
bloody history; above right, another god effigy typifies the Maya
obsession with deformity, while the fragility of the
Tepeu gourd painting below indicates why such artifacts
are rare and valuable.

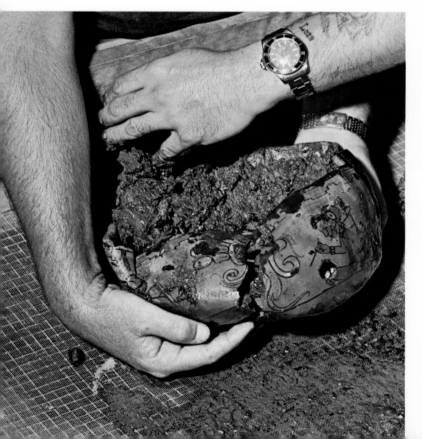

Again an underwater photo of divers recovering another ceramic vessel illustrates the high degree of clarification eventually achieved.

slightly more than five feet. Scott shook his head but said nothing.

We had come so far that it was almost heartbreaking to think of failure at this point. No one was really to blame, least of all Scott, who had singlehandedly organized the venture and worked himself to exhaustion seeing it through. It had been many weeks since I had seen traces of the high spirits which Scott and the rest of us had during the first weeks of the expedition. Just to see what his reaction would be, I reminded Scott of the "fountain incident." It took him a few seconds to realize what I was talking about, but once he did, he let out a hearty laugh. We forgot about the report for a few minutes and reminisced about that hilarious day back in September.

The trip to Yucatán had been something of an adventure itself, the task being to drive twenty-one vehicles in formation thirty-five hundred miles from Pompano Beach, Florida, to Chichén Itzá, Yucatán. In order to meet our timetable, we occasionally had to push the caravan fifteen hours a day, leaving us only a few hours for sleep before starting up the next morning. The driving schedule was complicated by our big tractor trailers, which were much slower than most of the other vehicles. Aggravating the problem still further was the movie crew that insisted on having us in perfect formation for the cameras. This meant at least an hour of passing and repassing furious drivers of other cars on the road until we achieved the desired formation. Then the camera crew had to zip ahead of us, find a place to shoot from and hope they could set up the equipment before the caravan sped past. The campers were equipped with showers, but we often did not have time to fill the water tanks and had to do without bathing for several days at a time. On one memorable occasion Austin got confused between the water and gasoline tanks and wound up showering with Amoco Regular.

As we were leaving a campsite near Baton Rouge, one of the tractor trailers got stuck in a muddy ditch and nearly overturned. Scott stayed behind to make arrangements for a crane to pull it out, but the job took so long that Scott and the big truck were nearly a day behind the rest of us. It was a crucial time gap because on the following day Scott had to be in Houston to pick up the filtration tanks and some other equipment. Without really knowing what to do, he took a chance and called the governor of Louisiana. The telephone rang in the governor's mansion at about seven-thirty in the morning.

"Hello, who's this?" Scott asked when someone answered the phone.

"This is Governor McKeithen. May I help you?"

Scott, dripping with mud and exhausted, had the difficult job of explaining to Governor John McKeithen about getting stuck in a ditch with a twenty-one-vehicle caravan heading to the Yucatán jungle.

McKeithen, who was having breakfast when the phone rang, indicated that Scott had come to the right man. His plan was this: Scott would be given a Highway Patrol escort that would let him cross the state at any speed he wanted. The truck, meanwhile, would be waved through without red tape at the weigh stations. The plan worked. Scott caught up to us that afternoon, the truck joined the caravan the following day, and the world of archaeology owes an everlasting debt to the governor who was not too busy to help someone calling from a phone booth and talking about the Yucatán jungle.

It was difficult enough to keep the caravan moving smoothly in the United States, but the language barrier made driving in Mexico just a little tricky for the monolingual members of the expedition. The journey into Mexico began with a bad omen. We had to spend twelve hours parked in the hot sun at Nuevo Laredo while Mexican customs officials debated whether we would be allowed to enter the country with our vast array of equipment. The fact that we were working for the National Institute meant nothing to them since departments in the Mexican government are very independent. When we finally did get rolling, we had problems with the Mexican gasoline which, though supplied free by Petróleos Mexicanos, was different in quality from American fuel. If one asks a gas station attendant for *"especial,"* for instance, he will get the lowest grade of gas instead of the highest.

Somewhat miraculously we pulled into Mexico City with the assistance of a police escort that prevented us from getting lost

194

more than once every five kilometers or so. CEDAM had arranged for a big news conference the following day at the Museum of Anthropology in Chapultepec Park. We were even given permission to park the twenty-one vehicles on the walkway in front of the museum. Despite our total exhaustion and lack of a shower in nearly a week, we tried to look our best at the news conference, which was followed by a semiformal lunch reception given in the museum by the National Institute.

After the speeches and picture-taking some of us wandered around the museum, a building which I have heard persons less prone to hyperbole than I describe as one of the most beautiful in the world. I shall say only that if the museum did not contain a single item, it would still be worth seeing. Its architecture and design are so beautiful that the museum's grandeur often overshadows its contents. The focal point of this elegence is a gigantic fountain in a wide courtyard. The fountain is built around a stone column about five feet in diameter which forms the stalk of its mushroom shape. At the top of the stalk, three stories up, the water pours down like rain, splashing onto the stone floor of the courtyard and then disappearing into drains.

Scott, Jack Kiefer, our still photography team of Joyce and Charles Irwin, and I wandered around the museum for more than an hour. We got several sneers from the guards who did not think too highly of our wrinkled clothes and dirty bodies, but once we explained who we were and what we were doing here, they gave us red carpet treatment. Finally it was time to leave. We walked out of the Maya Room and into the courtyard. A cool wind brought some of the fountain spray in our direction. We stared at the fountain for a few minutes and realized that we all had the same ridiculous idea.

Before the guards had a chance to say anything, the five of us were dancing around under the cascading water. We let it run through our hair and into our faces. It was the first refreshing shower we had had in five days. The performance was so good that a troup of Mexican boy scouts ran out of the Toltec Room to catch the final act, which consisted of the five of us running in single file around the circle in which the water fell. The only embarrassing part of the venture was having to walk out through the museum's rather formal lobby, nodding sheepishly as we did so to some of the same officials who had attended the luncheon.

Scott was sleepy by the time we got through reminiscing about the wild time we had getting to Chichén. Dori knocked on the door with some papers and the mail, but Scott said he would get to them in the morning.

"You know," he said as I was leaving the room, "if we have to leave Chichén now, it's not going to be much of a picnic driving back. I'd hate to have to face the same newspapermen who wrote those stories about what we hoped to find on the hemisphere's biggest expedition."

10

Scott improved substantially during the next couple of days although he had little good news from the campsite to bolster his spirits. Visibility was holding steady at about five and a half feet, but it seemed impossible to increase it beyond that distance. No matter how carefully the divers worked on the bottom, too much mud was being stirred up for the filters to handle.

On Saturday, one week after Scott had taken ill, he got a report after dinner from Harold Martin. Two of the firehoses had scraped on rocks and ruptured that afternoon. Filtration would be halted until the hoses were repaired.

Scott's only concern was the length of time it would take to replace the hoses. Harold said that work started as soon as one break became apparent but that the rupture in the second hose was not noticed until divers went to investigate the first leak. Harold's problem was that he had given some expedition members the day off to go into Mérida, leaving him with only a skeleton crew. Scott told him to have Avelino round up some Mayas if more hands were needed, but Harold doubted they could be useful right now. Only a limited number of people could work in the cenote at night without falling over each other. He said the two new hoses could be lowered and hooked up tonight but that he would have to wait for daylight to send divers in to make sure they still were not rubbing on the rocks. Scott gave the order to work through the night and to check with him as soon as the new hoses were attached, regardless of the hour. Harold left, but Scott could not sleep. The doctor had given him some sleeping pills, but he did not take them. Maybe he didn't want to sleep.

At 2:00 A.M. Scott got out of bed and went to the cenote. Harold and Avelino protested that he should not be up, but Scott said he was feeling great. Throughout the night he worked on the new hoses. He put on a wet suit and got in the well, which is no easy place to work at night. The ruptures had to be traced so that the correct hoses would be disconnected from the manifold on the raft. Al Datz, who had not slept in more than twenty-four hours, operated the crane that lifted the hoses from the water. In daylight the task would have been cumbersome. At night it was laboriously tedious.

Finally the lengths of new hoses were lowered into position, and the crane kept them high enough so they would not scrape again on the rocks. The new segments were linked up, tightened and then attached to the two manifolds. Shortly before dawn Scott and the night crew finished the job and were ready to start the filters in order to make sure the hoses would not scrape. The big pump was started, the filtration tanks were backwashed, and by daylight the filters were back in operation.

On Sunday afternoon Scott rounded up a couple of the divers who had stayed in Chichén for the weekend to check the distance between the hoses and the rocks. Inman figured that the loss of filter time, coupled with the activity in the water, might have brought the visibility back to four and a half or five feet. It was a setback we could scarcely afford, and my only hope was that it was not the one to break the back of the expedition.

Doctors could say what they wanted, but it was obvious that Scott was well. Later Sunday afternoon he watched Bill and Jerry

198

give diving lessons to the archaeologists at the hacienda pool.

Segovia was a particularly good pupil. He was a better than average swimmer and had no trouble in mastering the techniques of the equipment. Folan did not really need any lessons. He dived often on the 1960–61 expedition and had already gone to the bottom several times in the last two weeks. Jerry Griffin was fascinated by the diving apparatus but apparently was no better in the pool than Victor. The three of them would have gotten A for effort in any school, and I am sure they realized the necessity of their learning. It would not do, however, for them to learn only the minimum requirements, for Scott would not take any chances on an accident, especially after the near-catastrophe with chlorination.

Bill expected Victor to become a great diver, but on Monday in the cenote the archaeologist was a different person. I watched Victor on the raft as he slowly put on his diving rig and climbed down the ladder that led from the guard rail. For reasons known only to him, Victor found it impossible to let go of the ladder. Had he done so, he would have glided gently into the water and his weight belt would have pulled him slowly to the bottom. However logically he could convince himself that diving in the well was no different from in the pool, he could not bring himself to let go.

"There's no hurry. We might be here for a long time," Scott said as he extended a hand over the rail to Victor.

Folan was already on the bottom watching Jeff and Jack feed the airlift. Griffin, who had been only an average pupil, turned out to be fearless in the water.

"You and I can go down later on this afternoon, okay?" Scott said to Victor, who nodded gratefully in reply.

It was several days before Victor got as close to the water as he had been on Monday, but later in the week he managed to get in the water. Finding that he would not plummet to the bottom with the heavy diving rig and weight belt, he swam around for several minutes before hoisting himself back onto the raft. Scott congratulated him and took the occasion again to ask me when I was going to learn to dive. Again I evaded the question by asking Scott if he had seen the latest jawbones to be retrieved from the bottom.

We walked over to the bucket by the screening tables and pulled them out. Like many others we had found, these had the front teeth missing. After finding so many jawbones in the same conditions we had all but ruled out coincidence or natural means of extraction.

It was later in the same afternoon that immense rain clouds began to build up in the north. I had seen a few clouds in that direction during the morning and thought we would probably get a light shower about noon. By four o'clock, however, it still had not rained, and the bank of dark nimbus clouds looked monstrous. Chuck Irwin had wanted to photograph some of the skulls and jawbones that afternoon, but he told us it was too cloudy to get the quality of pictures he wanted. Just as Chuck was explaining this to Scott, I felt the first big drop on my shoulder. Scott had felt one also. He looked up and frowned. Before we signaled for the basket to be lowered, a clap of thunder echoed through the well. This, I suppose was the sound that answered the ancient Mayas' prayers to Chac, but to us it sounded like a curse.

Minutes after the first torrents struck the raft, we saw brown streams of mud tumbling down the sides of the well. Although we were on the raft, we could visualize the campsite turning instantly into a field of mud which would flow down toward the precipice and accumulate into large pools near the edge. If these pools finally overflowed, the mud would cascade down into the cenote. We could see this process already developing as pools of brown water were forming within the well itself. Several Maya workers, unimpressed with our filtration system, had joked about Chac's ability to pour more than two hundred thousand gallons of mud into the well any time he chose. It seemed that the god had a malicious sense of timing.

Nearly drowned out by the thunder in the well, Scott yelled again for the crane to bring us to the top, trying meanwhile to wipe the water from his face with the back of his hand. Finally, just as another of the mud pools on top broke loose and spurted over the cliff, the crane set the basket down on the deck of the raft.

Scott paused to look at the circles of brown silt growing larger in the cenote, far from the intake to the filters, which could not have handled them anyway. On the way to the top, he signaled the crane to stop every fifteen feet or so. Then dangling close to the vines and trees that still clung to the walls, he peered dismally at the waterfalls of mud which, in less than five minutes, had undone at least five days of filtration.

Pablo Bush was in the command shed when Scott got out of the basket and sloshed his way toward the intercom. He picked up the phone and pushed the switch to ring the bell on the raft. He ordered the filtering continued despite the rain and asked Bill to have a couple of divers inspect the hoses near the rocks. He figured that rain would increase the current in the cenote, thereby making it more likely that the hoses would scrape. Scott betrayed his disgust with the rain by slamming the receiver down as he walked from the command shed. I could hardly blame him.

"No one can remember it raining this hard in November except during a hurricane," Don Pablo said as we ran to the archaeologists' shed. Once we got there, Don Pablo said, "A couple of the workers have an idea that might be worth looking into, and I don't mean sacrificing to Chac." Scott looked interested.

It was probably too late to do much good now, Pablo said, but we might be able to put the debris that we were taking out of the well to good use on top. He said two of the laborers thought we might keep the mud for cascading into the cenote by building dams out of the debris along the precipice. Unintentionally, we had aggravated the problem ourselves several weeks ago when we took away part of the soil around the edge of the well to level the ground for the crane and filtration tanks. That had only made a steeper slope near the cliff. The workers' plan was essentially to replace this earth and to build up the ground near the edge.

Scott glanced at the steady streams of water pouring into the well, one of which was trickling almost under his feet through the archaeologists' shed. He said he doubted that dams could be built high enough to contain the water from a big rain like this one. Moreover, he was not sure that mud could be prevented from slipping through a dam constructed mainly of rocks. Don Pablo was not convinced either but told him the Mayas said the mud itself would clog up the spaces between the stone. As far as the height of the dam was concerned, Don Pablo said, we had ample debris and plenty of time now that diving operations would probably have to be halted until the water was reclarified. Scott said the plan was worth trying.

They went back out into the rain to find Avelino, so work on the dam could start immediately. When the foreman was told of the plan, the three of them walked around the campsite, choosing places where retaining walls would do the most good and surveying in disgust the damage that the downpour was causing. Scott said they should also have a long talk with Wade and Inman since the rain had caused a tragic setback in filtration. The rain had further harassed the camp by undermining the garbage areas around the campers. Streams of water carried the trash into the center of the site, and flies were bound to start swarming as soon as the air was dry. Scott wanted the trash cleared away before nightfall for fear it would attract the animals which so far we had been lucky in warding off.

The streams of water continued down the slope of the site until they hit the foundation of the ancient building at the end of the sacbe. Don Pablo was afraid it might also be undermined despite the reconstruction job that Piña had ordered several weeks ago.

Jerry Kemler was putting sheets of plastic over machinery that could be damaged by the rain, but there was never enough plastic to go around. Scott told him to dismantle some of the plastic awnings over the campers if the shortage became desperate.

While Jerry was worrying about protecting the machinery, Al Datz was walking around looking helpless as the water eroded the soil beneath the crane. He told Scott and Don Pablo that the situation could be serious because the soil under the crane was being shifted by the torrents of water. About a week ago we had

"... leaning out over the altar platform. ..."
Note the vegetation on the cenote wall in the background.

carefully packed soil on the crane legs to weight them down, but now this soil was also being washed away. It was essential that the legs have this extra weight to prevent it from tipping when heavy loads of rocks were hoisted from the well. With his crane sitting on the edge of the cenote, Al was taking a big risk in operating it without the protective weight. Problems caused by the rain mushroomed: until the crane was weighted down again, we could not bring up fill for the dams. Al said the only way to solve the problem was to have workers roll over some stones that had already been brought topside, and in the meantime he would bring up small loads of debris so work on the retaining walls could begin. Fortunately there was also quite a bit of debris on the outskirts of the campsite that could be brought back for the dams.

Just beyond the crane we saw Otto leaning out over the altar platform as he precariously held on to the protruding rock from the adjacent structure. The platform, probably more than six hundred years old, was beyond the stage of being undermined. The tons of water that had splashed on it over the centuries had only helped to fuse the limestone and mortar with which it was built. A thick layer of soil and grass made the actual platform difficult to see from the top, but from the raft it could be seen jutting out over the precipice like a single stratum of stone. The rocks that formed the platform had apparently fused to the limestone bedrock. If that were the case, it would last as long as the walls of the cenote themselves.

Otto pointed out a place in the platform where he said the archaeologists planned to start digging tomorrow. Restoration work had already begun on the building at the end of the sacbe, and the altar platform was next on the list. Otto said his only problem might be finding workmen willing to be hoisted out over the edge of the well to reach the farthermost stones. Scott suggested he get the same men who helped Sam chip away part of the wall for the personnel lift.

Victor interrupted the conversation between Otto and Scott. He needed Otto's help at the archaeologists' shed since many of the bones had been left out to dry in the sun earlier in the

"Restoration work had already begun on the building
at the end of the sacbe. . . ."

day. Victor wanted them brought in immediately and covered with
tarpaulins. I glanced toward the shed and saw Yoko trying to
stretch a tarpaulin over one of the tables. The wind was fighting
her. A Maya worker finally ran over and took the other side of
the cover, which they unfolded like a bedspread over the bones
that had lain under water for centuries. Another workman, Avelino's son, gathered large rocks to hold down the tarpaulin. Otto
went about putting all the pieces of ceramics under a table where
no one would be likely to run into them.

Scott and Don Pablo jumped down the rock embankment that separated the archaeologists' area from the filtration tanks. Inman, his arm still red from handling cyanuric acid, was adjusting the automatic chlorinator. Wade was at the edge of the well with Bob Drake, peering at the brown pools below with the same look of disgust that I had seen in Scott and Don Pablo. Wade wore a straw had that had accumulated enough water to make the brim sag. When Scott called to him, Wade turned, the movement upsetting the water that had settled in the hat. It splashed over on his shoulder and ran down his side. Scott laughed for the first time in hours.

"Okay, what do we do now?" the expedition leader asked.

Wade was slow to produce a reply. He finally said that it was possible for the filtration equipment to catch up with the increased turbidity. "But what's bothering me," he added, "is that we have no guarantee that even after we catch up it won't rain like this again."

Scott said the point was academic. If it rained like this again, we would have to call the expedition off. But he said that even assuming the skies cleared in twenty-four hours, we would have to clarify the water in a couple of days in order to have enough time to complete excavations before our money ran out.

Don Pablo told the filtration team about the plan to build the dams, but the water experts voiced the same doubts that Scott had expressed earlier.

Inman said we had to go on one assumption, that it was not going to rain like this again. The entire expedition had been scheduled for late fall specifically to avoid heavy rains, and he agreed with Scott that we were completely unprepared to deal with a freakish quirk of nature.

Wade broke in at the end of Gordon's remarks. "Our team here just finished talking about trying a completely different approach to the problem. Let's get under the shed and talk about it," he said.

We climbed back up the embankment to the archaeologists' shed and chose seats with our backs to the wind that was whipping the rain under the roof. Wade started the conversation by saying that the big brown pools of mud in the the cenote were nothing new.

"We have them every day. This time they just happen to be on the surface of the water instead of near the bottom where they're caused by the airlifts," he said.

The problem was still the same, and it was a little ironic. The very devices that we were using to bring up a fraction of the sacrificial treasure were keeping us from bringing it all up.

Wade said he thought there was a solution, or at least one approach that had not yet been tried. He said we should shut down operations completely for three or four days, during which time the Purex engineers would make an all-out attempt at flocculating the water. This meant pouring in chemicals that would cause suspended particulars of mud to aggregate and form larger particles with a density greater than that of water. When this happened, Wade said, the particles would fall to the bottom. Afterward, filtration and chlorination would resume and continue around the clock. He said it was necessary to shut operations down because it was imperative not to disturb the water during flocculation or the subsequent treatment.

Although the plan made sense, it was another gamble. We would be losing several days' work at a crucial time in the expedition. Scott said that if he took Wade's suggestion and the water still failed to clear, we would have passed the point of no return and be forced to abandon the well permanently. Another thing bothered Scott: what guarantee was there that the filtration equipment could maintain clarity once it was achieved? Wade said the answer was based on the total turbidity. The filters could not now handle both the mud stirred up by the airlifts and divers as well as the normal amount of turbidity in the well. What his plan would basically accomplish was reducing to a minimum the normal level of turbidity, after which the filters would be free to cope with the excess created by our activity in the water. If necessary, he said, a second treatment could be worked in during a shorter period of time later in the expedition, possibly on a Sunday when no one was working.

The plan did not appeal to Scott so much as it represented the only approach that we had not yet tried.

The rain lasted through the evening and into the night. Maya workers had gathered rubble for the dams until quitting time. They would have been asked to work later except that by then it was so dark they could barely see. Workers began building the retaining dam in the area worst hit by the rain, a slope that had become a river of mud between the personnel lift and the crane. Before half the section was built, we had an idea that the plan was going to work. The water had already started to pile up in front of the wall, and the river shrank to a fraction of its former size.

Scott went directly to his room after dinner to talk further with Wade, Don Pablo and several other expedition members. It was the consensus of those present that Scott needed a good rest and that the crew could certainly use a long weekend. Wade suggested we all go away for a few days, leaving only his team and a skeleton crew of Mayas at the well. Scott was all in favor of a hiatus, but he did not like the idea of leaving Chichén. Expedition members, he said, were welcome to the time off, but he told Wade that he would like to stay around to see the operation through. Only after several minutes of persuasion did Don Pablo convince Scott to take a holiday himself. After all, Don Pablo argued, there was really nothing for any of us to do that the Purex people could not do alone. Moreover, if the clarification experiment was successful, we had better be rested up for several weeks of hard work. To top off his argument, he offered us his island home on Cozumel for the weekend.

Scott finally smiled and asked Don Pablo how soon we could be in Cozumel.

As for the rest of us, I think we wanted a long weekend very badly. The plan to suspend operations and undertake intensive flocculation and filtration was an experiment that might fail. No one particularly wanted to be around to witness a failure.

The rain ended some time during the night, about 2:00 A.M. according to the watchman. In midmorning the campsite was customarily filled with activity, laundry women bargaining to take in washing, machinery drumming incessantly in the background and orders being given in three languages.

Now it was quiet. The trash heap that the flood created had been completely cleared away by workmen, who were given the rest of the day off. The sun began to bake the mud as soon as it got high enough over the trees to reach the ground. The skeleten crew of Mayas worked quietly on another section of the dam. At 9:00 A.M. Gordon Inman and Bob Drake drove down the sacbe, got out and walked across the campsite. They glanced at the low irregularly shaped indentations in the mud which we had all learned to recognize as snake tracks. The serpent had slithered not more than five feet from the watchman's cot, apparently to feed on the rats that had been attracted by the trash heaps.

Wade had intended to start flocculation that morning, Friday, but decided to give the fresh mud a few hours to settle on its own. Meanwhile, he and Wayne Vanderlow got the chemicals in order. At three-thirty in the afternoon they dumped six hundred pounds of aluminum sulphate into the cenote. Then they mixed two pounds of a high-powered flocculant called Purfloc into a fifty-gallon tank. The mixture became the consistency of honey and was spread evenly around the well. Then the men waited. They hoped that the rain had ended for good and that the flocculant would have the expected effect.

The Purex team got up before dawn on Saturday. They had worked into the night to connect a fresh tank of chlorine to the automatic chlorinator. They were tired in the morning but too keyed up to realize it. When the men arrived back at the well, they walked down by the precipice to look at the water. Daylight had already reached the top but there was not yet enough light in the cenote for them to see whether the flocculation had been successful. Wade, Inman, Drake and Vanderlow stood by the edge, had a smoke and continued to wait. As sunlight crept down into the god's home, it showed the men what they did not want to see. At first they thought the water looked murky because of the weak light, but as the day brightened, they were sure that the mud had not yet settled. Wayne brought up a water sample and analyzed it. Many of the particles had precipitated with the help of the chemicals, but smaller ones were still in suspension. In other words, the process *was* working although more slowly than anticipated.

There was nothing else they could do now. Wade, realizing now how tired the team was, suggested they take the rest of the day off and get some sleep. They had talked earlier about cleaning some of the equipment during the afternoon, but sleep overcame them as soon as they reached their rooms.

On Sunday they waited until it was light enough to see the water clearly before going to the well. At midmorning the crane lowered the men onto the raft. Footsteps echoed around the cenote. The water appeared dark but clear, and it was obvious that the remaining suspended particles had sunk to the bottom. Analysis of the water confirmed the observation.

The pump was started immediately and once again the deafening sound of the engine filled the cenote cavern. On top, the men put the chlorinator into operation. Eight pounds of chlorine per hour began mixing with the water as it flowed back into the well. The water analysis ironically revealed that the well was becoming too alkali for the chlorine to have maximum effectiveness. Wade decided to add muriatic acid in hope of neutralizing the alkalinity but without increasing the acidity to a dangerous level. Then, with the chlorinator and filters working around the clock, the men waited.

They had fewer than twenty-four hours before other expedition members would return for the new work week. One of the filtration team stayed at the site at all times to backwash the filtration tanks, but more often than not all four were at camp. They could not allow anything to go wrong now. Clouds gathered before dusk, but the air was dry and rain failed to come. Inman thought it would be a good idea for the team to spend the night at the well just in case manpower was needed in a hurry. None of the team got much sleep that night. When they were not backwashing the filters, they inspected the chlorinator or repeatedly consulted the night watchman on the chances of rain.

11

THE PLANE was late taking off Monday morning from Cozumel, but finally around nine-thirty the turboprops whined, and the craft lifted above the whitecaps in the Yucatán Channel.

Cozumel had been just the medicine we needed. Some of us stayed in Don Pablo's house, which was now repaired from Hurricane Beulah's damage. Others stayed at hotels on the island where the tourist season had just begun. I do not think any of us had had so much fun since one night in Mexico City two months earlier. Every tourist we could find got thrown in the pool, and if Norman Scott is not remembered for opening the time capsule of the Mayas, he will be remembered for stacking champagne glasses on top of each other higher than anyone else had ever done in Cozumel and possibly all of Mexico. A threat to throw the hotel owner himself in the pool put an end to the Saturday night party.

The divers had a postman's holiday, but Gypsy turned it into an exciting weekend. For many years there had been stories about black coral in the Caribbean, but it has been only since the mid-

1960s that the location of the coral beds became common knowledge among divers. Gypsy helped Bill, Jerry, Austin, Jeff and Jack find an area where the rare coral grows off the Cozumel coast. There, under more than 125 feet of water, are the black bushes of coral that look something like inverted weeping willow trees. The limbs are rubbery but resistant to all but the sharpest knives. Divers managed to cut off small pieces, and when the pieces were dried, they became hard as stone. When polished, the coral looks like black pearl or ebony. Ancient Mayas probably would have deified the substance, but it is unlikely that black coral was known to them. Even if it had been, they would have found great difficulty in working a material which is harder than flint.

As the plane passed low over boats in the channel, I was reminded of stories about women who in ancient times made pilgrimages to worship at Cozumel. The shrine of Ix Chel, goddess of motherhood, was located on the island, which women could reach only by chartering a canoe to take them across the dangerous channel. Women tried to visit the temple of Ix Chel at least once in a lifetime, and many of them were undoubtedly claimed by the channel. Maybe Ix Chel was at odds with another god, such as the North Star God, called Xaman Ek, or the God of Wind, whose name we do not know. Athena's feud with Poseidon would provide an interesting parallel in Greek mythology.

A few minutes' flying time from the Yucatán coast was the border between the territory of Quintana Roo and the state of Yucatán. The country looked even more desolate from the air than from the ground. We looked for roads but could not see any, and the thatching on the scattered clusters of huts blended with the scrub jungle. The ruins at Cobah looked like a bombed-out village. Although we could not see it, we knew that to the north was the road from Mérida to Isla Mujeres that also ran through Chichén Itzá. Excavations indicated that an ancient sacbe ran south of it through Cobah, but the jungle long ago covered the paving that Mayas had put down by hand.

Cenotes looked like freckles on the face of the land. An air traveler not acquainted with Yucatán would take the grayish brown sinkholes for ponds and expect to see streams flowing into them.

In fact, there were no streams, and even the cenotes were far apart, giving a dramatic picture of how scarce surface water is on the peninsula. It was about ten o'clock when we came in view of the road. Then near the horizon we saw the tops of the Caracol and the Temple of Kukulcán grow larger as we approached the landing strip.

Suddenly all of us leaped to the left side of the plane. It was as though we had never seen Chichén before. The sacred well gleamed like an aquamarine.

The pilot must have been startled too. He decided to circle once more. When he did, the left wing pointed down into the crystal clear water, set like a jewel between the white surface of the sacbe and the green of the jungle. We could see directly into the well, where its white sides turned bluish green as they disappeared into the water. But then we noticed that nothing completely disappeared in the water: we could see the bottom of the cenote itself!

We went by foot directly from the airstrip to the well, and by the time we got there most of us were running flat out along the dusty white road. Inman and Wade were sitting in the archaeologists' shed. They looked exhausted. Wayne was on the precipice backwashing the filters. Close to him stood Avelino and the Maya workers, who had arrived as usual for work without realizing what they would see. Now they stood gaping at the bottom of the well which their ancestors thought was bottomless.

Visibility was more than thirty feet, and Wade told us it could probably be extended farther by additional filtration. One could not imagine the well being any clearer. On the west side we could see the retaining wall on Thompson's bank extending some five to ten feet under water. The firehoses could be seen just as clearly as they looped down from the cliff in the water. More startling than these sights, however, was the now-visible conical shape of the cenote, its sides growing steeply deeper toward the center.

Scott was so pleased that he announced we could use the rest of the morning for a swim. One would have thought we had got our fill of swimming at Cozumel, but the well looked too inviting to pass up. We rushed to the campers for our swim suits, and Chuck ran for the underwater photographic gear.

Meanwhile Scott walked to the archaeologists' shed and shook Wade's hand. Wade was quick to point out that there still were many variables in the formula for success. Our main job now was to keep the water clear, and the maintenance of clarity hinged on many factors. The airlifts still would have to be used with the greatest of care, and divers must continue working without fins. Chemical treatment would have to be kept up on a rigid timetable, and filtration would begin as soon as the workday stopped at five in the afternoon. Altogether, the job of keeping the water clear would require many extra man-hours. Scott thought this was a small price to pay for the chance finally to get at the heart of the sacrificial treasure. His gambles had paid off, and the winnings looked attractive.

That same morning the divers decided to do some exploring that previously had been impossible. I watched Jack as he plunged off the raft. At that point the cenote could not have been too different from the Yale University swimming pool he was accustomed to. Jack headed first toward the filter outfall through which the clear, chlorinated water was rushing in. The effect from the top was beautiful: although the aluminum pipe had been carefully sealed, some air was still leaking in; the outfall line forced this air into the cenote, where the tiny bubbles were sprayed out under the blue water.

Jack swam through the spray of bubbles and then drifted toward the walls. When he turned, he told me several important aspects of the well that he had learned. There were several large openings in the upper walls, but when he had stuck his hand in, he could not detect a current or even a change of temperature which would be indicative of a cold underground stream flowing into the warmer cenote. In the lower walls, near the area where mud begins to collect, Jack spotted a dark hole some three feet in diameter. He said that as soon as he reached it, a chill went through his body although no actual current could be felt. It was difficult to judge the position, but Jack guessed the

With the water clear, divers provided Don Pablo with more and more skulls.

hole was slightly to the north of the area beneath the sacrificial platform.

What he had found, of course, was one of the openings that connected the sacred well to the water table of the Yucatán Peninsula. It was holes like that one which had frustrated our efforts to drain the well. When the cenote was full, there was enough pressure on the holes to keep the underground streams from rushing in, but once we had removed part of the water, the pressure was reduced and the water flowed in. That still did not mean that there were not pumps capable of draining the well nor that someday someone might actually do it. Other divers explored the walls many times, determining that there were at least a half-dozen similar cold-water holes, one of which had a faintly detectable current. That meant that many times the pumping capacity that we possessed would be needed to drain the well.

Piña Chan was scheduled to arrive Thursday for a big meeting with Scott, Folan, Segovia and Don Pablo. Kirk would also attend if he were able to get back from Fort Worth. I had an inkling of what the meeting might be about: now that we were successful in clarifying the water, we had to work out a system for excavations. I could not foresee any conflict although I knew Scott and Kirk would want to use the fastest possible method and that this might not be the one archaeologists preferred.

Seeing the well clarified and considerably more tractable than when we arrived, I made a monumental decision.

"Jerry," I said nervously one day, "will you teach me to dive?"

The following afternoon we were at the pool at the hacienda. Jerry had told me to get the two diving rigs which he had brought up in a pickup truck. I ran to the vehicle and saw what must have been a couple hundred pounds of diving equipment. That scared me. Since I am naturally prone to sinking, what chance would I have with a weight like that on my back?

"Well," Jerry said, "let's see how well you swim."

I used my own stroke, known as an inverted New Zealand crawl, to negotiate a few lengths of the pool. Jerry looked unimpressed. He instructed me to put on a mask, snorkel and fins to get used to the apparatus. Child's play, I thought. After another couple of lengths with these devices on, Jerry told me to flood the snorkel and then clear it. After I had gone under water to let the snorkel tube fill up, I ascended with the intention of blowing the water out as I had been instructed. I had forgotten one thing however. I did not have any breath left. Nonetheless, with Jerry's patience, I mastered this technique after a few more tries. By the time he told me to put on the wet suit jacket and diving rig, I was worn out. My body sagged as I hoisted the heavy gear on my shoulders. Trying to look professional, I gave my head a jerk forward to toss the hoses and mouthpiece over my head. Unfortunately I lost my balance in the process and fell in the pool.

"Now that you're in, put everything on and just swim around a little," Jerry said.

Much to my amazement, I found that the heavy gear was not only weightless in the water but that the jacket and air tank were actually buoyant enough to pull me to the surface. I found myself in the awkward situation of having a full diving rig on without being able to get under water. I tried very hard to dive to the bottom of the pool, but the attempts must have looked pathetic. When I swam back to Jerry, he had a weight belt ready. That might have helped except that the belt was too heavy, and for the next few minutes I found myself walking on the bottom of the swimming pool without the slightest idea how to get back to the surface. Only absolute faith in my instructor prevented outright panic. I finally got out by walking on the bottom to the shallow end of the pool, emerging like a sea monster on a beach. Once the weight belt was adjusted to the point of neutral buoyancy, I began to like diving very much. One is as weightless in the water as an astronaut in orbit. The effect is fascinating, and I swam around enjoying it for several minutes.

Next came the lesson on clearing the mask under water. The ability to do so is necessary whenever a mask accidentally fills with water. The technique is simple in theory: all one has to do is tilt the head and blow, or snort as divers call it. During the first few attempts I accomplished nothing but taking several deep breaths through my nose, completely forgetting that the air hose was attached to my mouth. After a half hour or so more of practice, however, I was able to get all but a few drops of water out of the mask. The next lesson consisted of learning how to put on and take off the diving rig under water, and needless to say I had little difficulty taking it off. Diving back in and putting it on under water was another matter. Only with hours of practice did I come close to learning how it is done.

It was near the end of the afternoon session with Jerry that I learned something I had always been curious about. I was at the bottom of the pool when I suddenly had the urge to sneeze. I stifled the urge for several minutes before deciding I had better come to the surface. Too late. Half way up I sneezed so hard I thought the whole rig would come off. When the sneeze was over, I realized that nothing too bad had happened. I had taken a big breath from the mouthpiece and sneezed exactly as I would have done anywhere else. The problem under water is that one has to clean the inside of the mask immediately after sneezing, and that,

"Let go of the pipe," they kept saying.
But the author had a certain understandable reluctance on his first diving attempt.

too, was a simple matter now that I knew how to take a mask off, put it back on and get the water out—all below the surface. Other body functions, I understand, are somewhat more complicated under water.

The next day, Wednesday, I ventured into the well for the first time. From that experience I have learned never to ridicule anyone who is the slightest bit timid of the water. Only after maximum coaxing from Jeff was I brave enough to follow an airlift pipe down to the bottom of the well.

Despite the blue-green appearance of the water from above, the bottom still looked brown and dirty. The aura of death had not been filtered out.

Entranced by the realization of where I was, I decided to sit near the airlift nozzle and watch the other divers at work. Jeff and Jack were on the altar side of the raft while Bill and Austin were working the lift. Jerry Griffin was watching them. Gypsy had remained in Cozumel, but our two other Mexican divers, Luis Concha and Hernán Gutiérrez, were just going to the surface after a turn at the airlifts themselves. Beyond the airlift was the outfall line from the filters, with its constant spray of bubbles forming a background for my view of Jeff and Jack.

Jeff scooped up a handful of mud near the nozzle and let it sift through his fingers. He saw what looked like a large bead, but it had slipped through his hand before he could grab it. He plunged his hand back into the mud and felt around for several minutes. I could tell from the expression on his face that he was having no luck in retrieving the object. I was about four feet from him and saw his wrist scrape against something sharp as he withdrew it from the bottom. I at first assumed that it had scraped against a limb but then saw Jeff reach back in that direction. He pulled out of the mud an object that looked something like a branch but was pointed at one end. As he brought it closer for me to see, I could determine that it was a carved object although its material and function were beyond my knowledge. I had never seen anything like it before.

I followed Jeff to the surface to ask Victor about the relic. The archaeologist recognized the material as carved stag horn and the figure on it as a stylized turkey. However, he was also at a loss to name its function. The object was about seven inches long, a plausible length for a knife, but the end was not sharp. Above all, in a land where people revered the exotic quetzal bird and where warriors chose the eagle as their symbol, why would any-one want to carve an animal as lowly as the turkey?

I found Scott topside talking with Otto and Folan in the archaeologists' shed. I told him about the unusual discovery, but he did not seem impressed about anything we brought from the well except gold, and the truth was that we were bringing very little of that metal from the cenote. We had about six gold bells, several pieces of leaf and some small ornamental discs. Apart from that, the only gold we had found was in alloy form with copper. Scott had read many times De Landa's statement about gold in the sacred well, and I suppose he felt cheated to find anything less. Archaeologists, however, seemed more than satisfied with what was coming to the surface. The unusual nature of some of the sacrificial treasure appealed to their scholarly curiosity.

While Scott was talking to Folan, I spotted a ceramic face which I had not seen before. The figure retained blue paint throughout, and the pupils of the eyes were black. Jutting out from the face were two appendages that gave the figure an almost insect appearance. When Folan told me that the figure represented the diving god, I immediately considered it a good omen. One day after I learned how to dive, we discovered an effigy of the diving god.

Later when I told Victor about it, he laughed. I had learned about the more familiar Mayan deities, but I had not done my homework on the lesser ones. The diving god has nothing to do with water diving, he said. Rather, archaeologists know of the deity primarily from the Temple of the Diving God at Tulúm, a holy city on the coast near Cozumel. Stucco decorations on the temple depict the god descending, or diving, but Victor said no one is certain as to the purpose of the descent although he appears to be diving from heaven. The appendages on the ceramic which we found represented the arms of the god. As far as I was able to learn, the effigy of the diving god from the well was the only representation of the deity found outside of Tulúm.

Kirk arrived back in Chichén, or "Chicken Town" as he called it, on Thursday afternoon, and the big conference was scheduled for that evening. I was not included in it, but from what I learned, the positions were something like this: Segovia wanted us to undertake systematic excavations of the entire well, exploring each area stratum by stratum (assuming distinct levels existed). Kirk wanted to concentrate on the site below the altar area in an attempt to improve the quality of the finds, without which it would be difficult to justify the expense of the expedition. Don Pablo wanted money for CEDAM, and Kirk was afraid he would withhold his valuable influence from the expedition unless the money were paid.

"I'm ready to yank this expedition out of here right now if these people are going to pull any monkey business," Kirk said after the meeting, at which no decision was reached.

He knew that the richest finds were probably under the altar and thought it might be scientifically interesting but hardly profitable to concentrate excavations anywhere else. Scott agreed. Piña and Victor thought it would be foolish not to undertake slow, methodical excavations now that we had the ability to do so.

"I understand their position, but if it's one thing I don't have, it's time to scratch around in the mud for a year or two," Kirk said.

At the root of the controversy was the uniqueness of the expedition itself. It represented the first time that industry and commerce had gone into the business of sponsoring an archaeological expedition. If that expedition were not successful, it would be doubtful that industry would ever get involved in archaeology again. To the scientists, of course, it was a new experience to work with businessmen on an expedition. A compromise was reached the following afternoon. We would concentrate excavations in the altar area, and then, if the finds were rich enough, continue the work systematically throughout the well. Don Pablo got some extra funds for CEDAM, and although Kirk resented having to pay him, he chalked it off to the manner in which business is done in Mexico. And while there was no friendship

221

between the two men, Kirk respected Don Pablo's acumen in business and his influence in government.

Scott had tried to be prepared for any outcome of the conference. Although he had not announced it, he had a plan in mind to render any decision somewhat academic. He wanted to extend the expedition into the next year. In a sense, he had no choice. We had only two or three weeks to go before our money would run out, and in that time it was doubtful that meaningful excavations could be accomplished. His plan was to go back to the industries that had originally sponsored the expedition and convince them, on the basis of what we had already found, to expand their contributions. In addition he figured there was a good chance of getting new industries to participate. He and Kirk mulled over the idea some time before Kirk finally approved the plan.

It was a fortunate decision because in the next few weeks our finds were impressive but hardly monumental. Scott, still disappointed at not finding more gold, was convinced it *could* be found if given enough time. Several excellent ceramics were found during this period, undoubtedly the best ever to come from the sacred well. One day at the screening tables I saw Otto examine a sliver of material which I thought was pottery. He told me he had thought so, too, but that on closer observation it turned out to be part of a gourd, one end of which apparently was painted. When I asked him what it meant, Otto told me that some of the finest Mayan painting was done on gourds by the Tepeu artists. The one sliver did not mean there was any Tepeu in the well, he said, but it was a strong indication that there might be.

It was interesting for me to note how excited an archaeologist could become over a sliver of gourd that may or may not have been painted, and how unimpressed a Texas millionaire can be over anything less than a king's ransom. What all of us had to remember was that if it had not been for Kirk's faith in the project and his determination to see it through, the archaeologists would not have even the sliver of gourd.

Once the big controversy was solved, Kirk began spending more time in Chicken Town. I know he liked it there for many reasons.

He seemed to enjoy anything to do with nature or the out-of-doors and took every opportunity he had to leave his oil business in Fort Worth to go hunting and camping. While the expedition might have been something on the order of an ultimate camping trip for him, he was beginning to show more than his usual concern for its success. Above all, he liked being in Chichén because Ann Campbell was there. Neither of them seemed suited to big-city life. With money to travel wherever they wanted, Kirk and Ann seemed to be happiest when sitting on the veranda of the hacienda or mixing a bullshot after work at the cenote.

Kirk even decided to give a party before we left, but when he told me about his plans, I was aghast.

"Don," he said, "I want to give a party for everyone around here. I've never given a party for a whole country before."

Neither have many other people, but the invitations went out—by word of mouth, of course. Kirk had decided to have the party at the well. He wanted a bonfire, Mexican food and a piñata filled with candy for the children. A band was summoned from one of the "bigger" towns, and liquor brought in by the caseload.

The method of transmitting the invitations was startlingly successful. People came from Valladolid to the east and from as far away as Xocchel, some fifty miles to the west. Women wore the satin *huipiles* they had received as wedding presents, and men put on their cleanest white shirts and white trousers.

The family that served meals to tourists across from the gatehouse in Chichén was hired to fix food for "several hundred people," an order that was beyond the imagination of the hacienda staff. It took five days to get all the food brought to Chichén, and on the afternoon of the fiesta I stopped by to watch its preparation. The meat was cut and laid out in the courtyard behind the family's restaurant, but I did not recognize it immediately as meat since it was covered with several layers of flies. I winced at the sight and then reeled back as I smelled the odor of fresh meat baking in the sun. The family kept several animals in the same area, including a chained up ocelot, and the odor of their elimination was nearly as strong as that of the meat. Sickened at what I had seen, I decided to forego anything to eat at the party, preferring to have dinner first at the hacienda if I were feeling up to it.

The bonfire had warmed the cool autumn air at the campsite by the time our guests arrived. Jerry had strung up as many lights as he could find, and the music from the band could be heard all the way to the Temple of Kukulcán. The music varied from improvisations on themes from Radio America to the old songs of Mayab. Avelino and his wife performed the *jarana,* the traditional dance of Yucatán, while the rest of us gathered around in a circle. It was his moment of glory and probably the only chance he would ever have to dance on the holy ground where his ancestors were once sacrificed to Chac.

I was so caught up in the festivities that before I realized what I was doing I walked over to the food stand, grabbed a *taco* and a couple of *papadzules* and began eating them. I was half finished before I remembered the circumstances in which I had last seen that same food.

Scott had a surprise for the party, and he called everyone to the side of the well to witness it. When we were all peering into the blackness of the cenote, he gave a signal. Instantly the blackness disappeared, and the well began to glow from the depths of the water. The sacred well was being illuminated with underwater lights. One by one the lights went on until the cenote fairly dazzled us with color and brightness. It was as though we were peering into the heart of an emerald.

Scott's show, however, was a little ironic. We proved with one gesture that technology had conquered the barriers to the Mayan time capsule while at the same time we had neither the time nor money to remove the contents from the capsule. The Mayas at the party reacted to the lights as Scott had anticipated. They ooed and aahed for several minutes at the wonder of what our machinery and science had performed, but I felt like asking the expedition leader what he planned for an encore.

When the next act did come, it was a letdown. Scott made the announcement that the expedition would soon stop, ostensibly for the Christmas holiday but actually to give us time to raise the money needed to continue excavations. For those who doubted we would return, Scott said that our machinery would remain at the site. I wondered privately if we had the funds to remove it.

The days between the party and our departure were somber ones. Work went ahead in the water, but I think all of us lacked the initiative that had spurred us earlier in the game. The bleakness of the situation disappeared momentarily one day when divers pulled from the well a wooden object that looked like a turtle. In fact, we thought it was a carved turtle until Victor pointed out that the object was a low wooden stool that rested on four legs. What we thought was the head of the turtle was actually the head of a serpent on one end of the stool. Following Victor's hand with our eyes, we saw the outlines of a face inside the serpent's open mouth It was the head of a man. The figure apparently represented Kukulcán, but Victor said he could not determine the function of the stool or the reason it had been sacrificed. We had become so interested in the mystery surrounding the object that we had overlooked another aspect of the find. The wooden stool was the first piece of ancient Mayan furniture ever discovered.

Scott hoped we would have a spectacular find in the last days before we left, but in his mind the wooden stool would not qualify despite the virtual ecstasy that the archaeologists expressed over the discovery. The goal of the expedition had been described as finding the sacrificial treasure of the Mayas, and I admit it was still difficult to understand why a wooden stool would be treasured now or a millennium ago.

We were all sad when the day came for us to leave Chichén Itzá. Being there for nearly three months had changed our way of living. After all, how many people pass a thousand-year-old pyramid on their way to work each morning? As we drove past the ruins and out of the ancient city, I could not help thinking of the immense amount of work that would have to be done in the coming weeks to raise funds for the expedition's return. I had had nightmares about a guide showing tourists through Chichén and pointing out our abandoned equipment as "the ruins of an expedition, one of the finest examples of the style to be found anywhere in the hemisphere."

Scott had taken his ultimate gamble. If we were unable to convince industries to extend their sponsorship, it might be all we could do to return and remove the half-million dollars' worth of equipment and machinery.

Expedition headquarters shifted from the banks of the sacred well to a little office between the garage and swimming pool of Scott's home in Pompano Beach. The office was not big enough, and before long the entire house was filled with some of the same people who had been used to working in the middle of a jungle. Dori kept up the difficult job of bookkeeping, and Ann handled the files. Jeff, Jerry and Austin were around to take care of the heavy work, and a new member was added to the team. Karen Melba, a twenty-one-year-old girl from a neighboring town, became our secretary, taking over from Bill McGehee's wife, who had handled secretarial duties at the site. Chuck and Joyce rounded out the nucleus group which kept the business of the expedition going while Scott tried to get the expedition itself going.

It often appeared that he had chosen a hopeless task for himself. In addition to finding new companies that wanted to capitalize on associating with an expedition, we had problems with the Mexican government because our agreement with the National Institute of Anthropology and History had expired and a new agreement had to be executed. This was made doubly difficult because the director of the institute, Dr. Eusebio Dávalos Hurtado, died unexpectedly after Christmas. None of us had had any dealings with his successor, Dr. Ignacio Bernal, who for all we knew might disapprove our plans for underwater excavation. It was no easy job to convince dozens of people to help us continue excavations, which even in Scott's mind were not especially successful at this point.

Scott made so many trips to New York and California that several stewardesses came to recognize him. He would spend a

226

week or two lining up a dozen appointments and then have Dori or Karen squeeze them into a two-day schedule. With an oversize briefcase flapping in the wind, Scott would catch a plane early in the morning and begin his round of appointments before noon.

"Hello, I'm Norm Scott. Let me give you a fast rundown of the largest expedition ever conducted in the Western Hemisphere."

The man sitting behind the desk at such-and-such a company would watch him open the oversize briefcase and take out color drawings and photographs of the expedition. Then the inevitable question would be asked. What were we finding in the well? Scott would produce color photographs of some of the artifacts we had recovered so far, and often to his amazement the man behind the desk would lean forward, take a slow look at the pictures and say his company might indeed be interested in contributing funds. The industries saw that they could benefit since their product would be publicized with the vast amount of publicity the expedition was receiving. Some businesses such as the Purex Corporation saw an opportunity to test new equipment and techniques. The Ford Motor Company, which had supplied vehicles and industrial engines, planned to kick off its 1968 line of trucks with the publicity generated by the expedition, and its executives found several other ways to capitalize on the venture.

The list of our sponsoring firms read like a stockbroker's list: aside from Ford and Purex there were Johns-Manville International for the diatomaceous earth, Ryder Systems for the three tractor trailers and one smaller truck, Pan American Airways for assistance in flying personnel in and out of Yucatán, the Onan Corporation for our generators, W. R. Ames Company for aluminum pipe, Dow Chemical for Styrofoam, Evinrude Motors for two-man diving units called Aquanauts, Rolex Watch Corporation for diving watches, Wallace & Tiernan for the automatic chlorinators, American Oil Company for fuel and oil on the American side of the border and Petróleos Mexicanos for the same commodities in Mexico, Pacific Pumping Company for our centrifugal pumps, Seamless Rubber Company for wet suits and diving gear, Clark Cortez Company for our three large self-contained campers, E. R. Squibb & Sons for medicine, Sullivan Machinery

Company for compressors and Grove Manufacturing Company for the crane.

Those companies had joined the expedition at the outset. It was far more difficult for Scott to convince other firms to join the venture at what he hoped was the halfway mark. For two months it appeared that the money was simply not forthcoming. Moreover, the expedition funds ran the risk of depletion because it took some $6000 a month just to keep the staff and office going in Pompano.

By the end of February I would have given better than ten-to-one odds that we would not return to Chichén Itzá. Even members of Scott's nucleus staff began making plans in case the return were impossible. Dori could go back to work as a stewardess, a job she gave up nearly five years ago to go off with Scott and Kirk to search for the wreck of the *Genovesa* off the Jamaica coast. She was now twenty-five and had been on at least one expedition a year for the last four years. Expeditions had become a way of life for her, and it would be difficult, if not impossible, to change it. Jeff and Austin thought about going back to school, but they realized that few universities could teach as much in one semester as they could learn at Chichén in a month. Joyce thought she might go back to teaching, and Chuck shopped around for other photographic assignments. As for myself, if the expedition did not continue, I had decided to move to England where I had once lived and where a magazine now offered a job.

I never asked Scott what he would do, and he never volunteered the information. He was the great-great-grandson of General Winfield Scott and went about planning his life in a military routine that would have made his ancestor proud. He also had more energy than any five other men. Scott had played halfback at the University of Virginia and had been a Navy pilot. As a civilian, he went into the swimming pool business in the Washington, D.C. area and then took a fateful vacation to Puerto Rico back in the 1950s. It was on that vacation that he first went exploring around the wreck of a sunken ship. When he returned to Washington, he decided to became an amateur treasure hunter. Two years later he was a professional one. Scott's brother, Sam, was the chief

228

pilot for Central Airlines, which was owned by Kirk's family. Through Sam the two men got together. Kirk liked the idea of trying to make treasure hunting profitable and decided to back Scott's search for the *Genovesa*. The association had endured through several other expeditions, including the working of five wreck sites for the Bahamas government. Scott impressed me as the type of man who made a habit of landing on his feet. If Chichén were a failure, he and Kirk would pick up the pieces, and a few years from now I could imagine getting a call in London. It would be Scott, asking if I wanted to serve as historian for an expedition to the Sea of Tranquillity. The location of that particular sea would not bother him a bit: he was the kind of guy who would always shoot for the moon.

During the first week in March I stopped by the BOAC office to buy a one-way ticket to London. My reservation was for the end of the month. Toward the end of that week, however, I got the first indications that Scott might be having some success. Although it was difficult for him to understand, the pictures of the sacrificial treasure were having the desired effect. Johns-Manville agreed to contribute another $5000, and several new firms joined the venture, including Nikon and Aloe Creme Laboratories, whose ALO-Cosmetics, tanning aids and medications are based on gel from the tropical Aloe Vera plant, known as a medicament even before the Chichén Itzá period. The Florida firm was interested in the expedition's using their moisturizing products and testing their newest sunshine skin care product. The industrial commitments grew, and it soon appeared that we were in reach of our goal. Renewing our agreement with the Mexican government was the final hurdle to overcome, and this time we were lucky. Kirk's attorney in Mexico, a close friend of Dr. Bernal, paved the way for a basically identical agreement to the one we had got in 1967. BOAC refunded my money, I canceled my reservation and booked space on a flight to Mérida. We were going back.

12

BILL AND I took the same plane back, and, when we arrived at the Mérida airport, we saw Gordon Inman leaving. His work at Chichén was done. Gordon had preceded us to the site by several days to reclarify the well, which had regressed to its original turbid state during our absence. That was the way we should have done things in the first place. At the outset of the expedition, the Purex team should have got to the cenote ahead of us, clarified it and then notified us when it was ready. However expensive, the expedition was a learning experience for us and a lesson from which I hope archaeologists can benefit in the future. Anyway, Gordon was smiling, and that told me that clarification was again successful.

We looked at Thompson's old gear with a little more assurance as we passed the gatehouse this time. Felix, who headed the security staff at the ruins, was so glad to see us that he returned Austin's motorscooter. Another good omen, I thought.

Once at the site, Scott stripped the expedition of unnecessary jobs. He pronounced the death of the personnel lift, which was still inoperative. No one really cared because we had become accustomed to being hoisted up and down by crane. Morning meetings were shorter and more to the point. We knew which questions to ask, and Scott could now anticipate problems. We had become more professional, and a new attitude of expertise pervaded the group. We knew what the hardships would be and we came prepared. We had missed the life at Chichén, and it was great to be back, even if it meant cold showers and hard work.

Divers immediately began work on the hydrolift to see if it was at all worthwhile to use in excavations. Bill and Jeff took it far toward the center of the well to see what kind of a hole it could dig. After three days of working with it, they had pierced more than fifteen feet of mud, about three times the amount that Scott and Folan thought existed in the cenote. Now the best guess at the ultimate depth was more than twenty feet. Since no artifacts of significance were found at fifteen feet, and because the hydrolift was stirring up a dangerous amount of mud, Scott doubted it would be used for the remainder of the expedition. Moreover, archaeologists had approved the airlifts but not the hydrolift for recovery, and Scott did not want to muddy the waters in another sense of the phrase.

We had been at work for three or four days when I saw Jeff and Victor talking excitedly as they were being hoisted to the top. Victor was carrying a bucket in his hand. The two men got out of the basket and walked to the command shed, where they had spotted Scott.

"Take a look at this," Jeff said.

Scott reached into the bucket of water and drew out two pieces of pottery. They shone as the early morning light hit the wet surfaces. Piña and one of his students walked over from the archaeologists' shed. The chief archaeologist gave a low whistle when he saw what Scott had pulled from the bucket. The expedition leader held the pieces in his hand and turned them over several times. They were splendidly painted Tepeu ceramics. Otto, who was not with us for the second half of the expedition, had predicted we might find Tepeu although none had ever been discovered in Yucatán. In a world of otherwise drab brown pottery, the sacred well had yielded a technicolor insight into the ancient Mayan world. In the picture on the vessel fragments a warrior frowned, a nobleman looked haughty, and a laborer appeared weary. An artist more than a thousand years ago had depicted it all. Red, blue, yellow, aqua, white and black sparkled as Scott turned the ceramics over in his hands.

"Is this any good?" Scott asked finally.

In slow but clear English, Piña replied, "Norman, this is one of the best ceramics ever found in Yucatán. It is marvelous."

Scott looked a little incredulous, but later in the day the archaeologists explained a great deal about ceramics and polychrome painting in Mayab.

For many centuries Maya women had created very plain pottery. Eventually the vessels which went to the more important households and to the priests were decorated with simple designs, some painted, others incised or molded. Somewhere around A.D. 300 a potter in the Guatemala lowlands hit on the idea of multicolor designs, and a couple of centuries later someone else decided to abandon the geometric designs for representational art work. The development culminated in Tepeu ceramics decorated with multicolor paintings that depicted the life of the Maya man rather than the gods which he worshiped.

Development of design was slow and pottery making itself was laborious. Women had to find time for the craft among such other duties as raising children, making meals, preparing steam baths for their husbands, cleaning house and weaving. A mental block against the wheel prevented men from moving stones with ease and women from making pottery more quickly. It is difficult to figure out how to make a pot without a potter's wheel. One's first instinct usually is to mold it, but without a wheel it is nearly impossible to achieve a high degree of symmetry. But working with a piece of clay in one's hands, eventually, like a ten-year-old child in art class, he would start to coil it.

A Maya woman patted out a base for her pots, then pressed it by hand to get it even and firm. From this base she began coiling the wet clay. If the work was done at home, the potter had to keep the children from spilling the bowl of water that she kept

232

close by to moisten the clay. She had to schedule her work so the clay would not harden if she stopped half finished to fix food. Thick coils were easy to work with but they did not produce a very marketable vessel. Generally speaking, the smaller the coils in proportion to the size of the vessels, the more prized it was. Only cooking pots and other utilitarian ceramics were especially heavy. By changing the diameter of the coils, the Maya woman changed the shape of the pot. As the potter piled one coil on the other, she dipped her hands in the bowl of water and then kneaded the coils together. The more time she could spare to do this, the more even the walls of the vessel became. Eventually the coils disappeared and the product looked as though it had

". . . they never produced two vessels alike. . . ."

been made from one piece of clay instead of several dozen coils.

If they had thought of the potter's wheel, Mayas could have produced more ceramics in much less time. But by using the coil method, they never produced two vessels alike and achieved an individuality which would have disappeared with the wheel.

After the vessel was finished and the coils kneaded together, the woman fired her work, usually in a community kiln that burned grass, wood or charcoal. While it was firing, she probably had time to go back home and catch up on her housework. When the bowl or case had hardened, she let it cool and then put a design on it. Designs grew richer and more complicated, and it is doubtful that women did all of this kind of work. Much more time came to be required to paint one Tepeu vase than could be afforded by women. It was also a good bet that whoever the Tepeu artists were, they had seen or maybe even worked on some of the great murals. They covered their pottery or gourds with stucco and then began the painting, the identical system which the muralists used. Regardless of the base material, the Tepeu artists created something of a mini-mural, which most antiquarians consider about as good as anything of the type Greece produced and better than most ceramics from Rome.

Scott held the two fragments that fit together to form a segment about three inches wide and five inches long. The surface was still wet and shiny. His thumb accidentally touched a red stripe, and part of the pigment flaked off on his finger. Segovia decided that as soon as the fragments were photographed, they would have to be kept in water. For reasons that chemists may some day discover, water in the cenote was an excellent preservative for certain materials. Preservation, however, lasted only as long as the objects remained in water from the well.

It seemed sacrilegious to think this way, but when the two fragments were joined, the colors suggested those in a comic strip. But this was a marvelous comic strip out of the dim past.

The picture was banded in red, and the background was white. The principal colors were a greenish blue, black, white and brown. The artist had depicted a merchant, a Maya businessman, protected by warriors. Near him was a woman carrying goods. The

234

man's face was black, and the archaeologists had no immediate explanation for that fact. On his head was a large hat that first appeared made from quetzal feathers because of its blue-green color. Examined more closely, however, the hat looked woven.

Scott reached into the bucket and took out a third fragment. a narrow piece four inches long but less than one inch wide. This one pictured a warrior with an ornament, apparently made of bone, piercing his nose. He wore an elaborate headdress, part of it made from the skin of a jaguar.

These three fragments apparently came from the same vase and were found in about four feet of mud. Later in the day, near the same area, Bill discovered a larger fragment from another vessel. This one measured about six by five inches and had formed a section near the base of a magnificent vase. At the bottom of the fragment, apparently near the base of the vessel, was a band of red, followed upward by a band of green and a small, quarter-inch-wide band of black. The background above the bands was white, and on it the artist had painted a group of men, probably noblemen, who wore flamboyant white sandals and clothing of elaborately designed fabrics.

Archaeologists were so excited at the finds that they almost overlooked something on one of the pieces that had come up earlier in the day, the fragment that showed the merchant. They now realized that the woman who accompanied him was carrying a striped ceramic vessel that was only known to come from Yucatán. How then could artists in the Guatemala lowlands know anything about striped Yucatecan pottery? One answer was that they did not, that the vase was locally made and that the Tepeu style was more widely known than previously suspected. This answer was all but rejected because nothing else in the painting depicted anything typically Yucatecan. A more plausible explanation was that the striped urn had reached the lowlands through trade routes that were more active than formerly recognized. The Tepeu vase might actually have been commissioned by a merchant who had brought the Yucatecan pottery to Guatemala for trade.

The next ten days were filled with excitement. I was on the bottom of the well one day watching the divers operate the airlift when I saw an unfamiliar figure in the water. As the man swam closer, I realized it was Victor. Once he decided to make the fateful plunge, he became an expert diver with no trace of the fear that had gripped him earlier. I suppose that going where the action was was irresistible now for Victor since the action was at its peak. Several death masks with black paint had been found, along with a couple of unusually shaped lip plugs. A ring of unbelievably intricate workmanship came up in the airlift one afternoon and astounded those who saw it. The ring was made of a low-grade gold alloy, but the material was hardly important. The primitive craftsmen had taken thin strands of the metal and intwined them, giving the impression that the ring had been woven from gold threads. Victor said Aztecs might have made the ring, which could have passed on by trade to Mayab for sacrifice to Chac. The ring was only one of several that was brought to the surface during these days. Also coming up were dozens of skulls and bones, again the majority being those of children. Artifacts entered in the catalogue now numbered more than one thousand, and some of those units represented many fragments lumped together under one number. Of all the treasure found so far Piña considered Tepeu the most important. He had already told his colleagues in Mexico City about the find.

There had been several changes in personnel, but none of the new members seemed to have any difficulty adjusting to the fast pace. Rex Gerald replaced Jerry Griffin as the representative from the University of Texas. Folan was no longer with us since he had to resume his duties with Canada's Department of Indian Affairs and Northern Development. Piña, of course, remained in charge of the expedition, but in his frequent absence Victor supervised day-to-day operations. Victor's great responsibility undoubtedly was another factor that had brought him finally to the action at the bottom of the cenote. Otto Schondube and Yoko Sugiura had gone back to Mexico City, but assisting now in the cataloguing operation were four other girls—Amalia Cardós de Méndez, Talia Shay, Ana María Crespo and Guadalupe Ferrer. Jeff's wife, Kay, had joined us to pitch in with typing and office duties.

Talia was an Israeli girl, who had sighed in disbelief at the comparative opulence of our expedition. After seeing a stereo phonograph in the air-conditioned office-Cortez, she told me that on her first dig the archaeologists had been forced to borrow money for food and ask villagers for a place to stay. To her, commerce and archaeology were mutually exclusive.

Work on top went along as fast as it did in the well. Restoring the foundation of the building at the end of the sacbe was completed, and in the process several sacrificial ceramics were found, all of a fairly late period. Defoliation was completed around the well, giving archaeologists a chance to excavate a small altar, the ruins of which had been discovered almost directly opposite the altar near camp. The smaller one apparently was a later construction than the main sacrificial shrine. It rained briefly after we returned, but the dam that was built in November held fast, and only a negligible amount of mud found its way into the cenote.

Scott seemed slightly more optimistic about our finds, but the rings were the objects that most impressed him. Piña and Victor, on the other hand, glowed with pride at all the results of the excavations.

Through Tepeu paintings and the other art treasures from the well archaeologists got a dramatic view into the life of the ancient Maya. The multicolored pieces of pottery produced the effect of being able to look into the past. And after all, that was what archaeology is all about. Tepeu let us see both the man and his works; it was a window on the past. We began to appreciate the fact that the sacrificial treasure was not a monetary treasure but a fortune in knowledge. People from many walks of life had come as pilgrims to make sacrifices into the sacred well and the cenote's contents mirrored the pilgrims themselves. The well's treasure enabled us to do what had not been possible even six months earlier. We could reconstruct, partly from direct evidence and partly from inference, the history of Chichén Itzá when the holy city was the most important center in Mayab.

Let us consider three days in the year A.D. 999.

"Restoring the foundation of the building at the end of the sacbe . . . several sacrificial ceramics were found."

On this sacrificial ceramic face found under the building foundation is the Mayan look still seen in today's Yucatecan faces.

Ah Ceh had made up his mind that he was going to enjoy the day. He had been used to helping his father work the fields or hunt game, but today he was in Chichén Itzá looking forward to a holiday.

It had taken Ah Ceh's father more than a year to make arrangements for his young teen-age son to be interviewed in Chichén for a position as a student priest. These posts were usually reserved for the higher classes and Ah Ceh's family was among the "lower people." Ah Ceh's mother, however, was related to the Mexicans who had recently come from the west to the holy city, and that relationship gave Ah Ceh the advantage he needed for wangling an interview. His appointment with an assistant priest or *nacom* had been set for the day before, but it was unexpectedly canceled, apparently because the day of his birth was incompatible with the appointment date. The postponement gave Ah Ceh an extra day in Chichén.

The boy's family lived thirty miles from the holy city, and it was only the third time that he had ever come to Chichén. Even on the last visit, some four years ago, he could not remember the city being so large or so busy. People virtually fell over each other as they made their way through the maze of temples and the expansive courtyards. He had to be careful where he stepped for as a commoner he could walk only on the *sacbeob* and not on the red pavement that covered the holy ground around the temples. That rule caused much hardship for the thousands of workers who were in the process of building new temples and making additions onto old ones. In earlier years the priests dispensed with the rule for the workers, but the new priests from the west were stricter about the law, and in many areas the red paint had been removed so that laborers could have access.

Ah Ceh had left the house of his mother's relatives early that morning. He did not know them well, and did not particularly like them. They spoke with a heavy western accent which to his surprise was being affected by many residents whom he knew to be natives of Mayab. His mother's relatives had improved their lot since his last visit. They had not only a larger house but one built almost entirely of rock and mortar. Moreover, it was closer to the temple area than their old house had been, and that was truly the sign of higher status. Ah Ceh had learned, however, that almost anyone who possessed western blood and a moderate ambition could advance himself now that the Mexicans were in control of the city. His aunt asked him if he had brought anything from home as a sacrifice, and much to Ah Ceh's embarrassment, he confessed that he had not. No matter, his uncle said; they could go to the market and buy something worthy of sacrifice. This would be a further embarrassment to Ah Ceh for his father had given him only twenty cacao beans for the trip, and ten of that was for an offering when he entered the temple to be interviewed by the nacom.

His own family was not poor, but the growing season had been especially dry this year, forcing his father to support his family by hunting. Ah Ceh liked to join his father on hunting trips, and was constantly reminded that his name meant The Deer. That name, his formal one, was seldom used, however, for fear it would become "worn out." Instead, Ah Ceh was known by his nickname, Ci'uk.

Now he walked along the sacbe that ran toward the market. He planned to wander around and take in the sights during the morning. Then at about noon he would meet his uncle for the only unpleasant chore of the day. His uncle had suggested that they do their shopping together for sacrificial offerings. At least some of Ah Ceh's cousins might be along, and he especially liked one of them, Ix Ek, a girl with a beautiful round face and large limbs.

He did not get on very well with her brothers who persisted in ridiculing his head deformity. Ah Ceh's father had created the deformity in the manner typical of Mayab. The style was not popular among the westerners, and his male cousins laughed at it. Ah Ceh had been deeply hurt when he first heard the laughter for his father was very proud of his son's flat forehead, a shape which he said favored the gods. When viewed from the side, Ah Ceh's head slanted back sharply above the eyes, giving it the appearance of being pointed on top. The flattening had been achieved only after a long period of nightly squeezing of the head between two boards as Ah Ceh had slept. One of his cousins had asked whether the process was painful, and Ah Ceh took delight in lying about the immense pain which he had endured with stoic devotion to the gods.

When he reached the marketplace, he noticed many other people with flattened heads, but most of them were older than he. Evidently, he thought, the custom was dying out. What caught his attention most at the market was the size of it. The marketplace alone was larger than the village where he was born. The newcomers had repaired the paving and regimented the activities so that merchants had to remain in specific areas according to the nature of their produce. The scheme worked well because all those who sold one product were close enough to one another to know the prices of their competitors.

Ah Ceh entered the southwestern gateway to the market, just beyond which the artists and craftsmen had their stalls. Several goldsmiths worked from cast pieces, changing it into leaf and other ornaments in conformity with the style of Mayab. To the south of the goldsmiths were the potters. Few of them were actually making pottery at the market, but one woman was fashioning a mold for a vessel which her customer wanted made to order. She would take the mold home and finish the vessel at her leisure. Several women and a couple of men were painting designs on the pottery, but Ah Ceh did not think they were particularly skilled. Farther toward the center of the marketplace were the people who sold animals, both dead and alive, and Ah Ceh thought of his father when he saw a fresh load of game being brought in. There were also honey and complete hives of bees, commodities that Ah Ceh had not even realized were for sale. One woman asked him if he wanted a sample of honey and he accepted; after all, it was hardly up to him to tell her that he did not have any spending money. He wished very hard that he did have some because he saw a deer hide that was painted orange and blue—ideal, he thought, for his mother's bed. The price of eleven beans, however, was quite beyond his reach.

The market was so crowded that Ah Ceh could barely walk without bumping into someone. The pace of the activity was

242

greater than he could have imagined. One man was trading vanilla pods from the south for fish from the north, while another trader was trying to sell salt from Tulúm to preserve the fish. Nearby, another merchant was getting angry because he had just bought salt from the same man at a higher price. Another section of the market was devoted to cloth and feathers, some of which were being woven right in the marketplace. Nearby was the area reserved for clothing and sandals.

Before he realized the hour, it was time to meet his uncle at the appointed place by the shell merchants. Ah Ceh quickly asked directions and then ran to the location where his uncle was already waiting. Unfortunately neither Ix Ek nor the other cousins had accompanied him.

Ah Ceh's uncle showed him the area of the market where holy items were sold. As they approached, Ah Ceh saw row upon row of jade rings, earplugs, lip plugs, pendants and beads. Next to the rows of jade was copal or *pom,* the price of which varied with the reputed quality of the incense. Several wealthy traders, who painted their faces black as a symbol of their profession, were just bringing in a shipment of gold. The uncle looked interested.

Talking to one of the elegantly dressed traders, the uncle learned that the man had just come from the coast, where a merchant from the south had sold him three of the most exquisite gold bells ever seen. The uncle picked them up and looked them over. He was especially attracted to one of the ornaments, a bell of purest gold that bore the effigy of a god stylized as a bird on top. The uncle said the bell would be a suitable gift for Chac, a god that should especially be propitiated in view of the recent lack of rain. Ah Ceh also knew that sacrifices to Chac had increased in popularity in recent years. When his uncle inquired as to the origin of the bell, the trader told him it came from lands to the south, where such metal is common and where craftsmen worship the god with which they had decorated the ornament. The price was seventy-five cacao beans, which the uncle nonchalantly withdrew from a leather bag he kept under his clothing.

Sensing that his nephew had not nearly enough money to buy an offering of his own, he offered to lend Ah Ceh however many beans he needed. The boy refused politely, explaining that he would come up with a gift of his own one way or another and that a personal sacrifice would mean more to Chac than a borrowed one. The uncle admired his piety and said he hoped that such feelings would serve him well during his interview tomorrow with the nacom.

Ah Ceh did, however, let his uncle treat him to lunch at the market. He was so hungry that he fairly gulped down the mixture of corn mush and chocolate and asked for an extra piece of dried venison.

On the advice of the uncle, Ah Ceh spent much of the afternoon sight-seeing. He looked at the temples and gawked at the workers as they rolled heavy stones on logs over the roads that led to the construction sites. It seemed that everywhere he turned there was building going on. He asked the names of the largest temples but discovered that not even all the residents of Chichén knew the names. Nor did Ah Ceh have to know such names for the interview tomorrow. His being chosen or rejected for the priesthood theoretically should be based on the numerology of his birth and the dates of major events in life; in his own case the latter included only the attainment of puberty since his father had not yet made arrangements for a marriage. In fact, however, the decision of the nacom would probably be based on how much influence his family possessed and the amount of money his relatives were prepared to deposit in the temple coffers.

The day was nearly over when Ah Ceh realized he had not yet bought an offering for sacrifice to Chac. He rushed back to the market, but most of the stalls were already closing. Dejected over losing his last chance to buy an inexpensive offering, he wandered aimlessly around for a minute and then saw the merchant with the colored deer hides. The merchant also sold antlers and had some horn fragments lying on the ground. Ah Ceh walked over and inquired how much one of the single antlers cost. The man, who had probably considered the fragments unsalable, asked Ah Ceh what he wanted it for. When the boy told him he wanted it as a sacrificial offering for Chac, the merchant laughed aloud and handed the piece of stag horn to the boy. He wanted no payment from a boy as pious as Ah Ceh.

Ah Ceh borrowed a flint knife that night at his uncle's house and began making his own offering to Chac. He would carve the stag horn into a beautiful shape worthy of sacrifice. It no longer mattered if his rich cousins knew he had no money with which to buy a ready-made offering. A sacrifice to Chac could take on value by the time spent in its manufacture as well as money spent on its acquisition. Ah Ceh, who was unfamiliar with the art of religious carving, chose an object with which he was well acquainted, a turkey, the bird he had caught often on hunting trips with his father. It was an omen of good luck to his family, and he figured that an effigy of the bird would be considered by Chac as a worthy offering. His difficulty was that the piece of stag horn was flat in shape and only about seven inches long. It would ordinarily have been impossible to sculpture a turkey in such a space, but Ah Ceh decided to stylize the bird as he had seen other animals stylized in stone. As he worked into the night, the bird took shape, which was also the shape of the stag horn itself. Finally, an hour before dawn, the carving was finished. Ah Ceh returned the knife to the cooking area of the house and tried to get a little sleep before the household was awakened by its slave.

The carved stag horn was tucked into Ah Ceh's clothing when he went to the temple the following day for his interview with the nacom, and he made a point not to lose it during the ritual of changing clothes before he entered the temple.

Ah Ceh had expected to be questioned in one of the smaller shrines, but he soon learned that he would be taken directly to the main temple, a pyramid-shaped structure with several tunnels leading into its interior. Construction was going on to increase the size of the pyramid, and workers were talking so loudly that he could barely hear the directions being given him by the several assistants to the nacom. Once inside the tunnel, Ah Ceh underwent another change of attire and a purification ceremony at which pom was burned so closely to his body that he could feel the heat. Ah Ceh wondered at the time if the same ritual was given to everyone just in order to speak with the nacom.

He thought that this ritual seemed overly elaborate but then he considered the change that had come about recently in the leadership of Chichén Itzá.

When he was finally taken to the nacom, Ah Ceh saw a very plain man, hardly the person to command such a complex ceremony. The man spoke gently, almost in a monotone. Behind him in the shadows of the stone room were several assistants who beat rhythmically on drums. The nacom asked the boy to identify himself, and this time he gave his formal name, Ah Ceh, The Deer. The nacom asked if that was why he carried the piece of stag horn, but Ah Ceh explained that he had only recently carved the piece of antler as an offering to Chac. The nacom smiled and proceeded to ask questions about his birthdate, his family's birthdays and the date of his puberty ceremony.

The nacom was the lowest order of priest, but he had important functions in the holy city. Above him were the *chacs,* who should not be confused with the water god. Next in the priestly hierarchy were the *chilan,* who were so holy that slaves were employed by the temple to carry them on litters whenever they walked anywhere except on holy ground. It was the function of the chilan to act as go-betweens for man and god. A chilan was the one who read the omens and decided who was to be sacrificed. Above the chilan was the *ahkin* himself, but now in Chichén Itzá that post had been combined with the office of the temporal leader, and the man who held both offices was the man-god, the being whose name was only whispered but whose image was being carved and sculptured on every new monument in the city. He was the man who was not a man. He was the god who was a serpent with feathers. He was Kukulcán.

Knowing the order of the priests, Ah Ceh was very much surprised to see a lavishly arrayed chilan enter the chamber in which he was being questioned. The drums beat louder in the background and then stopped. The chilan spoke. He asked for Ah Ceh's name and then asked him for more specific dates of events in his life—when were his parents married? When was his maternal grandfather born? Ah Ceh fortunately had memorized the dates from the time he was a young boy. Two chacs entered the chamber dressed in robes of feathers only slightly less elegant than those of the chilan. The chacs conferred with their fellow priests as Ah Ceh marveled at the ritual responses with which they spoke to one another.

Now the question period appeared to be over. Another ceremony of purification was performed: more incense, more cleansing and more changes of garments. The identical ceremony was performed twice and then a third time, during which the drums began beating more loudly than Ah Ceh had ever heard them. Suddenly at the far end of the chamber a figure appeared out of the shadows. As he approached the light in the center of the chamber, the man turned and mounted the altar to sit on a throne which the chilan had rushed in when the drums were beating. The man was tall, and a headdress of pure quetzal feathers doubled his height. His robes of rich cloth and snake skin were so magnificent that Ah Ceh felt as though he was dreaming. Only the man-god himself could wear vestments like these.

The drums stopped again. Ah Ceh was not dreaming. As he looked timidly at the man on the altar, he realized that he was face to face with Kukulcán.

One by one the lower priests and attendants shuffled quietly from the chamber until only Ah Ceh and the man-god were left inside. The burning pom had left so much fume that Ah Ceh feared for an instant that he was going to faint. Then he thought his weakness might have been brought about not by the incense but by the presence of the man-god. The farm boy and the plumed serpent had been together several minutes before the god spoke.

"You have been chosen," he said.

Ah Ceh was almost paralyzed with awe as he listened to the holy voice. Then he began to wonder why the news of his selection was delivered by the ruler himself. He had once talked to a boy who was chosen for the priesthood, and he remembered the boy told him the news of selection had come to his father by a lower official who wanted a few cacao beans just for having brought the news. Perhaps, Ah Ceh thought, his dates were so favorable that the priest had made a special occasion of his case. His thoughts were interrupted by the voice of the man-god.

"I shall ask you many questions," he said.

The plumed serpent asked questions about Ah Ceh that he never expected anyone to ask. The man-god wanted to know everything about him and the dates on which the seemingly most trivial events occurred. The hours passed. Ah Ceh knew that it was now night, but still the questioning continued. When the holy ruler finished, he asked if there were any questions that Ah Ceh wanted to ask.

The boy was speechless. He knew of no one else who had ever had a chance to speak with the plumed serpent, much less ask him questions. He thought for several minutes before asking the ruler, "Why was I chosen?"

Kukulcán answered slowly. "You were chosen because the rain must fall and crops must grow. You were chosen because the days of your life and your family have ordained you for sacrifice. You were chosen because Chac must be nourished. You have been chosen because I have chosen you."

Now Ah Ceh knew what he had dared not even suspect. He had been selected not for the priesthood but for sacrifice.

"You will sleep now until Itzamná, the God of Heaven, lets the sun shine once more," the ruler said. He then summoned his attendants who performed a short ceremony on the departure of the man-god. Ah Ceh was too shaken by what he had been told to pay much attention to what was happening.

He was waked the next morning by a man he recognized as an assistant of the nacom. A final purification ceremony was held in a chamber where pools of blood stained the floor. These were pools made by devout men who pierced their own bodies to let blood flow for the gods. In this chamber Ah Ceh was bathed and covered with blue paint. It was not yet dawn when the attendants began dressing him in the finest clothes he had ever seen, save those the high priests themselves wore. Around his neck went several necklaces of copper bells that rang in Mayab only at the time of death. His wrists were encircled with bracelets of human teeth. His body was draped with feathers and richly woven cloth, with gold and jade, with obsidian and ornaments he did not recognize.

The light all but blinded Ah Ceh when he stepped into the daylight. He and several lower priests formed a procession from the dressing chamber to a smaller temple where musicians had assembled. Ah Ceh stood there, painted blue from head to toe, as a crowd of priests gathered around him. The music began. Men blew on conch shells and others beat drums and rattled bells. A crowd of pilgrims, mostly farmers, formed around the priests and soon grew to several hundred. When the music grew louder, the priests turned to the big pyramid. High up at one of the tunnel entrances the man-god appeared. At the raising of his hand, the procession began heading toward the sacbe. Two chilan in litters headed the procession, followed by Ah Ceh on foot. Next came the lower priests, followed by the musicians and finally by the pilgrims. Ah Ceh looked for his parents in the crowd, but he dared not turn around too often. He hoped very much that they were among the pilgrims, for they would be very proud of him. Maybe, he thought, his father had actually sent him to Chichén as a sacrifice but did not tell him for fear he would be disappointed if not chosen. Actually, Ah Ceh would have considered being chosen as a sacrifice too much to hope for. It would bring rain to the fields and give him direct admission into heaven.

When the procession reached the end of the sacbe, his outer garments were taken off, and Ah Ceh was led to the holy steam bath by the edge of the sacred well. The fire was already hot, and water was poured on the hot rocks as the priests led Ah Ceh to the entrance. The steam was very hot, but Ah Ceh endured the pain without flinching. This was only the final act of purification before the real pain began.

As he came out of the steam bath, Ah Ceh saw several pilgrims making sacrifices of their own, each of them paying a priest to help with the ritual. The pilgrim would hold the object he wanted to sacrifice, and the priest would break and kill it. Then the pilgrim would stand on one of the side altars and give the object to Chac.

Several of these minor sacrifices had taken place by the time

Ah Ceh was reclothed and led to the altar. Out of the corner of his eye he saw the nacom whom he originally met yesterday. The priest had found Ah Ceh's carved stag horn and was saying the ritual of sacrifice over it. He watched the nacom throw it in the well just as another priest asked him to lift his feet for the ceremony in which he was given gold sandals. Once the gold sandals were secured on Ah Ceh's feet, a priest removed his tooth bracelets and told him to open his mouth. Then with several blows from a gold instrument the priest knocked out Ah Ceh's front teeth, which were given to an assistant who would string them later into a bracelet for another sacrificial victim.

Ah Ceh was told to lie down on his back over something that looked like a stone mound on the altar. This maneuver was somewhat difficult because of his heavy clothing, but Ah Ceh performed it as gracefully as he could.

With his back arched up over the mound, his head dangled toward the ground. Blood from the sockets that once held his teeth dripped over his eyes. He had blinked no more than twice before he felt the cold plunge of a gold-plated knife into his chest. Had his eyes not been covered with blood, Ah Ceh might have gotten a glimpse of his own heart as the nacom gave it to the officiating chilan.

Prayers and words of supplication were said over the heart as the music grew louder. When the music seemed to be at its height, two of the chilan picked up Ah Ceh's body and carried it to the edge of the altar. When the body was given to Chac, the music stopped.

A few pilgrims walked to the edge of the sacred well to watch the red pool of blood on the surface of the water. Ah Ceh's body floated down toward the bottom, his sacrificial clothes already loosening in the water and his gold sandals slipping off his feet.

13

BILL McGEHEE reached into the mud near the airlift nozzle and withdrew a thin, flat piece of metal. The object was too sturdy to be gold leaf, but Bill was sure the metal *was* gold despite its tarnished condition. Cupping it gently in his hands, he swam to the surface. As he brought it out of the water, he recognized the shape of the object and realized he had found the sole of a gold sandal.

Victor examined the gold sheet and noticed that unlike the sole of a used shoe, this one had no indentations in areas where the ball and heel of the foot would have trod. He deduced that while the sandal might have been worn, it was never stepped on. That deduction helped considerably in the fictional reconstruction of the three days in the life of Ah Ceh. If the sole that Bill found had come from a used sandal, it would be evidence that Ah Ceh and other sacrificial victims were either dressed at the well or dressed at the temple and then carried by litter to the cenote. Since I have seen paintings of priests being carried in this manner but not of sacrificial victims, I chose to believe the former case to be true, that victims walked to the well with some of their sacrificial clothing on but then put on more, including sandals, once they arrived at the site. Victor said the condition of the sole precluded the possibility that it could have been worn even for the comparatively short journey from the temple area to the well.

Later, Piña Chan outlined his conception of the sacrificial rite on which I based the death of Ah Ceh. As more and more treasure from the time capsule was brought to the archaeologists' shed, it became possible to weave many stories around a plausible chain of events as they might have occurred shortly after the Toltecs took control of Chichén Itzá.

Another diver found a second sole of a gold sandal, but it was smaller than the first, indicating the victim was probably not more than seven or eight years old. The skeletal material which we brought from the well indicated that Ah Ceh, as a young teen-ager, was considerably older than the average sacrificial victim.

During this week divers brought up many important objects, including a second wooden stool decorated with a man's face inside a serpent's head. For the historical record, that made the second piece of ancient Mayan furniture known to exist.

Tepeu, much of it painted on gourds, continued to be found in the mud, giving us a still clearer insight into the lives of the people who once inhabited the scrub jungles of Yucatán. On one Tepeu gourd the artist depicted a porpoise in pale green against a dark green background that suggested the ocean. The rendering was one of the most sophisticated I have seen, the artist having captured the childlike smile of the sea mammal with accuracy and humor. For some reason, however, he painted the porpoise with a red ring around its neck, an almost whimsical addition which archaeologists were at a loss to explain. Was the red band a standard stylization? Did Maya fisherman capture porpoises by roping them? Was the porpoise a pet kept at one of the coastal towns such as Tulúm? Or did the artist merely think that a red band would look good on a porpoise? The last hypothesis might be very plausible since Tepeu painters were artists first and painters second. Their rendition of glyphs, for example, is somewhat poor because only the priestly classes were instructed in the art of glyph writing. Their separation from the priests evidently gave Tepeu artists a good deal of freedom which was not available to temple sculptors, and if they wanted to put a red band around a porpoise, there was no one standing over them to say otherwise. Still another piece of Tepeu gave us a sharp picture of the sandals noblemen wore in classical times, a style that probably did not change much as the Mayan civilization moved northward to Chichén Itzá.

The Hon. Fulton Freeman, U.S. ambassador to Mexico, inspects the serpent's head found in the sacred well.

Serpent-head carving on the Temple of the Warriors
similar to the one found in the well.

Also coming from the well was a large serpent's head, similar to those at the base of the Temple of Kukulcán. The find immediately raised many questions. The foundations around the rim of the well appeared much too small for a building that would have been decorated with a serpent's head of that size. How, then, did the head get to the bottom of the cenote? Archaeologists later had some interesting speculations.

During the time these discoveries were made, the water in the well remained remarkably clear. Our only real problem was an ironic one. Scott had brought in several trunkloads of spare parts and medicines, but customs officials demanded a prohibitively high duty on it. It did no good to tell them the material was needed to complete an expedition which would benefit Mexico because the Customs Department barely recognized the existence of the National Institute of Anthropology and History. After four days of negotiations, we convinced the chief customs agent to let us bring the equipment into the country on the condition that we post a bond of several thousand pesos. Even after the bond was posted, we had to go through another day of red tape before being allowed to bring the goods to Chichén. The difficulty with customs should have raised a red flag for us because we still faced the problem of leaving the country with a half million dollars' worth of equipment. But right now such fears were far from our minds.

The archaeologists informed me one day that the remains of sacrificial victims now totaled more than four hundred. It was difficult to arrive at an accurate count because when a right and left shin bone of the same size turned up, how could one say whether they came from one or two victims? A fair number of the skulls that came from the well were flattened, indicating the deformity was practiced to a limited extent in northern Yucatán or that victims had come from elsewhere, either as pilgrims or captives. When one looks at a deformed skull, by the way, it hardly looks like the head of the haughty men with aquiline features so often seen in sculpture or paintings. Only when the skull is turned to a profile position does the pointed-head appearance become apparent. The Mayas obviously were after this

255

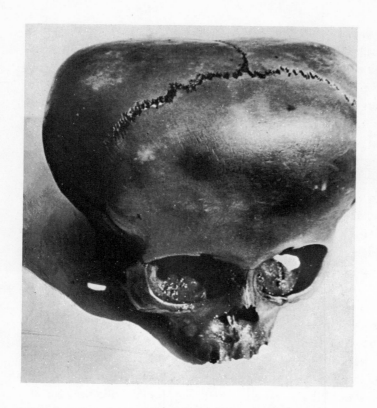

Mayans deformed the heads of their children
to give them a classical profile, but beautiful features
did not save this young child from being sacrificed to Chac.

long profile look rather than the round face which the deformity
also caused. To accentuate the acuteness of the profile, noblemen
put on false noses, probably made from wax or rubber.

I could not help developing a theory of my own about the
long-term results of the Mayas' passion for physical deformity.
They tattooed their bodies, put holes in the earlobes large enough
for an egg to fit through, pierced their noses, revered hunchbacks,
squashed their heads, let blood from their penises and even considered cross-eyes so beautiful that children wore a ball of wax
dangling in front of the eyes to affect the occular affliction.

Today young Yucatecan visitors pose on an artifact from the cenote.
Once youngsters like these had their hearts cut out
to appease the god of rain.

Was it surprising, then, that a people so prone to grotesqueries would find a plumed serpent appealing? The image of a rattle snake with quetzal feathers was just the beast that would appeal to their sense of the strange. When a man believed to be the incarnation of this strange beast marched into Chichén Itzá with a retinue of devout followers, was it surprising that the resident priests allowed him to take control? Hardly. In fact, any other reaction would have been out of character.

That, of course, is only a theory, which has yet to be tested or even explored in great depth. It certainly does not put the Mayas in the best of light, and people are usually ready to think the best about the primitive tribe that for so long was described as peace-loving and intellectual. As the contents of the time capsule revealed, however, the ancient Maya might have been intellectual, but among other things he put his intellect to work finding ways of slaughtering children. Don Pablo once protested that the Mayas should not be condemned for these bloody sacrifices, and I agreed since many surrounding tribes performed similar ones with equal zeal. Nevertheless, the ancient Maya was as bloodthirsty as most of his neighbors, and the excavations of the sacred well proved this beyond any doubt.

While divers continued to recover the sacrificial treasure, work was proceeding fast in other areas. Now that the several-yards strip of land surrounding the well had been defoliated, Segovia directed laborers to cut down the jungle along the sacbe. The magnificent extent of the holy road was revealed in the process. The sacbe was actually much higher than it had appeared in the midst of the wood; workmen centuries ago had made it at least ten feet higher than the surrounding ground, giving the populace a dramatic view of the processions from the Temple of Kukulcán to the sacred well.

Preliminary restoration was completed on the small altar across from the main sacrificial shrine, and several ceramic offerings were found buried beneath it. As these excavations were conducted, I realized something that had not been apparent before defoliation. We had previously assumed that the small altar was *directly* opposite the big one, but now we could see that it was slightly less than 180 degrees across the circumference of the cenote. Since the Mayas rarely if ever designed anything capriciously, I thought the relative position of the shrines was unusual and probably significant in the scheme of sacrifices. It was not until the expedition was nearly over that we had some definite ideas about the odd positioning of the altars.

Almost going unnoticed in the other activity, Victor had been supervising the unloading of large stones that the crane lifted from the cenote. The object was to sort out construction stones from the other boulders. Sorting was not difficult when we worked with carved stones, but when they were not carved it required a keen eye to spot the Mayas' building blocks which were often irregularly shaped. Since the sorting also required a large space in which to work, Victor chose an area near the rear entrance to the campsite. As the weeks passed, the collection of construction blocks grew. Workers had been trained to do much of the actual sorting, and now there were several distinct piles for stones used in pillars, arches, facades, walls, foundations and other construction areas. With these neatly arranged piles growing each day, the sorting area reminded me of pictures I had seen of men moving a European cathedral, for reconstruction block by block, to some little Midwestern town in the United States. The cathedral arrived in thousands of crates containing numbered building stones with which the edifice was to be reassembled. Newspapers took pictures of the bewildered mayor looking at the crates with an expression that meant he was thinking something like, "How in the world are we going to put this thing back together?" For the seventeenth-century masterbuilders of Europe, the task of reassembly would be easy while for the Midwesterners it would be immensely difficult. Our problem with the building blocks from the cenote can be appreciated when one considers that they did not come in numbered crates, there were no architectural drawings of the buildings from which they came, and that construction techniques have changed considerably in the last one thousand to twelve hundred years.

However confusing the stones looked, they were an immediate help in another type of reconstruction. By studying the ancient

259

building blocks in light of other treasure from the well archaeologists could reassemble the events in another period of Mayan history.

Let us look at several days in the year A.D. 1205.

Ah Balam realized he had the most important decision of his life to make. It would affect him, his wife and their children. As a soldier, he was accustomed to making decisions, but this one would decide not the fate of a battle but of his life and possibly of Chichén Itzá itself. Ah Balam was a nacom, not the priestly official who had the same name but the military chief of Chichén Itzá. Now that the very existence of the city was in danger, the fate of many people in Mayab rested on his ability to make the right decision in the next few days.

Ah Balam, whose name meant Jaguar, had been chosen nacom two years ago. Now, in the last year of his three-year term, Ah Balam often wished that he had not been selected at all. But who, he kept asking himself, would have realized even two years ago the state of events that were now taking place? Times are changing, the younger men on his advisory staff would counsel him, while the older priests would tell him that time is the only thing that does not change.

On the advice of a chilan who told him to expect great changes, Ah Balam had moved his family from their house in the newer section of Chichén to the house of his father, which was close to the temple area. He thought his wife, Ix Chen, and his children would be safer there; in case of emergency they could seek sanctuary in one of the temples. He was glad now that he had made such arrangements because an outright attack on Chichén appeared possible and the temples might be the only place where the family of a military nacom would be safe.

His family meant more to Ah Balam than all the honors that were ritualistically heaped on him each year at the war festival. He had three sons and two daughters; another son had died at birth. He also possessed two slaves, both of them recent gifts from his counterpart at Izamal. He doubted he could trust the slaves yet dared not say anything that would offend the giver. As another precaution he made a point never to discuss state affairs when the slaves were known to be present. He did not even like the woman slave to accompany his wife to the small cenote for drinking water. There was something treacherous in her eyes. But he was stuck with her, a gift from the man he could not offend.

Ah Balam decided to confide in his wife about some of the problems the city could expect in the coming days. He walked with her one morning to the sacred well to bring up holy water for use at the small shrine to the god Ek Chuah which they kept in their home. It was in honor of Ek Chuah that Ah Balam painted himself black during the war festival, but the god was also the patron of merchants who painted themselves the same color during their own festivals. Ix Chen carried two large pots with which to bring up water from the sacred well. When they arrived at the end of the sacbe, Ah Balam gave the attendant priest an offering and, in return, the couple were purified. Ix Chen let the pots down into the water by a rope that was kept near the steam bath. While the vessels filled with water, Ah Balam talked.

The trouble which was now upon them had begun two years ago in the month of Pax during which Ah Balam officiated at his first war festival. Painted black and dressed with exotically colored skins and feathers, he had been paraded through the holy city on a litter. He would experience the rite three times during his tenure in office, but he remembered that his emotion in the second festival was not nearly as strong as it had been when the office and rites were still new to him. His fellow warriors of the Jaguar Cult had made a special show of the occasion since it was the first time in twelve years that one of their number had been chosen nacom of war. Even members of the Eagle Cult were joyous on the occasion because Ah Balam's father-in-law had been one of them. On the night before the festival Ah Balam had gotten drunk with several of his old comrades. They had wound up at a house of prostitution on the outskirts of Chichén, but that was to be his last night of indulgence for three years. The position of nacom for war required living in honor and obeying the holy law.

Ix Chen forgot about the water jugs as Ah Balam reminded her of the events that had occurred soon after the festival. Not more than seven days later the ruler invited Hunac Ceel of Mayapán to witness a ceremony at the well. Ceremonies had changed in the last centuries and now few victims were killed during the rite. Instead, they were thrown in to receive the words of Chac. When they had heard the voice of the god, the human offerings were brought up from the cenote for a nighttime ceremony. The ahkin and the lower priests gathered around them to hear what the god had to say. It was this type of ceremony to which the ruler of Chichén Itzá had invited his counterpart, the True Man of Mayapán, Hunac Ceel.

The events of that day were well known. All of the human offerings died as soon as they hit the water although some residents of Chichén maintained they died of poison the priest could have put in *balche* which they had first drunk. When it became obvious that there would be no prophecy from the offerings, Hunac Ceel himself volunteered to go into the sacred well. Before anyone could protest, he jumped from the altar into the water, where he remained for several hours. A ladder was lowered for his return, and when the nighttime ceremony was held, Hunac Ceel told the priests that the gods had named him to rule over Chichén Itzá. In order to appease the local priesthood he appointed as viceroy Chac Xib Chac, the ruler of Chichén who had invited him to the holy city in the first place. Many residents said the two men had plotted the coup together for some time, but they still wondered what Chac Xib Chac would get out of the bargain.

They discovered what he would get a year later, when the two men met again at the wedding feast of the True Man of Izamal, who was named Ah Ulil. Until that time the viceroy of Chichén had defended his actions by saying that peace could be maintained by a balance of power among the three cities—Chichén, Mayapán and Izamal. The older men in Chichén naturally did not like to see the holy city lose the undiluted domination it had enjoyed for many years, but they had to admit the pact seemed to be working well. When the feast was held, Hunac Ceel found his opportunity for wrecking the alliance. He gave Chac Xib Chac a plumeria blossom which he said was from Ah Ulil's bride. Since that is the flower of love, Chac Xib Chac stopped the wedding and claimed the bride for his own. The ruler of Izamal was outraged and asked Hunac Ceel's assistance in defeating Chichén Itzá. That was precisely what Hunac Ceel had hoped for.

Ah Balam grew tense as he related the story to his wife. It had been nearly a year since Hunac Ceel promised assistance to Izamal in defeating Chichén, and while the city waited for the threatened invasion, its residents often compromised their loyalties. Already many government officials and priests from Chichén had switched allegiances. In the dark of the night they had moved their families from the holy city to Mayapán, a municipality growing in strength each day. The dominant Itzá families of Chichén either hoped for a pitched battle with Mayapán or reconciled themselves to a fate which only gods could have written. A few of them even invoked the name of the all-but-forgotten god, Kukulcán, whose temple now was only rarely used. Ah Balam was a member of those families whose ancestors had come to Mayab from the west several centuries ago. Now an upstart in the new city of Mayapán was appealing to the old Maya families to overthrow the Itzá and the city from which they ruled.

As a professional soldier, Ah Balam told his wife that Mayapán had more than enough power to subdue any defense which he could put up. He fairly whispered that remark and looked around after he had made it to see if anyone was in earshot. His dilemma was this: should he undertake the defense of an indefensible city, or should he, too, switch allegiances in order to avert the destruction of Chichén? Ah Balam's voice shook as he spoke. The fate of Chichén Itzá rested on the course of action which its leaders would take in the next few days. As the nacom for war, he would play a principal role in deciding that course.

Ix Chen looked up with tears in her eyes. She knew Ah Balam was in a torturous position regardless of the choice he made. If he decided to undertake the defense of Chichén Itzá, he would in effect be ordering its destruction. If he decided to negotiate with the leadership of Mayapán, he would forever be pointed out as a man who betrayed Chichén Itzá. Ix Chen was silent as she began to pull the water jugs from the well. Ah Balam took the rope from her to hurry the job, but he pulled too hard, causing one of the pots to catch on a limb beneath the surface. One vessel came up full, but they did not worry about the one that had broken off. Such accidents had happened before, and some women interpreted them to mean that Chac had taken a vessel as an offering.

As they walked back up the sacbe, Ah Balam and his wife looked back at the well. A dozen or so pilgrims were just approaching the altar, and another group was walking toward them along the holy road. Ix Chen remarked how odd it was that while other temples were falling into disuse, the well continued to draw pilgrims from throughout Mayab. Ah Balam's bodyguards joined the couple at the top of the sacbe, and the group walked slowly past the market and toward the home of Ah Balam. Only the wealthy merchants now used the market while the poorer tradesmen set up stalls under trees close by. The couple turned and looked toward the temples before they took the road to their house. They saw the morning sun gleaming on the limestone of the temples and thought of the centuries it had taken the workers of Mayab to construct them. Ix Chen could tell that her husband had made his decision. Neither of them could tolerate witnessing the destruction of the city where they were born and where their ancestors had settled. Ah Balam said it must be saved at any price, even at the cost of his reputation.

Ah Balam sent one of the few warriors he knew he could trust as an emissary to Hunac Ceel. A meeting was arranged the following week between Ah Balam and the nacom of Mayapán. T'ho was chosen as the site for the conference, at which the outcome could easily have been predicted. Ah Balam guaranteed not to offer resistance to the occupation of Chichén Itzá on the condition that its temples, shrines, priests and residents would not be harmed. The representative from Mayapán agreed.

It was less than ten days after the conference that the first troops arrived in the holy city. A contingent was assigned to guard the house of Ah Balam, who feared retaliation from a few priests and a band of loyalists who had already gotten word of his settlement with Hunac Ceel. Now that the troops were in Chichén Itzá, it was up to Ah Balam to convince the high priests and other military leaders to go along with the entente that had been reached at T'ho. Most of them appeared willing, but a small group held out. Their actions were critical since Ah Balam could not risk having his subordinates break the agreement he had so painfully reached. He ordered the temporary arrest of those he suspected of undermining his plan.

Ah Balam was shaken when many more troops than agreed on arrived in the city. The foreign soldiers, many of them mercenaries, were rowdy, and there were many infractions of the truce. Ah Balam sent pleading messages to Hunac Ceel, but the True Man of Mayapán did not reply.

The situation grew desperate. Ah Balam left his home with four bodyguards to survey the damage that was being done in the holy city. He saw immediately that the reports had been true. The foreigners were removing Chichén residents from their homes and sending for their families in Mayapán to move in. The homes of residents who refused to leave were burned to the ground. Shrines were being hideously defiled, and temples were being torn down for building materials. Ah Balam himself witnessed the desecration of the Temple of Kukulcán. A band of drunken soldiers lopped off one of the serpent's heads near the base of the pyramid and began rolling it down the sacbe. They were shouting something about throwing the head into the cenote.

The market was in turmoil. Several groups of faithful old women were buying pom offerings, which they rushed to the few priests who remained in the temple area. The priests hastily made glyph inscriptions into the incense, and the women ran down the sacbe to sacrifice it into the well. Ah Balam knew the sacrifices were too late.

There was a faint hope that he could rally enough support among his own warriors at least to stem the tide of destruction. He ran to the home of the old nacom who now headed the Eagle Cult, and the man agreed to help after tongue-lashing Ah Balam for his stupidity in trusting Hunac Ceel. The next morning a band of loyal Chichén soldiers met on a field near town and proceeded to march toward the Temple of the Warriors. Their plan was to occupy the temple area and to destroy the headquarters which the Mayapán army had put up.

When they arrived at the Temple of the Warriors, the soldiers discovered that it, too, had been destroyed. The majestic columns had been toppled and the main altar desecrated. Since most of the Mayapán soldiers were looting the residential section of town, the loyalists encountered little opposition at their makeshift headquarters. Chichén warriors seized two standard-bearers in the shapes of jaguars which flew the flags of Hunac Ceel, and in reprisal they rolled the standard-bearers down the sacbe for sacrifice into the sacred well.

Ah Balam and his warriors occupied the temple area for only a matter of hours before the invaders regrouped and forced them to retreat. Ah Balam knew that the one short-lived display of the defense would be the last. There was not enough manpower for greater resistance, and the will to protect the holy city had been broken along with its temples. Ah Balam walked calmly down the sacbe, not even concerned that an enemy soldier might spot him. He did not care now if he died, for the cause on which he had pinned his fate was now lost. Survival would mean becoming a lackey to the treacherous Hunac Ceel, who would probably order his death in any event. The Chichén residents whom he met on the sacbe turned their heads when he passed. Neither, he thought, was there a point to living in disgrace among the people whom he had tried to save.

At the well Ah Balam saw foreigners from Mayapán destroying the magnificent buildings that had encircled the cenote of sacrifice. He watched painfully as a group of teen-agers climbed atop one shrine and toppled two large stones into the water. They continued their destruction by tossing in a smaller block where the others had fallen. Ah Balam feared the reprisal that Chac

"Chichén warriors seized standard-bearers in the shapes of jaguars. . . ."

would send for the wanton act. He searched his clothing for an object worthy of sacrifice. He had only a few spears left and a knife. He flung them into the well. Then from his finger he took an Aztec ring that had been given up many years ago after battle in the west. The ring was made by Aztec goldsmiths who had drawn out the metal to look like thread and then woven the ring from these threads. Ah Balam had intended to give it to his son, but now he did not hesitate to give it to Chac. There was no priest at the well to purify or kill the offering, but Ah Balam repeated the ritual as best he could remember.

He turned toward the sacbe and saw Ix Chen running toward him. Together they stood for several minutes watching the destruction of the sacred buildings around the cenote. Ix Chen had come with a message. She said the Mayapán warriors were on their way down the sacbe with orders to kill Ah Balam in reprisal for the uprising. She said the children had been sent out of town. She described the burning and looting she had seen, and Ah Balam realized they were witnessing the very thing he had staked his life to avoid, the destruction of Chichén Itzá. Ix Chen said there were no soldiers left to defend the city. That left the couple to face Mayapán warriors who were only minutes away.

They turned toward the sacred well, repeated the ritual prayers to Chac and waited for their inevitable fate.

14

ALTHOUGH the story of Ah Balam is fictitious, it could never have been posited without the building blocks from the sacred well. There undoubtedly was a military nacom of Chichén Itzá who, after Hunac Ceel's coup, had grave decisions to make. If anyone had tried to prevent the sacking of the holy city, construction stones in the cenote testify to his failure. The Mayapán standard-bearers are evidence that pillage did not cease when that city brought Chichén under its domination. It was mere supposition that the ring of entwined gold was thrown in during this period of turmoil, but judging from the ring's manufacture, the supposition could not be far off. The turtle-like stools might also have been sacrificed into the well during this time, and it is fascinating to wonder why furniture that was used by priests wound up in the home of Chac.

The plumeria is a very real flower that is known in Spanish as the *flor de mayo,* a name that translates Mayflower despite its appearance a month earlier, at least in Yucatán. Since the Maya chronicles tell us that the plumeria played a part in Hunac's treachery, we can surmise that the wedding feast took place in April or May. Since we know from other sources the war festivals also were held in May, the chronology in the story of Ah Balam is plausible.

The *flores de mayo* had been in bloom several weeks before Scott announced that the expedition was near an end. He made the announcement with a reluctance I could not understand. Although we had opened the Mayan time capsule, Scott still seemed to doubt the value of a treasure which did not yield easily to monetary evaluation. Nevertheless, he had stretched our operating funds to the limit, and it would soon be time to say that the job was done and to head home.

When we finally realized the problem of getting our equipment back to the United States, Scott began to think of faster and cheaper ways of transportation. If we worked at the well much longer, we would not be in position to afford a two-week overland journey along the route by which we had come. We considered every possibility from hiring a cargo plane to selling the equipment and flying home. It was a matter of deduction that led Scott to think that shipping the equipment might be the most efficient means of transport providing we could get the proper government clearance, a difficult item to come by in view of our having entered the country at Nuevo Laredo. Incredibly, even the customs agents in different cities are somewhat independent of one another. After considering and then rejecting the port of Progreso, Scott decided to try Campeche. A shipping company was contacted in Miami, and the firm's representative quoted us a price that seemed reasonable. All we had to do was figure out a way to load our many tons of gear and vehicles onto two shrimp boats. I was slightly reassured when I discovered that the boats were not fishing boats but vessels used to transport frozen shrimp from Campeche and other ports to Miami. They reputedly had ample deck space for our vehicles.

From the only telephone in Chichén Itzá I called a representative of the shipping company in Campeche, but the Miami agent had failed to tell him anything about the big deal already agreed to by letter. It was not the easiest task to explain to a provincial shipping agent that his company had contracted to transport the equipment from the largest expedition in the hemisphere. I nevertheless got my point across and arranged a meeting for him and Scott in two days. The timing was important because if we could not conclude an agreement for transportation from Campeche, we would have to go overland, and we would soon lack sufficient funds for the latter course.

We were very lucky in our race against time because some business associates of Jack Kiefer's father were visiting the area

Austin and Sam Scott III "racing against time" to ready equipment for the journey home.

in a charter plane. They told Scott he could have use of both their plane and pilot while they stayed on Cozumel. The pilot, Frank Sullivan, was a likable young man with a good reputation for skillful flying in less than ideal conditions.

Scott and I left in the plane shortly after dawn and stopped in Mérida to pick up the American vice consul. Scott figured that since we were going to be talking with the customs agents in Campeche, it might strengthen our position to have our own government representative along. The man in the shipping office was predictably overawed by the size of the job, but with the help of the vice consul we convinced him it could be done. From the dimensions of the ships we judged that there was going to be difficulty getting all the vehicles aboard, especially the crane, but it looked like a good gamble. The customs officials and port captain could have made trouble for us (for such is often the way of doing business in Mexico), but the men were sympathetic to our cause.

Our business in Campeche took us longer than we anticipated, and it was after four o'clock when we finally got a taxi to the airport. Our tardiness was critical because Mexican aviation rules make it illegal for single-engine planes to fly at night. According to our flight plan, we would now have a few minutes of night flying. Knowing that the tower would refuse us permission to take off, we leaped from the taxi, dashed to the plane, revved up the engine and took off before the men in the tower realized what had happened. It was a chance we had to take. We could hardly afford to spend the night in Campeche, and all of us had faith in Frank's flying ability. There would, of course, be no opportunity to stop in Mérida to let the vice consul off. He would have to come to Chichén and return to Mérida the following morning.

Darkness began to close in, but we were not particularly worried since we possessed two sets of charts and an extra land map. Ideally, we would have followed the highway, but that route was so long that night would have fallen long before we reached Chichén Itzá. Instead, we had to use two railroad crossings to guide us toward the road from Mérida to Chichén. Once we spotted the road, we figured we could get to Chichén for a safe landing, regardless of the hour. The airstrip there was not lighted (residents put out smudge-pot flares when they knew in advance of a night landing), but the runway was paved with white lime-stone pebbles that could easily be seen against the black jungle.

We had no trouble in seeing the first of the two rail lines, but the second never appeared. The pilot and three passengers peered out from all sides of the plane, but nothing in sight even vaguely resembled the straight railroad that was depicted on the charts. We began to doubt the accuracy of the maps and looked for other landmarks.

Coming up on our right was something that looked like a village, but as we approached, we realized that it was actually the ruins of Kabah. A couple of minutes later we spotted the restored ruins of Uxmal. We knew we were on the right track, and Frank set his heading accordingly. Our next landmark would be Mayapán. It was ironic to reflect that four twentieth-century men in a modern aircraft had to rely on landmarks made by people who refused to use the wheel.

We passed what we thought was Mayapán, but the road to Chichén did not appear. It had become so difficult to see that Frank was flying as low as he dared. We had no more than five minutes before complete blackness would be upon us. Frank banked the plane and headed in a direction which seemed to me to be far from the road.

As the seconds ticked by, we made preparations for a crash landing. A few farmers in the area were clearing land, and Frank hoped their fires would point us toward some of the cleared ground. Another alternative was to head for the coast and land on the beach.

Now it was dark, and we had to think seriously about the alternatives. We had settled on trying for a farm when Frank raised up in his seat and pointed ahead to the right. It was the road.

The pilot banked to the right and followed the lights of the half dozen or so cars that we saw. Then out of the darkness ahead of us emerged a white strip of light. The Chichén airstrip

"A cameraman wanted to take Kirk's picture alongside several rows of skulls and ceramics. . . ."

fairly glowed in the dark, and Frank headed the plane directly for it. We were very lucky passengers.

The last days of the expedition were touched with pride and sorrow. We did not want to leave Yucatán, but we had a deep feeling of accomplishment over what we had been able to do there. Camera crews went back into action to film the last phase of the venture, and we found ourselves being asked to pose with the treasure that had come from the well. Such commercialism in a scientific venture would have been unthinkable even a few years ago, but now it seemed natural. Kirk returned to Chichén to be with the expedition for the final days, and I will never forget the shrug he gave when a cameraman wanted to take his picture alongside several rows of skulls and ceramics. Kirk was a Philistine who, without really realizing it, had spent many thousands of dollars and countless hours toward the understanding of Mayan culture. He grinned at the cameraman, put down his bottle of beer and obligingly posed as the man with the camera directed.

In the last weeks of the expedition archaeologists had not been able to catalogue the treasure as fast as it was being brought from the well. Now, however, in the final days the rate of recovery slowed considerably, indicating the last of the sacrificial offerings were at last being found. Victor spent much of his time sorting bones and preserving ceramics at the storeroom in the gatehouse. I was surprised that he was no longer rushing the relics back to Mexico City, but Victor refused to explain the change in procedure.

Two days before the end of the expedition, Victor joined Gypsy, Don Pablo and me for lunch in the little restaurant operated by the family that had cooked the food (and probably the flies too) for Kirk's party. I had actually come to prefer their food over the hacienda's, and for a while Scott had considered employing them to handle all our meals. Victor had been working so hard that he scarcely had time to enjoy a leisurely meal. Now he leaned back in his chair and ordered a cold beer. Don Pablo also looked pleased and relaxed, and of course Gypsy never looked any other way. The expedition had done more than anyone expected, Don Pablo said. Victor nodded, and I naturally concurred.

Aside from finding the first Mayan furniture, we had brought up more than two thousand sacrificial offerings and the remains of possibly a thousand victims. Photographs of the ring of entwined gold and another showing the face of Chac had been printed throughout the world, and replicas would soon be made. They were probably two of the most unusual rings in the world and would presumably go on display at the Museum of Anthropology in Mexico City along with row upon row of carved jade, golden bells, copper bells of death, painted ceramics, copal incense, offerings of rubber, ear and lip plugs, gold sandals, sacrificial ornaments, jaguar standard-bearers, flint projectile points, the bones of victims and one stylized turkey carved on a piece of stag horn.

Victor considered the Tepeu pottery the most important find, and few of us would argue for it was in the paintings of Tepeu artists that the time capsule was truly opened. The mini-murals had opened up a world of the Mayas that had been hidden since the Spanish priests burned their books and told them that Jesus Christ was another name for Chac. Now this window on the past would be wide open in museums and books. One look through the window would take the viewer back more than a thousand years and let him see not effigies of gods or the pyramids but the faces of the people who worshiped and built them.

But without the remains of the victims themselves, Victor said, we could still not tell what went on in the minds of the pyramid builders. We thought with amusement of romantic stories about virgin maidens thrown into the well. We had destroyed that myth once and for all; no longer would anyone call the cenote the well of virgins. The evidence had come to us in such forms as femurs, tibia and crania, and when it was all in, we *did* know something about the mind that worked out the art of sacrifice. Now we knew that the Mayas were not the intellectual pacifists they were once made out to be and that under Toltec domination they developed a child-slaughtering cult to rival the bloodthirst of most other native inhabitants of the Americas.

With the building material we recovered from the sacred well, it would be possible to reconstruct buildings that once stood around the cenote. Victor, however, said this would be an immensely expensive undertaking since there were still many building stones in the well. Yet from the material we found, an artist could come close to re-creating the magnificence of the well be-

Symbolically, we destroyed the "heart of the expedition"—dismantling the Styrofoam raft.

fore the surrounding buildings were destroyed. It occurred to me that although the structures were either torn down or allowed to crumble, the well itself remained a holy place—probably the holiest—in Mayab. Its presence was the reason Chichén Itzá was settled in the first place, and it was the only shrine of the city which was absolutely indestructible. The well that spurred the founding of the city undoubtedly saved Chichén from being abandoned several times during its cataclysmic history. The well and the city were one. I told Victor that I would like to see the day when the Mexican government or a foundation agreed to finance the reconstruction of the buildings around the sacred well. It would be one of the most splendid restorations ever undertaken.

Although I did not mention it at lunch, I had a notion about the well which I planned to advance later. After noticing that the small altar was substantially off the 180 degree mark from the main sacrificial platform, I began wondering whether astronomy played a part in determining the design of the cenote structures. It would be surprising if it did not, for astronomy governed everything else the Mayas did. I am convinced that many mysteries of the Mayas could be solved with the help of a detective astronomer such as Boston University's Gerald Hawkins, who recently applied his science to Stonehenge with history-making results.

Don Pablo said that our expedition itself had made history in many ways. Notwithstanding that it was the largest search-and-find venture ever undertaken in the hemisphere, the expedition was a milestone in underwater archaeology, Don Pablo said. People have been accustomed to thinking of an archaeological site as a roped-off piece of desert where men in pith helmets dig little holes. That certainly was once a typical archaeological site, but the science is changing. Now a site may be fifty feet under water. The tools that we tested and the techniques that we pioneered at the sacred well will let archaeologists go into areas that have been closed to them—the oceans, rivers and lakes of the world.

Although it was sometimes resented, we made history in another way. We proved that industry and science, which have joined forces in many other fields, can work hand in hand in archaeology.

278

Commercialism, which scientists instinctively abhor, is not mutually exclusive with archaeology after all. If an archaeologist can get a corporation to dig his holes in exchange for controlling publicity on what the hole yields, how is science compromised? Students like Talia might resent others getting rich from the bones of neolithic peasants, but if it were any other way, the bones might still be buried.

We talked so long at lunch that we were all tired out. I drank another beer, said good-by to my companions and then headed back to the hacienda for a nap, waking just in time for a shower before dinner.

This was our last dinner at the hacienda and Victor had an announcement. He said the National Institute had come to an agreement with landowners here to build a museum at Chichén Itzá. So this was why he was not sending any more artifacts back to Mexico City, I thought. Victor said the Barbachano interests, which had acquired the land long ago after Thompson left the country, agreed to contribute toward the construction of a museum to house artifacts from this section of Mayab. The treasure from the sacred well would be the principal collection. Yucatecans were especially happy over the news because they had become tired of seeing relics of their past shipped off to Mexico. Now these would stay in Yucatán, and the treasure from the well would become an attraction to both students and tourists.

When Scott heard the news about the museum, I think he began to become aware of the true value of what he had found.

It was in the heat of the day when our caravan began to move up the sacbe and wind around the temples toward the highway. It had taken us three days to pack the equipment, disassemble the raft and get the vehicles ready for travel. Our schedule called for an eight-hour drive to Campeche, where we would spend the night. The first of the two ships was scheduled to arrive in port the following day.

The ship, however, did not arrive that day or the next. We were told that it was on the way, but Scott became anxious when it still had not arrived by the third day. Arrangements were made

Tearing down the base of the personnel lift
was harder than erecting it in the first place.

with the customs officials so there was nothing for us to do but wait. We tried to enjoy ourselves by swimming in the pool at the hotel where we stayed, but the smell of chlorine somehow put us off. We had so many farewell dinners at the hotel I cannot in my memory distinguish one from another.

It was sadly ironic that just as we were trying to enjoy ourselves we heard the news about Gypsy and Frank Sullivan, who had flown on to Cozumel to join his party. While he was there, he and Gypsy met two airline stewardesses who were fascinated by the clear waters around the island. The men, only too eager to show them around, acquired an eighteen-foot catamaran and in-

Loading the last truck before the caravan began to move.

vited them to go out in the channel. When we got the news, they had not been heard from in two days. A storm had come up in the treacherous channel, and no one held out any hope.

The first of our two ships arrived on the fourth day. The work of loading it took our minds off the tragedy in Cozumel, but each morning we would dash to the lobby of the hotel for a copy of the Mérida newspaper which had carried a small story about the accident. It was in that article that I learned Gypsy's real name, Alberto Gavilondo.

The first ship departed as soon as it was loaded, and on the following day the second arrived. It became apparent that our vehicles would fit on the decks only in theory. In practice there was not enough space. Scott made hasty arrangements for the crane and several other vehicles to travel overland while the ships sailed across the gulf to Miami. Miguel González would drive one of the trucks and help out as an interpreter for the other drivers. Although they left a day after the second ship sailed, they would not complete the thirty-five-hundred-mile trip until more than a week after the ship was due to dock.

Scott left on the second vessel, and on the morning he departed, he received two envelopes from the United States. When he found time to open them, he read two long letters from museum officials who congratulated him on the expedition and wanted to know how they could exhibit some of the treasure from the sacred well. Scott mulled the letters over at lunch and I could tell by his expression that now he understood why the contents of the time capsule were so important. Everybody wanted to look through the window on the past which we had opened. Scott folded the letters and put them in his pocket, finally confident that he had found something more valuable than gold.

On board ship we slept in the vehicles that were strapped to the deck. The pace was slow, only eight or nine knots an hour, and there was little breeze. Whether because of the heat or whether we had other reasons for going out on deck, we all spent much of our traveling time leaning against the rail and scanning the sea. Maybe by some miracle the current in the channel had carried Gypsy and Frank into the gulf. It was impossible not to

"They wanted to talk to Norman Scott,
the man who had opened the time capsule of the Mayas."

keep a lookout. There was no sign of the catamaran, and we had no choice but to give up hope.

The trip across the gulf was sad and monotonous, but on the fifth day we arrived in Miami—unshaven and unwashed. To the bystanders it must have seemed funny to see the reporters rush up to a shrimp boat, but this is exactly what they did. They asked for Norman Scott. They wanted to talk to the man who had opened the time capsule of the Mayas.

INDEX

285

181–83, 198, 202, 206, 209, 213, 230

Irwin, Chuck, 74, 75, 195, 200, 214, 226, 228

Irwin, Joyce, 74–75, 195, 226, 228

Itzá Indians, 19–20, 62, 78

Ix Chel, shrine of, 212

Jade, 113, 114, 159, 170, 172, 180

Jarana (dance), 224

Johns-Manville International, 227, 229

Johnson, F. Kirk, Jr., 30–31, 42, 59, 75, 88, 103, 106, 149, 150, 152, 163, 164, 192, 216, 221–23, 228, 229, 274, 275

Kantil snakes, 92–94

Kemler, Jerry, 27, 33, 50, 72, 87, 96, 131, 138, 145, 171, 174, 176, 202, 216–18, 224, 226

Kiefer, Adolph, 38

Kiefer, Jack, 38, 130–31, 138, 145, 171, 172, 177, 180, 183, 195, 199, 212, 214–15, 219, 271–72

Kingsborough, Lord, 46–47

Kukulcán. *See* Feathered Serpent

Leyden Plate (jade piece), 15

Lincoln, Abraham, 107

Link, Edwin, 48

Lothrop, Samuel, 157

Lupita, Señorita, 186–87

McGehee, Bill, 33, 42, 72, 97, 99, 106, 132–38, 164, 177, 179, 180, 182, 187–89, 198–99, 212, 219, 226, 230, 231, 235, 251

McGoo, Billy, 40

McKeithen, Governor John, 194

Martin, Harold, 24–25, 27, 33, 56, 72, 99, 106, 138, 139, 140, 144, 180, 183, 184, 187, 197–98

Mayab, meaning of, 18

Maya Indians: achievement in calendrics, 15, 16
commercial empire of, 169–71
compared to Orientals, 161–62
currency, 169–70
fear of snakes, 129–30
goldwork of, 155–58

northward migration of, 17

origin of, 14–15, 127–28

physical characteristics of, 162–63, 255–58

zero concept of, 16

Melba, Karen, 226, 227

Moctezuma I, Emperor, 64

Moctezuma II, Emperor, 46, 64

Morley, Sylvanus, 164

Mozart, Wolfgang Amadeus, 147

Museum of Anthropology, 195, 276

Nahuatl language, 157–58

National Geographic Society, 30, 32, 48, 70, 180, 185

National Institute of Anthropology and History, 49, 57, 87, 106, 155, 167–68, 192, 194, 195, 226, 255, 279

Nikon Laboratories, 229

Onan Corporation, 227

Pacific Pump Company, 35, 227

Painter, Beasom, 42, 56–57, 61, 75, 97, 101, 108, 109, 111, 129, 132, 136, 150, 151, 182

Pan American Airways, 227

Peabody Museum, 48, 49

Peregrina (song), 141, 144

Petróleos Mexicanos, 194, 227

Physical deformity, passion for, 255–58

Piña Chan, Dr. Román, 57, 66–67, 88, 106, 131, 132, 140, 141, 144, 145, 179, 180, 202, 216, 221, 231, 232, 236, 237, 252

Platform of Venus, 22–23

Plumeria (flower), 269–70

Pop (calendar month), 22

Pottery, 164–66, 170, 187–89, 222, 231–35, 237, 276
coil method of, 232–34
development of design, 232

Projectile points, 112–13, 276

Purex Corporation, 34, 35, 36, 38, 67, 68, 83, 87, 133, 183, 209, 227, 230

Purfloc (flocculant), 209

Pyramid building, 142

Pyramid of the Sun, 19

287